THE LOST WRITINGS

THE LOST WRITINGS
JAMES CONNOLLY

Edited by Aindrias Ó Cathasaigh

Pluto Press
LONDON · CHICAGO, ILLINOIS

First Published 1997 by Pluto Press
345 Archway Road, London N6 5AA
and 1436 West Randolph, Chicago, Illinois 60607, USA

British Library Cataloguing in Publication Data
A catalogue record for this book is available from
the British Library

ISBN 0 7453 1297 7 hbk

Library of Congress Cataloguing in Publication Data
Connolly, James, 1868–1916.
    The lost writings / James Connolly : edited by Aindrias Ó
Cathasaigh.
      p.   cm.
    ISBN 0–7453–1297–7 (hbk)
    1. Ireland—Politics and government—1910–1921. 2. Labor
movement—Ireland. 3. Socialism—Ireland. I. Ó Cathasaigh,
Aindrias. II. Title.
DA965.C7A25   1997
941.5082'1—dc21   97–28160
                                             CIP

Designed, produced and typeset for Pluto Press by
Chase Production Services, Chadlington, OX7 3LN
Printed in the EC by Redwood Books

CONTENTS

ACKNOWLEDGEMENTS

James Connolly wrote this book; all I did was edit it – with a good bit of help. Thanks to the following (roughly in order of appearance).

For holding on to the articles, the staff of the National Library of Ireland. For getting the ball rolling, Pádraig Ó Snodaigh. For typing beyond the call of duty, Patricia McManus. For constant support and advice, Tomás Mac Síomóin. For financial support, the James Connolly Memorial Initiative. For reading and criticising, Pádraig, Patricia and Tomás again, as well as Mick Doyle and Brendan Donohoe.

Of course, none of the above bears any responsibility for errors of omission and commission: I managed them all by myself.

A. Ó C.

INTRODUCTION:
Connolly lost and found

James Connolly confronts us as one of the most impressive
socialist thinkers of his time. His life – from his early activism
in the Scottish socialist movement to his execution following
the 1916 uprising for Irish independence – is that of a crucial
figure in the development of the workers' movement during
one of its most intriguing phases. Connolly's theoretical contributions to that development mark him out as a man with
something to say, and a man worth listening to.

Like all the best Irish socialists, James Connolly was born in
Britain – in Edinburgh, on 5 June 1868, his parents having
emigrated from Co. Monaghan in the north of Ireland at the time
of the Great Famine. From the age of 10 onwards he worked in a
couple of dead-end jobs, but by 1882 was forced to lie about his
age and take the Queen's shilling. And it was in the uniform of
the British Army that he first set foot in Ireland. He deserted in
1889 for eminently good reasons – not only did he want to settle
down with the woman he'd met while off duty in Dublin, but he
was sick of the Empire he was made to serve.

Back in Edinburgh he got involved in the growing socialist
movement. By 1893 he was secretary of the Scottish Socialist
Federation and already ably wielding his pen for the cause. He
stood as a local election candidate with the declared intention of
becoming 'a disturber of the political peace'.[1] He got a respectable vote – so respectable that Edinburgh town council saw fit to
withhold his privilege of carting manure from the city's streets
on their behalf. An attempt to set himself up as a cobbler failed
when he proved unable to stick to his last, and emigration
seemed his only hope.

But then fate intervened in the shape of the tiny Dublin

Socialist Club, who were looking for an organiser. So in May 1896 Connolly was back in Dublin, where – after a bit of ideological weeding – he founded the Irish Socialist Republican Party (ISRP) together with a handful of Dublin workers, 'to muster all the forces of labor for a revolutionary reconstruction of society and the incidental destruction of the British Empire',[2] as he later explained. For the next seven years the ISRP played a small but significant part in the young Irish labour movement.

The party fell apart in 1903. The ostensible cause was financial – money Connolly had collected on an American speaking tour had been squandered – but Connolly noted an underlying resentment at the revolutionary politics he stood for. He returned to Scotland, where he played a central part in the founding of the Socialist Labour Party (SLP). But the fledgling party had enough problems without paying him his national organiser's wages, so Connolly set sail for the United States in September, hoping to build a better life for his growing family.

He joined the American Socialist Labor Party, which seemed to him 'the clearest and most revolutionary of the Socialist parties in the world to-day',[3] but he soon had a rude awakening. He crossed swords with the party leader, Daniel de Leon, and became more and more disillusioned with the American SLP's sectarian isolationism.

The founding of the Industrial Workers of the World in 1905 provided a chance to break through from sterile sectarianism to real socialist action. Connolly embraced industrial unionism heart and soul – the working class should forget their divisions and organise to beat the capitalists, to 'take and hold' the means of production. At the same time, race federations were springing up and gathering the various ethnic components of the American working class into the labour movement. Connolly tried to repeat the pattern by forming the Irish Socialist Federation in 1907 to bring the Irish workers into their rightful place on the battlefield alongside the other nationalities.

Although he became an organiser for the Socialist Party of America and author of a best-selling pamphlet, *Socialism Made Easy*, Connolly's thoughts still turned homeward. The newly-formed Irish Transport and General Workers' Union (ITGWU) was blazing a trail across the trade union movement, and the country's socialists had united in the Socialist Party of Ireland (SPI). The prospects for a fighting workers' movement in Ireland looked good, and Connolly returned home in July 1910 to join in.

Not long after landing he published his classic *Labour in Irish History*, a socialist analysis of Ireland over the centuries. He became Belfast organiser for the ITGWU in 1911, and the following year was involved in setting up the more broadly-based Independent Labour Party (ILP) of Ireland, as well as successfully proposing that the Irish TUC establish a labour party. But the employers of Dublin declared war on the growing forces of labour in 1913, locking out everyone who was in the ITGWU and a good few who were not. Together with the union's leader, Jim Larkin, Connolly was to the fore in the battle, which lasted six months before the workers went down to defeat.

But worse was to come soon after, when the British government announced its proposal to partition Ireland, setting up a Unionist statelet in the north-east. Connolly foresaw 'a carnival of reaction both North and South' as a result of this attack on the unity of Ireland and its working class: 'To it Labour should give the bitterest opposition, against it Labour in Ulster should fight even to the death, if necessary,' he wrote.[4]

The last straw was the outbreak of the world war in 1914, and the collapse of the international socialist movement, including his own organisation, the ILP of Ireland. Connolly was one of those few socialists dotted around Europe who stood their ground, opposing the war and their ex-comrades, who now prescribed mutual blood-letting to cement proletarian brotherhood. His hope was that the Irish working class would rise up against the war: 'Starting thus, Ireland may yet set the torch to a European conflagration that will not burn out until the last throne and the last capitalist bond and debenture will be shrivelled on the funeral pyre of the last war lord.'[5]

When Larkin went to the United States in October 1914, Connolly became general secretary of the ITGWU and leader of the Irish Citizen Army, a workers' defence force set up during the lockout. With these small forces, he determined that the war would not pass without striking some kind of a blow against British imperialism, and he concentrated his efforts on attempting to organise an uprising for national independence together with the Irish republican movement.

Their efforts came to fruition on Easter Monday 1916, when he led a rebel force, severely depleted by frustrated battle plans, to Dublin's General Post Office, where an Irish republic was proclaimed. For six days they held out, and Connolly was wounded twice before the insurgents, faced with an overwhelming British assault, threw in their hand.

The leaders of the Easter Rising were put up against a wall and shot, and even the fact of Connolly's acutely gangrenous leg did not spare him the same treatment. He was physically unable to stand upright when he was taken to Kilmainham gaol early on 12 May, but the British Empire wasn't one to stand on ceremony. He was strapped to a chair, and the firing squad put an end to the life of Ireland's greatest socialist.

That life was never the easiest, and getting his message across always proved difficult. But now that he couldn't even shout to make his voice heard, spreading Connolly's message would become an increasingly uphill battle.

The posthumous publication of James Connolly's writings hit its first snag before he was even posthumous. On 9 May 1916, as he lay dying in Dublin Castle, tortured by gangrene, he asked his eldest daughter Nora to see if his fellow socialist Francis Sheehy Skeffington could arrange to publish some of his songs. His immediate consideration was to scrape some money together for his wife and children – soon to be his widow and orphans – but he also wanted to see his work survive him, and knew that Skeffington would do the job well.

The problem was that Connolly's comrade had found a quicklime grave before him. On the third day of the Rising, having been taken prisoner while trying to prevent looting, Skeffington was shot on the orders of a British officer who was subsequently declared insane. The nearest Connolly would ever have to a literary executor was no more.

Connolly had always taken great care not only in writing and publishing his work, but also in attempting to preserve it as far as possible. His pamphlet *The New Evangel Preached to Irish Toilers* (1901), as well as the first part of *Socialism Made Easy* (1909), are collections of articles he had published earlier. The files of *The Workers' Republic* and *The Harp* contain many a reprinted article.

He was just as scrupulous when it came to his revolutionary predecessors. In 1897 he published some forgotten writings of the 1848 revolutionary Fintan Lalor, and a series of *'98 Readings*, which rescued from academic neglect many writings from the United Irish insurrection of 1798. In *Labour in Irish History* he noted that, while the heroic exploits of the United Irishmen formed the stock in trade of many a historian, the literature of the movement was all but unknown. One editor had suppressed many of their productions because of their 'trashy' republican and irreligious tendencies.

This is to be regretted, as it places upon other biographers and historians the trouble (a thousand times more difficult now) of searching for anew, and re-collecting the literary material from which to build a proper appreciation of the work of those pioneers of democracy in Ireland.

Future generations, he felt, might well conclude 'that the stones rejected by the builders of the past have become the corner-stones of the edifice'.[6]

Connolly was composing his own bibliographical epitaph. Fear of his revolutionary message would combine with intellectual dog-laziness and a fair dash of sheer bad luck to keep a fearful amount of his work effectively hidden from view for the next 80 years.

Thankfully, things didn't start off that badly. The year after Connolly's death saw Maunsel publish his 1910 classic *Labour in Irish History*, together with *The Re-conquest of Ireland* (1915), under the title *Labour in Ireland*. The recently re-formed SPI published *The New Evangel* the same year, as well as those songs, around the same time, in *The Legacy and Songs of Freedom*.

So, some of Connolly's works were available to the Irish working class during the most revolutionary period in its history so far. The theoretical demands arising from that period led the SPI to publish *Labour, Nationality and Religion* (which first appeared in 1910) in 1920. The Irish Transport and General Workers' Union (ITGWU) published Section II of *Socialism Made Easy*, combined with a 1914 article of Connolly's, as *The Axe to the Root* the year after.

The revolutionary left in Britain also felt the need of their former comrade's writings. The Socialist Labour Party published a version of *Socialism Made Easy* in Scotland. Though more complete than the ITGWU edition, it annoyingly left out parts of Section I.

Erin's Hope: The end and the means, Connolly's first pamphlet, from 1896, was now the only Connolly pamphlet not to be republished since his execution, a gap filled when it now appeared (for some reason) under the title *The Irish Revolution*. Connolly's son Roddy edited it in the name of the James Connolly Publishing Company, which ambitiously proposed to publish a complete, annotated edition of the 'Life, Works, and Letters of James Connolly'. But the far left, including Roddy Connolly's young Communist Party of Ireland (CPI), was by then fighting a rearguard action against the ebb of the revolutionary tide, and such a laudable project lay far beyond its scant resources.

One of the problems lay in the figure of William O'Brien, the effective leader of the ITGWU. Sheehy Skeffington's execution meant that he became Connolly's literary executor by sheer default. He does appear to have once had some good intentions regarding Connolly's writings – but they soon became paving stones to the proverbial destination. The project of making Connolly's work available was subordinated to O'Brien's own project in the Irish labour movement.

While far from alone, O'Brien was the leading embodiment of the labour lieutenant – ready to talk left as the occasion demanded and nod in the direction of the martyred Connolly, but happiest sitting round a table in the corridors of power negotiating 'on behalf of his members' with the great and the good. The worst manifestations of this spirit are to be found in the lost battles and clever deals spanning a long career, but James Connolly's writings also paid the price.

O'Brien had managed to gather together Connolly's letters and documents, as well as the only substantial collection in the country of Connolly's newspapers. He had them, and he was going to use them. So Roddy and Nora Connolly, two of the young Turks who were just after expelling him from the SPI as a reformist – before turning the party into the CPI – could whistle for them. The fact that the James Connolly Publishing Company was the child of Connolly's heirs, both literally and politically (the CPI, for all its faults, was the body trying to carry on Connolly's work), cut no ice with him.

He had other uses in mind for the writings. When Jim Larkin returned from America in 1923 after a nine-year absence, and the ITGWU split, O'Brien played the trump card he'd had up his sleeve. He published extracts from letters in which Connolly had expressed his frustration at the reckless and unpredictable twists and turns of Larkin's leadership of the union.[7] Perceptive readers spotted the deliberate mistake – that Connolly wanted a disciplined revolutionary spirit, whereas O'Brien wanted no revolutionary spirit at all – but the pattern was set: Connolly's writings were a political football that William O'Brien could take off the field when he felt like it.

A 17-year standstill then ensued, until 1941, when the Communist Party of Great Britain published *A Socialist and War 1914–16*, edited by P. J. Musgrave.[8] This was the first collection of articles by Connolly, as opposed to a book or pamphlet reprint. It consisted of 19 articles written by Connolly during the war, well chosen and well presented.

But, of course, the CPGB were not actuated by a disinterested desire to spread the Connolly gospel. They were attempting to draw a parallel between the two world wars. The Communist line at the time was that World War II was a war between two equally bad imperialist powers, pure and simple, just like its predecessor. So the introduction and footnotes to *A Socialist and War* compared the British government's attacks on workers' rights in 1914–16 with the same government's attacks in 1939–41.

The only problem with the line was that one of those imperialist powers was fascist, and the other – willing as it was to compromise with the Nazis – was not; and the fact that many on the latter side went to war in the firm belief that they were fighting to get rid of fascism. The Communists were forcibly reminded of Nazism's presence later in 1941 when Hitler, showing a most unbusinesslike lack of respect for the pact he had signed with Stalin over the grave of Poland, decided to invade Russia.

The line from Moscow hurriedly changed, and the Communist Parties proceeded to jump out of the frying pan into the fire. While the old line at least allowed them to stand up for workers' rights against wartime government encroachments, this backflip meant that Winston Churchill was all of a sudden a brave democrat leading a people's war against the very fascism he had admired not so long before.

Troublesome revolutionaries, who were of the belief that the working class was the real force that could overthrow tyranny, became something of a back number. *A Socialist and War* was consigned with indecent haste to the fires of oblivion. The first decent collection of Connolly was nice while it lasted, if only it lasted a bit longer.

By the end of the decade, however, things were starting to look up. Between 1948 and 1951 three volumes of Connolly's writings, edited by Desmond Ryan, were published: *Socialism and Nationalism, Labour and Easter Week* and *The Workers' Republic*.[9] Over 500 pages of Connolly, beautifully printed, were made available – and cheaply, thanks to an ITGWU subsidy. The fact that, after all these years, these volumes remain the highpoint of Connolly scholarship says something about them.

But it also says something about the standard of Connolly scholarship. For they are far from perfect collections. Desmond Ryan had shown in his works on the Easter Rising, on its political head Pádraig Pearse, and on Connolly himself a fine grasp of the history of the period Connolly worked in. But his understanding of Connolly's politics had its limitations – his biography of Connolly,[10] for instance, concluded that he would have accepted the Anglo-Irish Treaty settlement of 1921 rather than war against it – and his rather platitudinous introduction to *Socialism and Nationalism* did nothing to go beyond those limitations.

But far worse was the man standing at the editor's shoulder. Ryan acknowledged 'the co-operation and ripe judgment of Mr William O'Brien' upon whose 'unrivalled library of Connolly books, papers and manuscripts' the collections were based. And if that wasn't bad enough, the volumes appeared at a time when the ripe co-operator O'Brien and his ITGWU were going through a distinctly right-wing phase, even by their own standards.

They had just succeeded in splitting the entire Irish labour movement in two. As the ITGWU's dominance of the movement began to wane by the 1940s, they resorted to drastic measures, with the help of the right-wing Fianna Fáil government and the Catholic Church. The government made O'Brien, great follower of Connolly that he was, a director of the Central Bank of Ireland, and introduced a Trade Union Act which, had it not proved too unconstitutional for the Supreme Court itself to stomach, would have effectively deprived other unions of recognition. For its part, the ITGWU accused the labour movement of being run by a Communist plot no less, and, pausing only to ask the bishops to launch an enquiry into this nefarious conspiracy, set up a rival trade union congress and labour party, suitably cleansed of socialists, atheists and foreigners.

Vice, as always, paid homage to virtue: the publication of some of Connolly's writings was an attempt to take an intellectual high ground in the labour movement, to claim Connolly's mantle for the ITGWU and company. As such, the series was bound to bear the mark of its origin. So, because the ITGWU was at war with the so-called British unions, Connolly's articles on the magnificent support shown by British workers during the Dublin lockout of 1913 were not included. Because the ITGWU was cosying up to the Catholic Church, *Labour, Nationality and Religion* with its tales of ecclesiastical support for the rich and powerful was almost left out, and when it was left in was prefaced by a chronologically out-of-place article from years later – which just happened to be the most conciliatory to the Catholic Church of all Connolly's writings. And because the leaders of the ITGWU had become a comfortable bureaucracy feathering their own nests, Connolly's articles on the dangers of trade union officialdom and the need for a rank-and-file fight were mysteriously absent.

O'Brien's introduction to *Labour and Easter Week* was, let it be said, interesting to the historian of Connolly's last years. No such claims could be made for the introduction William McMullen, another of the ITGWU leadership, wrote for *The Workers' Republic*. He recalled his and Connolly's opposition to calling off socialist meetings in Belfast at the start of the war, but somehow neglected to mention that, at those same meetings, he himself had spoken against opposing the war. But as he had already disremembered enough to accept a Fianna Fáil nomination to the Irish Senate, perhaps his forgetfulness is not to be wondered at.

Desmond Ryan's editorial style had its own faults. Many of the articles were only extracts, usually without being presented as such. He saw fit to alter some aspects of the texts now and again. Repeatedly, he ripped the odd paragraph from an article, presenting it in the form of a footnote, which usually posed more questions than it answered – although constraints of space and the ripe judgment of William O'Brien may be to blame here.

But when all is said and done, the Ryan selections were a good start to the work of placing the publication of Connolly on a sound basis. Or they would have been a good start if they had been followed up: but for the next 17 years we'd have no choice but to put up with them, because they were all we were getting.

The late 1960s broke the log-jam. The fiftieth anniversary of the Easter Rising reminded people that Connolly was by far the most interesting and relevant of the men of 1916. The centenary of Connolly's birth in 1968 raised interest further.

But more importantly, these dates coincided with an upsurge of struggle across the world, from Paris to Vietnam to Derry.

When people were fighting to close down the carnival of reaction that Connolly foresaw, they were interested in what he had to say. When revolution was back on the worldwide agenda after decades of enervating stability, the revolutionaries were interested in what Connolly had to say. When Connolly's birth and Connolly's death were being commemorated, people were interested in what the man had to say in between. The external impulse of rebellion forced Connolly's writings out into the open.

In 1968, the small Irish Communist Organisation (ICO) began to publish a series of 'Connolly's Suppressed Articles', selections of his writings from the Scottish weekly *Forward*.[11] The prefaces to these typewritten pamphlets were resplendent with indiscriminate attacks on Connolly's various suppressors, but, although the ICO came dangerously close to placing Messrs O'Brien and Ryan on the grassy knoll when Kennedy was assassinated, their attitude was infinitely superior to the indifferent shrugging of shoulders displayed elsewhere.

(In 1971, the ICO suddenly discovered that all this time they had been labouring under the misconception that there was just the one nation in Ireland – when all along, they now said, there were two, one of them being an Ulster Protestant nation whose right to self-determination was being denied by the nasty anti-partitionists. After repenting 'the "one-nation" myth of Catholic bourgeois nationalism' and rechristening themselves the *British and* Irish Communist Organisation (B&ICO), they republished *Press Poisoners in Ireland*, recanting their own and Connolly's 'Catholic nationalist deviations'. Thankfully, the articles following the preface refuted the 'two-nations' myth propounded in it. The B&ICO started describing ever-decreasing circles around their own sectarian plughole, but not before a not inconsiderable number of the spokespersons of the Catholic bourgeoisie came round to their way of thinking. The B&ICO had published their last Connolly.)

Also in 1968, the CPI – who, to their eternal credit, kept *Labour in Irish History* and other Connolly writings in print after the ITGWU got bored with them – published *Revolutionary Warfare*, which contained Connolly's 1915 articles on street fighting.[12] In 1971, *Socialism Made Easy* was published in full, for the first time since Connolly's death.[13]

The only serious Connolly selection, besides the Ryan volumes, came in 1973 when Owen Dudley Edwards and Bernard Ransom edited *Selected Political Writings*.[14] It included 17 new articles, and editorially is still the most honest and rigorous effort. However, the predeliction of the editors (particularly Dudley Edwards, as evidenced in his earlier study of Connolly)[15] for a 'Christian socialist' interpretation of Connolly marred the selection somewhat.

In the early and mid-1970s, the Cork Workers' Club joined a good few dots in the picture of Connolly's writings. A *James Connolly Songbook* brought some more verse; *Ireland upon the Dissecting Table* gathered some new writings on the North; and *The Connolly–De Leon Controversy* republished a crucial debate in Connolly's development.[16]

This period also, however, saw a couple of collections that advanced the cause of publishing Connolly not an inch. *The Best of Connolly*, edited by Proinsias Mac Aonghusa and Liam Ó Réagáin,[17] consisted entirely of pieces lifted by the editors from the old ITGWU selections. P. Berresford Ellis's *Selected Writings*[18] was slightly better, the editor going to the trouble of borrowing from *Selected Political Writings* and the *Songbook* as well as the old ITGWU selections.

The Connolly–De Leon Controversy appeared in 1976, and there followed 20 years when the publication of Connolly's work ground to a complete halt. The same old story of indifference, complacency and fear of Connolly's message made for the longest barren period ever.

It wasn't for lack of things to publish: hundreds of Connolly's articles lay there, as did his letters, not to mention a play. For William O'Brien had finally shuffled off this mortal coil, and so found himself unable to maintain his vice-like grip on his unrivalled library, which passed into the hands of the National Library of Ireland.[19]

But instead of this work becoming available to the general reader, there was much running to keep still. 1986 saw *The Words of James Connolly*, edited by a great-grandson of his, James Connolly Heron.[20] It consisted of nothing more than odd paragraphs taken from writings already available and arranged under arbitrary chapter headings, and consituted a degeneration rather than a progression.

Another false dawn followed, although even false dawns

brighten things up a little. The East German Communist Party
offered to publish Connolly's writings on behalf of their Irish
counterpart, which willingly took up the offer. Lack of time
meant that all they could manage was a reprint of the ITGWU
volumes together with *Revolutionary Warfare*. But with touching
innocence, they decided to baptise the two stout volumes
Connolly's *Collected Works*,[21] thus perpetuating the cosy myth
that all Connolly's writings were available. But the CPI were
hardly to blame for the fact that turning the clock back 40
years consituted some kind of a step forward.

As if to crown this 20-year voyage in the wilderness, in
1995 Proinsias Mac Aonghusa presented a book of isolated
quotes, adding nothing to his earlier selection but claiming to
represent *What Connolly Said*, if you don't mind.[22] Appropri-
ately enough, it was the leader of the Fianna Fáil party who
was prevailed upon to launch the effort.

A tiny crack in the ice appeared finally in 1996, when the
James Connolly Memorial Initiative unveiled a fine statue of
Connolly in Dublin. They found room in the souvenir programme for a speech of Connolly's from 1911, together with an
article by the present editor.

Which brings us to this collection. Contained here are 65
articles and speeches by Connolly never before published, in
whole or in part, in any collection of his writings.[23] All
items are presented in their entirety, with nothing added and
nothing taken away.

Many aspects of Connolly come through in these writings.
He emerges in his rightful capacity: as an original socialist
propagandist and agitator, bringing forward and developing
socialist theory and practice in a living way. The international-
ism of his activities and his thoughts shines through. Even
1913 and 1916, the two biggest events in Connolly's career,
haven't been properly covered up to now – but here appears
Connolly the strategist of the lockout, and Connolly the revolutionary trying to strike a blow against the British ruling class
and its murderous war.

This collection means that the gaping hole in the publication of Connolly's writings won't gape so much. But it
remains a huge one all the same. Hundreds of Connolly's
articles have still yet to get beyond the National Library, as
have all his letters. And while this selection was based on

the same library's collection, there's a backload of Connolly's writings scattered throughout the papers of the working-class movement in Scotland, England, the United States, and maybe elsewhere.

This will not do. Connolly's work should be available to those he wrote it for. On the bus home from work, or after putting the kids to bed, or while waiting for the rent allowance, people should be able to read an article or two of Connolly's. They should be able to read, appreciate and think about Connolly's entire work as a socialist thinker. The ambitious project of Connolly's heirs has to be resurrected – a start has to be made on the Complete Works of James Connolly.

And no one ever said it was going to be easy. This world is run by people who have everything to lose if Connolly's revolutionary message is heard and acted on. Within the labour movement itself there is no shortage of those who fear to speak of 1868–1916. Excavating Connolly's writings will mean challenging, implicitly and explicitly, those who have an interest in keeping them buried.

Because this is no mere bibliographical problem: it's not just a question of how long it will take so many men to fill a hole. The reason for making Connolly's work available is to continue and finish that work. In a world built around exploitation and oppression, Connolly helps us to understand the causes of exploitation and oppression, and to fight against them. When push comes to shove, Connolly will be brought into the light as an element in building a movement that can enable the working class to drag the human race out of its present mess, and create a socialist society in Ireland and beyond. And some of the stones rejected in the past could well be the cornerstones in that edifice.

Aindrias Ó Cathasaigh
Dublin, 1997

Part One

The Workers' Republic 1898–1903

After coming to Ireland in 1896, Connolly found outlets for his propaganda for an Irish workers' republic wherever he could, but British labour papers and Irish republican papers were a poor substitute for an ISRP paper. As if to confirm Connolly's Marxist explanation of the dependence of the ideological on the economic, however, the party's financial position (or lack of it) precluded that. A loan of £50 from his old comrade Keir Hardie was needed before Connolly could finally realise the ambition.

The Workers' Republic was launched upon an unsuspecting world on 13 August 1898. The paper would always open with Connolly's 'Home Thrusts' column, discussing the issues of the day with a sense of humour that carried a vicious sting in its tail. The editorial would be an opportunity for Connolly to apply socialist theory to the world around him.

The paper made great strides, but often ran out of shoe leather. It had to pack up after two months, but returned the following summer, printed by the party members themselves. It was now written, edited, printed and sold by Connolly and his comrades – which led the Dublin printers to take umbrage, until Connolly convinced them that he was no more scabbing on them than he was scabbing on the barbers when he shaved himself in the morning. The *Workers' Republic* appeared most weeks until expiring in February 1900. Three months later it rose again, but retreated to a fortnightly in October – having come out, as Connolly remarked, so weakly it almost died – and a monthly from the following February.

Because it was produced, in Connolly's words, 'by the voluntary labour of men who during the day have been drudging in the service of a capitalist exploiter', it hardly set standards of technical excellence, but, again in Connolly's words, 'let the soundness of the doctrine preached compensate for the lack of excellence in the printing'. The great virtue of *The Workers' Republic* was that it set forth the clean, hard politics of the ISRP, lambasting anyone and everyone who stood between the working class and the socialist republic.

Connolly's writings in the paper deserve recognition above all for their pioneering position on the national question. While many socialists floundered on the issue, Connolly boldly proclaimed that a central part of the Irish working class's contribution to the international fight for socialism was the overthrow of the British Empire in Ireland. Not only should they take part in the national struggle, they should lead it, as all the other classes were too comfortable and afraid to overthrow anything, for fear that they might be next in line. The fight for independence, argued Connolly, had to be a part of the workers' fight for the ideal embodied in the paper's title.

The Workers' Republic reflects the enthusiastic activism of the ISRP, which put them at the forefront of protests against royalty and the imperialist war in South Africa, and made them something of a force to be reckoned with in the emerging Irish labour movement. Surprisingly in view of his later development, Connolly was given to downplaying the effectiveness of strikes and trade unionism in this period, often placing a higher premium on electoral activity. However, this was a fault common to socialists internationally at the time – and world developments in the socialist movement always found a place in the paper.

The demise of *The Workers' Republic* accompanied the demise of the ISRP itself. Connolly edited the last two issues of the paper from Scotland.

HOME THRUSTS

[20 August 1898]

The statement made by one of our contributors in last week's issue that the action of the '98 Executive in fixing the date for the Wolfe Tone Demonstration on 15th August, a generally recognised Catholic festival, would be fraught with evil consequences,[1] has already been justified.

The return of the Belfast contingent from Dublin to the former city was made the occasion of a sectarian outburst in the streets, in the course of which Protestant and Catholic belaboured each other in the most beautiful manner, in a truly Christian spirit.

> And proved their doctrine orthodox,
> By Apostolic blows and knocks.

He who could hit the hardest felt himself master of the soundest theology, and he whose blows did not flatten out his opponents' skull was, no doubt, afflicted by conscientious scruples as to his own orthodoxy.

And when Catholic and Protestant workmen absented themselves from work next morning in order to procure the needed sticking-plaster for their craniums, Catholic and Protestant employers stopped their wages accordingly with the most beautiful impartiality.

Commend me to an employer of labour for strict impartiality in his dealings between workmen of different creeds. If the Catholic employer can make more profit out of a Protestant workman than out of a Catholic, he does not allow religious scruples to bind *him*. Oh, no!

He straightaway discharges his co-religionist and engages the man who yields him the greatest plunder. And the Protestant employer is equally fair-minded (*sic*) in his dealings with the Protestant worker.

Harland and Wolff, Belfast, are great Protestants and Unionists, so are their workmen. But in the course of an industrial dispute in the shipbuilding trade a few years ago, the Protestant employer locked out the Protestant workmen and *starved* or attempted to starve them into subjection.

Mr Alderman Meade and the Master Builders' Association on the one hand and the building trades on the other point the moral on the Catholic side for Dublin readers, who have not forgotten the building trade dispute of '96.[2]

To the employing class, as a whole, we might indeed apply the terms employed by John Mitchel[3] to the Anglo-Saxon section of them. Listen –

> They worship money, they pray to no other god but money, they would buy and sell the Holy Ghost for money, and they believe the whole world is created, sustained, and governed, and can only be saved by the one true, immutable and almighty £ s d.

Wherefore, oh, my Belfast Brethren, should you make your city a scandal to Europe by insensate fights over religious dogmas, while as you spill each other's boozy blood throughout the streets, the ruling class in industry and politics calmly seat themselves firmer upon your backs and dive their hands deeper into your pockets.

Consider, do our masters fight over religion when their pockets are involved? No. The only union of Home Ruler and Unionist we have had in the last generation, viz, that over the Financial Relations Question,[4] was on a question not of principle, but of purse.

Not the purse of the people. Indeed with most of the working class a purse would be a mere superfluity, like breeches to a highlandman, or a conscience to a politician. They would not have any use for it, or know what to do with it.

For the Financial Relations Question does not concern the workers in town or country. Our wages as workers are fixed, roughly speaking, by our competition for employment. If there are many unemployed, our wages *will be* low; if there are few idle, our wages *may be* high; but whether our masters pay heavy direct taxation or none at all, does not affect our wages.

Ditto with the tenants in the country districts. Their rents are fixed by the Land Court in proportion, not to the value of the land, but in proportion to their ability to pay.[5] In estimating that ability, taxes are taken into consideration as well as prices of agricultural produce.

If, not merely Ireland's (?) over-taxation, but all taxes in Ireland were abolished tomorrow, the Land Court would see in that fact a reason why the tenant, his expenses being lower, could pay a higher rent, and would fix it accordingly.

The Financial Relations agitation is merely a fight between Irish capitalists and landlords, and English capitalists and landlords. The working people can not hope for anything good as a result of the struggle, except, perhaps, that it might end like the famous struggle between the Kilkenny cats – in the mutual destruction of both parties.[6]

The only Financial Relation with which the working class are concerned generally hangs out three golden balls.[7]

Oh, my prophetic soul, my uncle.

The Commemoration Banquet at the Mansion House[8] produced some curious results. I do not know whether it was due to the liquor or the excitement, or both combined, but certain it is that the speakers seemed to mix up their opinions and sentiments in the most wonderful manner.

Our Lord Mayor was especially felicitous (?) in his remarks.

'He was himself,' he assured the audience, 'descended from people who had to fly from their peasant home to the mountains to escape persecution.' He forgot to point out the moral, and so we can only guess at it. Perhaps he meant that in view of that fact he had made up his mind that he, at least, did not intend to be forced to fly to the mountains if acting the flunkey would keep him at home.

Therefore he hastened to make the astounding declaration – astounding in such a time and place – that 'he claimed that Irishmen could best govern themselves, *and could do it best under English Law.*'

Lord Mayor Tallon won't fly to the mountains if he knows it. The Mansion House is good enough for him. The mountains can wait.

Poor Wolfe Tone. Lived, fought, and suffered for Ireland in order that a purse-proud, inflated windbag should exploit your memory to his own aggrandisement.

Lord Mayor Tallon is also reported to have said that 'after many years of residence in Dublin he was as good an Irishman as when he entered it.' What did this mean?

Are we to understand that he considers the people of Dublin so bad a lot that he should be complimented for his tenacity in sticking to his patriotism in *their* company?

If not what does he mean? Perhaps that, however, is not a fair question. Perhaps the wine was good. Perhaps the capacity of our Lord Mayor for assimilating liquors is no greater than his capacity for talking sense.

Which is saying a great deal.

Mr John O'Leary[9] labours under the disadvantage of age, and, consequently, it is not safe to accept as literally correct any newspaper report of his speech. So I can only hope that his utterances at the banquet, as reported, were not his exact sentiments.

He is reported to have said, 'He infinitely preferred that Ireland should be under her own laws, and not English laws,' which was of course right enough. So say all of us.

But he went on, 'He did not mind whether it was a republic, an absolute monarchy, or a limited monarchy.' According to this theory, if the Queen of England were to come to

Dublin and get crowned Queen of Ireland the aspirations of Irish Nationalists would be realized.

Some of our theoretical revolutionists of the political type are fond of building great hopes on the possibility of an alliance between France and Russia against England. If this did happen and Russian troops landed in Ireland, kicked England out and then crowned the Czar absolute monarch of Ireland, according to Mr O'Leary's theory we would be free.

But perhaps I will be told this is not a fair assumption, because the Czar would not then rule by the free consent of the Irish people, but by the power of his bayonets. But does an absolute monarch ever rule solely by the consent of his people? Does he not always depend upon his bayonets?

Do our friends only object to tyranny when it is English? Would they hug their chains if they were guaranteed of Irish manufacture?

But if our friends think only of native Irish Kings will they please tell us where to get them.

Will the gentle and courtier-like Tim Healy[10] do?

How would this read in our newspapers. 'His Royal Highness Timothy I, King of All Ireland, held a levee at Dublin Castle to-day. Lords Harrington, Dillon and Redmond attended as pages-in-waiting. Amongst others present we noticed T. P. O'Connor, Esq,[11] who as bearer of the royal snuff-box was the object of considerable admiration.'

This you will say, dear reader, is only fooling. It is. But so is the talk of those people who talk of revolting against British rule and refuse to recognise the fact that our way to freedom can only be hewn by the strong hand of *labour*, and that labour revolts against oppression of *all kinds*, not merely against the peculiarly British brand.

The whole edifice of modern society to-day is built upon the oppression and plunder of labour. The Sovereign on her throne, the nobleman in his palace, the capitalist in his mansion, the judge on the bench, and the lawyer at the bar are all pensioners on the labour of the workers, are all seated like Sinbad's Old Man of the Sea astride the back of the worker riding him to social death.

The politics of the master class are only the quarrels of thieves over the division of the spoil. The politics of the working class are the organised efforts of the victims conscious of the thieving, to put an end to the system of society which makes it possible.

The mixed character of all speeches in connection with the '98 movement, at the banquet and elsewhere, proves conclusively that our middle-class leaders are afraid to trust democracy. In the midst of their most fervent vituperations against the British Government, there rises up before their mind's eye the spectacle of the Irish working people demanding Freedom for their class from the economic slavery of to-day.

And struck with affright the middle-class politician buttons up *his* trousers pocket, and shoving his hand deep into the pockets of his working class compatriots, cries out as his fingers close upon the plunder: 'No class questions in Irish politics.'

So our middle-class become Home Rulers, secretly or openly leaning to the British Constitution.

What is the difference between the Unionist and the Home Ruler? Answer: Starting from the postulate that we accept Mitchel's definition of the British Empire, as 'a pirate institution robbing and plundering upon the public highway' we must conclude that the Unionists wish to keep the Irish people as *subjects* of the British Empire, the Home Ruler desires to raise them to the dignity of *accomplices*.

And the Socialist Republican wishes to kick the whole Empire and all its fraudulent institutions into the outer darkness.

And once it is effectually elevated from off the face of this planet it has so long cursed by its presence, whether it goes to join the angels above or the politicians below is no concern of

SPAILPÍN.[12]

HOME THRUSTS

[3 September 1898]

The compositor fiend had his innings last week. Whether it was revolutionary enthusiasm or loyalist spleen which disturbed his brain we know not, but we do know that pages 3 and 7 and part of page 6 of our last issue presented to the readers a new species of grammar and orthography decidedly unknown to the writers of this paper.

The spelling was as vile as the principles of a hireling scribe on an Unionist or Home Rule newspaper, and the grammar was as doubtful as the patriotism of a politician.

We are assured by the printer that precautions have been taken to prevent the recurrence of such mistakes. We hope so. The fiend capable of such an atrocity as we complain of ought to be bound hand and foot and thrown among the wild beasts – in the City Hall.[13]

United Ireland, which still drags on its painful career, presumably by means of the donations begged from the country priests, takes us to task for our exposure of the double-dealing practised by certain leading lights in the '98 Executive, in the matter of speech-making and toast-drinking.[14]

It asks can we not 'recognise the distinction between the men who ostentatiously drink a toast which a Nationalist cannot with regard to himself honour, and the person who, though present when the toast is given, does not drink it, but treats it with calm indifference'?

How beautifully that sentence is worded. The *suggestio falsi* was never more cleverly introduced. Mr Harrington does not attempt to *prove* that the persons referred to did not drink the loyal toast, but he gently hints to them a way by which they can escape the censure they so richly deserve.

We can imagine these gentlemen as soon as they read the paragraph in *United Ireland* immediately chorussing, 'Yes, that's it, we were there of course but we did not drink the toast, we treated the toast with indifference.'

But swallowed the liquor with joy.

Now in order to prove the absurdity of this excuse let us put a parallel case. Suppose that at each of the functions referred to, viz, the Press Banquet at Malahide and Health Congress Banquet in Dublin, the convenors had put upon the list of toasts, *An Irish Republic*; would the loyalists present have sat in silence or allowed their names to go to the newspapers as participating in the function?

And if they had would *their* newspapers have remained silent over the matter as our Home Rule rags have done?

Is it too much to expect that our Nationalist politicians (so-called) shall at least be as consistent in their public actions as the Unionists whom they pretend to oppose?

Does not the howl set up by all those middle-class journalists when any of their number is exposed, and their little treacheries held up to the light of day, betray an uneasy conscience?

But *United Ireland* wants the *Workers' Republic* to be more impartial, forsooth. It asks what about Alderman Pile who, 'at a dinner recently not only drank the health of the Queen but proposed the toast himself and bubbled all over with delight when he saw his guests honouring it'?

Well, never in our wildest dreams did we imagine Alderman Pile to be a Nationalist. He owes his position in the Corporation of Dublin to the fact that that body is elected on a restricted franchise. He is a fitting representative of the middle-class who elected him.

Like yourself, Tim, my dear boy, he is not, nor, perhaps, ever would be elected to that body by the workers' votes.

But, *United Ireland* continues, 'Alderman Pile was, a few days before this loyal performance, co-opted on the Wolfe Tone Committee.'

Sorry to hear it, but not surprised. The Wolfe Tone Committee is the child of the '98 Executive, which at its inception was thoroughly honest and patriotic, but which is now dominated and controlled by the quondam members of Mr Harrington's United Irishmen Centennial Association.

It is a pity the Wolfe Tone Committee should so co-opt some men who propose and other men who drink loyal toasts, but after swallowing Mr Harrington's nest of wire-pullers, it should easily assimilate a common or garden Alderman.

Why do we insist so much upon outspokenness in such matters? Because there is just now a perfect land-slide in a loyalist direction in Ireland. Home Rule Lord Mayors shaking hands with Tory Lord Lieutenants,[15] Home Rule Editors drinking loyal toasts to-day and writing 'patriotic articles' tomorrow, Home Rule Corporations electing Tory Lord Mayors, the conquest of Ireland at last accepted and ratified by her sons.

Said Darby the Blast in Lever's novel, *Tom Burke of Ours*, 'Bad luck to the gintry, 'tis the gintry ever and always betrayed us.'

Since our Home Rule politicians were graciously permitted to associate with Lords and Earls on the Financial Relations agitation, all the virility and aggressiveness has gone out of our public life, and our politicians are now afraid to utter a single sentence which might not suit their new allies.

If this loyalist reaction is to be stopped and the tide of public feeling set flowing in a more healthy direction, we require strong, vigorous speech and action, both in public and private.

Therefore we say: away with middle-class leadership, which means middle-class compromise, middle-class trickery, middle-class time-serving, middle-class treachery. Room for the strong hand and clear brain of Labour.

We can assure our friends there is no trace of personal feeling in our attitude towards the middle-class politicians and their hireling scribes.

If we cherish any other feeling towards them than that of amused contempt it must be that feeling which animates the naturalist when he gazes upon some strange freak of nature – just newly caught and not yet classified.

The 'freaks' which abound in Irish politics to-day are in our opinion the outcome of the foolishness of so many of our countrymen in insisting upon a 'broad platform.'

They will have no exclusiveness, they tell us, and open out their ranks to all who like to enter, and no questions asked. Their organizations are run on the same principles as Barnum's menagerie. Pay the entrance money and you have the run of the show.

As a result they get what they want, a 'broad platform,' so broad in fact is it you can neither discover where it begins or ends.

For our part we are for a narrow platform, a platform so narrow that there will not be a place on it where anyone not an uncompromising enemy of tyranny can rest the soles of his feet.

And yet broad enough for every honest man. Eh, Tim.

Next for shaving.

'Roll on, thou deep and dark blue Ocean, roll.' So sang the poet in his most condescending mood. But I have never heard that the ocean rolled either faster or slower because of the permission thus graciously accorded to it.

And I am just inclined to think that the onward rolling ocean of Labour will pay as little heed to the bland advice which the Dublin dailies are so freely distributing on the question of labour representation.

Now that the scribes perceive the working men are determined on having their class represented they are all purring forth their approval of the step. As they are not strong enough to oppose they seem resolved to try what flattery can do to prevent the working men entering the Council animated with strong class feelings.

If they are so convinced of the value of labour representation, how many parliamentary seats are they prepared to hand over to labour candidates? Eh, my soft-spoken friends.

Now don't all speak at once. We know you all are in Parliament at an immense sacrifice to yourselves, and that you only remain there for your country's sake, so the opportunity of leaving it will be a perfect godsend to you. Who will hand up his seat to a *bona fide* representative of labour, chosen, say, by the Trades Councils of Dublin, Waterford, Cork and Limerick respectively?

What, no answer. You are still resolved to sacrifice yourselves for your country's good – on the cushioned seats and in the well-upholstered smoke-rooms of the British Parliament.

Heroic self-sacrifice, unselfish devotion!

The *Freeman's Journal*, commenting on the Bristol Trades Union Congress, declares that a period has opened in which the war between labour and capital will be waged in a more bitter and uncompromising spirit than ever.

It declares that the recent engineers' lockout[16] has proven the crushing strength masters can bring to bear when organized, and regrets the defeat of the unions, not, mark, because the *Freeman's Journal* sympathises with labour, but because, in its own words, 'they [the unions] have acted as the *most effective of all defences against the revolutionary ideas* that find such fertile soil in France, Germany or Italy. Their disappearance would not mean the cessation of the activity of the workers for their advantage, but the diversion of it into new and far more dangerous channels.'

I am glad to hear a capitalistic organ like the *Freeman* so openly admitting that Socialism is a more 'dangerous' foe to the exploitation or robbery of labour than trade unions are. But what shall we say then of the danger (to oppression) of trades unionism and Socialism *combined*, as they are on the Continent, and as they will be here when the Irish worker divests himself of the fear of politics in trade unions – a fear imported into this country from the conservative, slow-moving trade organizations of Great Britain.

The London correspondent of the *Freeman* also informs us that 'the Trades Union Congress is presided over, for the first time, by a Socialist, and moreover by an Irishman, Mr James O'Grady of Bristol.'

He then goes on to say – 'Mr O'Grady is possessed of sound common sense.' Of course, Mr Correspondent, that is why he is a Socialist.

Go thou and do likewise.

And be assured that the democracy of Ireland are not in the least afraid of 'revolutionary ideas' even if the old woman of Prince's Street[17] is.

If you shriek in our ears about 'Continental Socialism,' we
will shout back "tis better than British capitalism,' which will
be a comforting reflection to cheer the heart of a
                                                    SPAILPÍN.

THE INDEPENDENT *AND NEW MACHINERY*
[1 October 1898]

Our contemporary, the *Independent* newspaper, has lately introduced to its printing department some new machinery, which, it
has loudly informed the Irish public, is second to none in
Ireland, perhaps in Europe. We do not wish, in the smallest
degree, to disparage the enterprise or the management of the
Independent, but we think it right at this moment to offer to its
literary staff some free instruction in the elementary principles of
capitalist development; which free instruction, when thoroughly
assimilated, will, we think, somewhat cool their enthusiasm over
this achievement.

No one denies the right of a capitalist to introduce in his
business whatever new methods or new machinery may best
serve his purposes in competition with his rivals. Indeed in the
competitive field there is recognised no other law than the
survival of the fittest; ethics or religion are at all times deliber-
ately laid aside in the work-a-day world, and are only taken up
when the stern business of profit-making is interrupted by the
weekly Sunday holiday. Even then no preacher dare apply ethi-
cal considerations to economic questions; or treat of the former
in any other fashion than as mere abstractions having little, if
any, bearing upon the problems of civilization.

Socialists recognise these facts while denouncing them; our
enemies deny the facts while shaping their lives in accordance
therewith. This much being made clear to the reader it will at
once be perceived that our criticism is not likely to take the
form of merely railing against this new venture should it happen to displace labour; but will be directed towards another
point – a point probably even less understood than the one
alluded to.

Whosoever embarks in the competitive world must keep
pace with his rivals; should his industrial equipment fall
beneath the standard of his competitors he will go down in the
maelstrom of competition; his business will be drawn away
from him by the rival who better succeeds in satisfying the

public desires. If, therefore, one firm introduces into its business a machine capable of better work than its rivals, each of those rivals must also procure a similar machine or else see their business pass into the hands of their more enterprising competitor. They have absolutely no alternative. The public will go to the firm which suits them best and charges them least. Under pressure of this knowledge each firm so menaced hastens to procure machinery which will place it upon an equality with its rival; when this is accomplished and each firm stands similarly equipped and equal in productive capacity, they find that, as a result of all their anxiety and expenditure, they are exactly at the same point as they were before any such machinery was introduced. To use a homely simile:– Competition is like a crowd of people in the street striving to see some spectacle. One man gets a stool, and, standing upon it, sees better than his fellows; but should all the rest get stools and stand upon them, they would be at the same position for sight-seeing as if they all stood upon the ground.

In time, however, some one of the business firms we have spoken of – as typical of society in general – or some new competitor in the business, introduces some new machinery even better than the last; and if he is a wealthy competitor, his new machine cancels the value of all the old ones, and reduces them to the position of mere lumber. If their owners would save themselves from ruin they must equip themselves with machinery as good as this new product of the inventor's brain. Once again the weary circle must be retraced, until every firm is again equipped with the new invention, and, as a result, finds itself precisely at its starting point.

Each new machine invented renders nugatory the competitive value of all former machines; compels all the rivals of its owner to become owners of a like machine; and is generally in its turn replaced by an improvement making again a similar demand upon the owners of industry.

The *Independent* introduces, with a flourish of trumpets, an improved printing press. Shareholders smile in expectation of the long deferred dividend. But should it be found that this improvement accomplishes what it is intended to, viz, to draw advertisers away from the rivals of the *Independent* (the *Freeman's Journal* or *Irish Times*), the managerial departments of these journals will hasten also to introduce a similar machine; and so after the expenditure of much cash and energy, the competing daily papers of Dublin will find themselves again on equal terms, and not a whit better off than if such machinery had never crossed the sea.

Thus is the iron law of capitalism exemplified. Onward, ever onward, we are hurried by the pressure of economic forces; the greed of the capitalist, the competition of the market, the revolt of humane souls aghast at the atrocities of civilization, all working together toward the one end; and even when apparently in the fiercest antagonism contributing equally to produce a hatred of present conditions and so pave the way for the Socialist Republic.

THE SWEATING SYSTEM

[3 June 1899]

We are unfeignedly glad to see the members of the tailoring trade in Dublin bestirring themselves to put an end to the sweating system in connection with that industry. Unfortunately in a great many of our most important trades any discontent which exists is too often attributed to merely imaginary causes, and the money and energy of the workers frittered away in a foolish effort to win the co-operation of the employers in an attempt to better the condition of Labour.

In this move of the tailoring craft, however, there are to be found the tokens of a recognition on the part of the men that, from whatever quarter assistance may voluntarily come, from the side of the masters nothing can be hoped for, – except by pressure of the Union on the one hand or the threat of withdrawal of custom on the other. This fact helps to clear the air and will, no doubt, be highly beneficial to the men in so far as it will serve to solidify their ranks and compel them to realise that it is only by the financial and moral strength of their organisation they can hope to achieve success, and not at all by any reliance upon the goodwill of employers.

For the benefit of the general public we may here set down some of the principal factors in the dispute alluded to. The central grievance upon which attention is directed, if not the only one at present, lies in the employment of what are known as 'outworkers.' Such outworkers are men or women for whom the employer provides no workshop or other facilities, but who execute at home whatever work they receive. This system has a double disadvantage for those workers who work only in the shop, or as it is technically termed, on 'the board.' In the first place, it makes impossible any effective supervision of the conditions under which the work is performed – and thus opens the way for all manner of inroads on the 'log', or price list, and provides the employing class with a reserve of unorganised labour continually competing with the organised workers, and continually offering facilities to the employer in his struggles with his workmen. In the second place, whereas the regular union worker can only work for one employer at a time, and must take all chances incidental to the fluctuations of that employer's business, the outworkers can serve two or three firms at once and thus assure themselves of work, if not from one, then from the other. The result being that the union worker, having insecurity of employment to reckon with, must necessarily seek for such a rate of wages as will counterbalance such insecurity, but the outworkers having greater facilities for procuring work can, and do, accept lower wages. Add to this the fact that even if both sections of workers got the same wages IN CASH yet, owing to their peculiar circumstances, the outworkers would be the less costly to the employer as they would be providing their own workshop, fires, etc. Under such conditions it is no wonder that the regularly organised members of the tailoring craft regard the existence of the outworking, or sweating, system as a danger to their best interests. Indeed it were a wonder were it otherwise, for the facts herein set forth give but the faintest outline of the evils contained in the system of outworking. For instance the fact of such work being performed within the small compass of a working-class 'home' is fatal to the health of those employed upon it, and engenders fever and other contagious diseases which, through the medium of the garments, are spread throughout the entire community. Then, like all other 'home' work, it invariably leads to female and child labour – all the members of the family being pressed into the service. Thus a crop of evils of the most serious nature are fostered by this system of sweating against which our friends of the tailoring craft are now arrayed.

But what of the remedy? We might, were we so minded, placidly – and quite correctly – point out to our tailoring friends that the only remedy is Socialism, that nothing short of the public ownership and democratic control of the means of life will finally rid them of their industrial troubles; that sweating is but the natural child of Capitalism, and that to get rid of the one you must abolish the other. But this is not our attitude, nor is it the attitude of the scientific Socialist wherever he is found. Socialism is indeed the only permanent remedy, but Socialists seek for a mitigation of present evils even whilst pressing for the abolition of the source from whence they sprung. Indeed, Socialists are the most imperative of all in agitating for immediate reforms because we know that no measure of relief to the cause of Labour is to-day possible, which does not carry within it the germ of Socialist principles – is not in a greater or less degree an application to industrial life of the Socialist idea. Thus the only radical and effective remedy for the evils of sweating, viz the entire suppression of outworking, is perhaps too herculean a task for mere trade-union effort to accomplish, but lies well within the range of what the workers might accomplish by political action AS A CLASS. And as the regulation of industrial activity by the workers themselves, instead of by a dominant class, is the very essence of the Socialist conception so even that partial application of the principle which would be shown in the spectacle of working-class representatives in the House of Commons forcing this upon the employers, lies along those lines of progress we desire to travel. We would advise our friends to study that fact well, and then ask themselves why it is that our Home Rule representatives, so ready to serve the class interests of the tenant farmers, are so utterly indifferent to the class interests of the town workers.

Meanwhile in every effort their union may make towards abolishing the evils of sweating, the tailoring trade can count upon our heartiest co-operation.

HOME THRUSTS

[1 July 1899]

Peace, blessed Peace!

The Peace Conference summoned by the Czar of Russia is now sitting at the Hague – and the Czar is busy using military force to suppress the constitution of Finland.[18]

Peace, blessed Peace! Britain prepares for war with the Transvaal in the interests of the capitalist speculators who desire to exploit that territory.[19]

Peace, blessed Peace! The United States troops are busily engaged in massacring the Filippinos; looting their towns and burning whatever they cannot carry off.[20]

Peace, blessed Peace! Lock out in Berlin, lock out in Paris, lock out in Scotland, lock out in Dublin, lock out of workers by the masters, desirous of reducing their wage slaves to subjection.

Peace, blessed Peace! The Peace Conference is sitting at the Hague – and the Prince of Hades enjoys the joke.

When nations go to war the women and children are exempted from molestation by the contending forces, but in the industrial struggle – the CLASS WAR – it is the sufferings of the women and children upon which the capitalist class depends to defeat and subdue us.

You see, it works out in this fashion. There is no antagonism between the workmen and those by whom Labour is employed (eh, Mr McCarron[21]) but when the masters desire to provide their wives or daughters with some fresh luxury – a dainty diamond bracelet or a Continental trip – then the workers are called upon to submit to a reduction of wages –

Just to show their friendly feelings and their humble Christian spirit.

Sad to say, the workers most inconsiderately refuse. Some foolish idea about the duty of providing the necessaries of life for their own wives and children gets into their heads, and as a result of this little difference of opinion there is a lock out.

A lock out! You know what that means. It means that the master class as its weapon against the workers uses the powers of slow and maddening STARVATION. It means that your master in order to defeat you, takes the food from your table, the clothes from your body, the coals from your fires, that he condemns you, as far as in him lies, to hunger and misery, and that he calculates, with a fiendish ferocity, that you will submit to his terms rather than see those dear to you perish for lack of proper nourishment.

That is a lock out. During the lock out the masters want for nothing, the workers are in want of everything. A fair fight? Hem.

At the ballot box the master would only count as one against his workers; their force could, if properly used, ensure the triumph of Labour as certainly as on the industrial plane the power of the master's purse will nearly always win.

Yet it is upon the industrial field alone that the workers prefer to fight.

In the workshop they fight the masters – at the ballot box they elect the master or his lackeys to rule them.

Yet it is the men elected at the ballot box who make the laws which govern the fight in the workshop.

When will the workers learn that the political power they could wield as an organised body is the greatest weapon in their hands, that the field of politics is the only field upon which the workers can win emancipation from the domination of capital?

In other words, when will the workers copy the masters who, not content with their tremendous economic power, unceasingly strive to secure every atom of political power in order to entrench their class in its position of supremacy.

Let the workers organise to seize political power; let them remember that all industrial institutions can be moulded responsive to the will of the class wielding the governmental power, and, so remembering, let them direct their energies toward the only object worth striving for, viz, to wrest the private ownership and control of industry from the hands of a robber class, and prepare the ground for the harvest of freedom – the Socialist Republic.

Then we shall have peace. Not the peace of imperial hypocrites, military bullies, lying diplomats and commercial pirates, nor yet the peace of beaten slaves, but the peace of a free people, paying tribute to no exploiter, fully masters of their own destiny.

Peace, blessed Peace?

SPAILPÍN.

THE RE-CONQUEST OF IRELAND

[2 September 1899]

The movement in favour of the direct employment of labour by the County Councils, established under the Local Government Act,[22] has scarcely attracted as much public attention as it deserves. Our national press is, as a rule, so much wrapped up in the work of recording the gyrations of its political chiefs, and so little capable of realising the importance of any movement outside of, and uninfluenced by, the ordinary currents of political activity, that they can spare no space to chronicle the progress of a movement which, if consistently followed up, will do more to place the destinies of the people in their own hands than has been effected by all the political movements of the century.

It appears that throughout the South of Ireland the labourers are at present vigorously agitating against the system of letting out public works to private contractors, and in favour of the direct employment of all labour by the County Councils. This proposal, which virtually means that the labourers have emancipated their minds from the social superstition that a private, profit-hunting capitalist can do work better for the community than the community itself can perform it through its elected and responsible officials, has been already adopted by some of the County Councils, and is being discussed by others. The labourer thus finding in his hand one weapon of his emancipation – the ballot box – has already shown himself prepared to use it with an amount of political discernment not a little disconcerting to the men who fondly imagined that the parrot cry of Home Rule would still have its old effect in weaning the minds of the workers from any movement for the bettering of their position as a class. And this, be it noted, is only a beginning. As the movement progresses, as the labourer sees that the vote which has placed him in the position of being able to elect his representative on the local governing bodies, may also, if properly used, enable him to transfer himself from the employment of an irresponsible master to the servant of a public board, of which he himself is one of the masters, he cannot fail to observe that the arguments and fallacious reasonings with which each step in that direction is met by the propertied class, are exactly the same in every respect as those with which the demands of his nation for political justice have always been met by the enemies of national freedom. He will observe that the nationalist propertied class hurl against the labourer the same epithets, and allege the same incapacity for administration, as they have had hurled at themselves when putting forward their demand for legislative independence; he will also observe that the propertied Unionist will line up, solid as a rock, along with the propertied Nationalist in defence of their joint interest in the subjection of labour; and finally he will discover that in this apparently insignificant movement for direct employment of labour there lies a path to freedom not only for his class, but for his nation.

The subjection of Ireland which is represented to-day as a mere political question is instead an economic, a social question. It is only political that it may be economic. In

other words, the political machinery is only held by a
dominant nation in order that the social powers may be held
by a dominant class. The conquest of Ireland is founded
upon the dispossession of her people from all right to the
soil, and from all right to life except upon terms dictated by
the possessing class, in field, farms, or workshop owned and
possessed by that class. That is to say, that the subjection of
Ireland, like all other such subjection, is based upon the
economic dependence of the oppressed upon the oppressor.
The army, navy, and police are but the instruments with
which this class enforces its domination, and the political
subjection of Ireland to England means nothing more than
that the possessing class were astute enough to place the
control of those instruments of domination beyond the reach
of the Irish people. On the same line of reasoning it will be
seen that the cry for a 'Union of Classes' is in reality an
insidious move on the part of our Irish master class to have
the powers of government transferred from the hands of the
English capitalist government into the hands of an Irish
capitalist government, and to pave the way for this change
by inducing the Irish worker to abandon all hopes of bettering his own position, and to assume such an attitude of
meek resignation to his lot as a wage-slave as might convince the English government that he would make no revolutionary use of his political power, but would leave things
much as they are. The bitterness of the opposition to the
new labour movement is the outcome of the chagrin felt at
the failure of this plot to delude the Irish worker in the
interest of his Irish master. Instinctively the labourer feels
that every move which lessens his economic subjection to a
master raises him a step nearer to the heights of freedom;
he gradually recognises that in exact proportion as the workers take the control of the work of the country from the
hands of private individuals and vest it in the charge of
public bodies representing the Irish people, in the same
proportion does Ireland strike from off her limbs the shack-
les of slavery. By a steady pursuit of this policy the subjection of Ireland can be, in great part, reversed. The Socialist
Republican Party has, ever since its formation, based its
hopes upon the successful issue of this policy, and can not
but be delighted that the line of action it had sketched out
as the most immediately practical – sketched out after deep
study of the social and political conditions of this country –

is now being taken up by the labourers of Ireland. The fact that most of the men now pursuing this policy would repudiate all connection with Socialism is the greater proof of the insight, alike into human nature and political developments, possessed by the band of pioneers who formulated this programme of action, knowing the self-interest of the workers would force such action on, apart from all theorisings, or knowledge of its greater possibilities.

People who talk of difficulties in the way of Socialism do not, as a rule, realise the nature of the Socialist plan of campaign. The workers are a subject class, but the workers are in the majority; therefore the workers may, by voting together, oust from every public board the majority of their masters, and replace them by a majority of class-conscious workers – workers conscious of the fact that the workers are a subject class, and determined to destroy such class subjection – and this majority of class-conscious workers can vote to take every industry from the hands of the master class and vest it in the hands of associations of workers, serving under the public bodies. Being in a majority the workers are irresistible – when enlightened.

In the course of this socialization of society, this gradual re-conquest of Ireland, the public boards in question will eventually find their paths crossed by the capitalist Imperial government; then Labour, from a dominant local, will rise to the position of a dominant national party, and the fight for complete independence will be taken up by the working class already in possession of the internal government of the country, with all the prestige arising from that fact, and with all the leverage arising from the circumstance that whatever action they may take will have been forced on by a desire to protect the interests of the majority – the workers. Such a crisis, and it is unavoidable if this line of action is consistently followed up, would bring the question of what is called national independence home to the fireside of every worker as a fight for the security of their daily bread, and under such conditions the war for freedom will not fail for lack of an army of adherents.

Therefore every worker who studies the social and political conditions of the day must see that the Irish Socialist Republican policy, already so justified by the unconscious adoption here pointed out, is the only policy which blends in one irresistible force the interests of Ireland a Nation and the interests of the working class.

AMERICA AND IRELAND
Farmers' Demands

[21 October 1899]

As a general rule we refrain from taking notice in our
columns of the quarrels or discussions of the Socialist parties
of the world. We regard ourselves as being, at present, primarily a missionary organ, founded for the purpose of
presenting to the working class of Ireland a truer and more
scientific understanding of the principles of Socialism than
they could derive from a perusal of the scant and misleading
references to that subject to be found in the ordinary capitalist press. This task also involves, as a matter of course, the
criticism and exposure of all the quack remedies and political
trickeries with which our masters, or their ignorant imitators
in the ranks of the workers themselves, seek to impose upon
the people as cure-alls for our social evils. We have all along
acted upon the conviction that we must give the revolutionary principles of Socialism an Irish home and habitation
before we venture to express our opinions on the minor
matters dividing the party abroad. We can say now with
some degree of confidence that we have succeeded in that
task and that the Socialist Republican Party of Ireland is one
of the factors which will play a big part in shaping the
future history of this country, and being so confident we
now propose to say a word upon a subject at present under
discussion in the United States of America; and in which
the name of our Party has been cited as following a course
of action similar to that adopted by one of the disputants.

The matter is as follows:– There are in the States just now
two distinct Socialist parties – The Socialist Labor Party, and the
Social Democratic Party. The first named is the longest established of the two and has repeatedly run candidates for the post
of President of the United States, polling on the occasion of the
last Presidential contest 36,664 votes. The last named has only
come into existence since the last Presidential campaign, and is
composed for the greater part of men and women who, while
avowing themselves Socialists, disapproved of the policy and tactics pursued by the Socialist Labor Party. To the uninitiated in
the economics and philosophy of Socialism it is hard to explain
the exact point at issue, but it may be briefly summed up in the
statement that the Socialist Labor Party adhere uncompromis-

ingly to the policy of identifying themselves as a party with, and basing all their hopes upon, the struggle of the working class against every section of their exploiters, or employers. This involves opposition to every demand made in the interest of the master class, and an attitude of complacency, or even triumph, at the success of the great capitalist in crushing out his smaller competitor – this complacency arising from the, it seems to us, absolutely correct position that the crushing out of small capitalists by large ones will tend to increase the ranks of the working class, concentrate industry under centralised management, decrease the numbers of those interested in private property, and so make the ultimate attainment of Socialism easier.

In other words, theirs is the position known in Europe as the Marxist position, from its being first definitely formulated by the founder of Modern Socialism – Karl Marx.

The Social Democratic Party, on the other hand, look to the fact that the small middle class, and especially the farmers, still wield an enormous voting power, and, looking to the present rather than to the future, they have embodied in their programme certain 'Farmers' Demands' – proposals for legislation to enable the petty farmers to bear up against the competition of those mammoth farms for which the United States is so famous. The object being, of course, to win the votes of the farmers as a class.

Over those 'Farmers' Demands' a battle royal has been raging for some time between the two parties. The Socialist Labor Party denouncing them as reactionary and unscientific, the Social Democratic Party defending them as practical and useful. Lately some members of the latter party have themselves taken up the battle against those proposals being included in their programme, and demand their removal. In the course of this latter discussion in the columns of the *Social Democratic Herald* published at Chicago, Sept 25th, one writer, F.G.R . Gordon, in defending the proposals, cites our example as a party which, occupying an absolutely scientific position on Socialist doctrines, yet has its 'Farmers' Demands.' Here is the quotation:–

The Irish Socialist Republican Party have their Farmers' Demands; and their party has been endorsed as the par excellent Scientific Socialist Party.

No. 3 of our programme is, we presume, the plank alluded to.[23]

Now, we have no wish to be misunderstood by our comrades in America; we value our reputation as a straight Socialist Party too much to allow our name to be used as a cover for any kind of looseness in principles, tactics, or policy, even when it is used accompanied by flattery. Therefore, we would wish to point out to all whom it may concern that the cases of America and Ireland are not at all analogous. Agriculture in America has assumed already its company form, being in many cases administered purely on capitalist lines for the profit of non-resident owners; agriculture in Ireland is still in a semi-feudal form, the largest farm in Ireland would be classed as a petty farm in America, and the absorption of the working farmer by the capitalist managed estate of the non-resident farmer is practically unknown. Now observe this vital point of difference between the programme of the Socialist Republican Party of Ireland, and the programme of the Social Democratic Party of America. Both have demands for farmers, granted, but:–

(1) The Farmers' Demands of the Social Democrats of America are demands which aim at the perpetuation of the system of petty farming by legislation to protect it from the effects of the competition of farms managed on those lines most nearly approximating to the Socialist form of industry, viz, the lines of centralised capital, and agricultural armies. American agriculture, AS SUCH, is not in any danger as a source of support for the agriculturist. His status may be endangered, not his existence.

(2) The Farmers' Demands of the Socialist Republican Party of Ireland are demands which aim at preserving Agriculture in Ireland from being ANNIHILATED AS A NATIVE INDUSTRY by the competition of FOREIGN agriculturists. Irish agriculturists are not threatened with absorption, but with extinction and enforced exile.

In other words the American Farmers' Demands are in the interest of one particular form of agricultural enterprise, as against another; the Irish Demands are directed towards rescuing agriculture itself, and teaching the agriculturist to look to national co-operation as the factor he should count upon for help in his struggle to remain in the country of his birth.

Things which look alike are not always alike. The apparent identity of the Irish and American proposals is seen to be non-existent when you take into account the different historical and industrial conditions of the two countries. Given American conditions in Ireland, the Irish Socialists would wipe their Farmers' Demands from off their programme, but in Ireland as it is with the rags of a medieval system of land tenure still choking our life and cramping our industry, with perennial famine destroying our people, with our population dwindling away by emigrations, we consider it right to point out, even if unheeded, that it is the duty of the State to undertake the functions of manufacture and custodian of all implements required for the one important industry of the country – agriculture. This is all we demand in that nature:–

Establishment at public expense of rural depots for the most improved agricultural machinery, to be lent out to the agricultural population at a rent covering cost and management alone.

It is not a sectional demand, but is the outcome of a national exigency.

'The practical application of the principles' (of Socialism), said Marx and Engels in their joint preface to the Communist Manifesto,[24] 'everywhere, and at all times will depend on the historical conditions for the time being existing.'

Let our critics please remember that fact, and the Socialist Republicans of Ireland can confidently abide by the result.

DUBLIN AND THE WAR
Diary of the 'Troubles'[25]

[30 December 1899]

December 8. – Announced in London and Dublin newspapers that the Right Hon Joseph Chamberlain, MP, Colonial Secretary, would visit Dublin on the 17th and 18th December to receive a degree from Trinity College.

English newspapers eulogise Chamberlain's 'courage.'

December 11. – Special meeting of Dublin Corporation to consider a vote of sympathy with the Boers is rendered abortive by the Home Rule members treacherously absenting themselves.[26]

December 12. – Public meeting called by the Irish Socialist Republican Party 'to celebrate the British defeat at Stormberg.'[27]

Date of meeting 19th December, same date as Chamberlain's triumphal entry; place of meeting, College Green, beside Trinity.

December 13. – Reliable natives report the jingo enemy to be very wrathful at Socialist audacity.

December 14. – Irish Transvaal Committee summon public meeting to be held in Beresford Place on Sunday 17th, to denounce the action of the Dublin Corporation – and salute Chamberlain.

British garrison go into laager.[28]

December 15. – London *Pall Mall Gazette* declares that there is trouble brewing in Dublin in connection with Mr Chamberlain's visit and expresses the belief that the parties responsible for all the trouble are 'the Irish Socialist Republican Party which is composed of a number of the most extreme and least reputable representatives of the nationalists of Dublin.'

London *St James' Gazette* hopes 'that the police will see to it.'

Irish Daily Independent reminds us of the 'rights of hospitality.'

December 16. – Reported at British Headquarters that both wings of the Irish Revolutionary forces were gathering behind the kopjes.[29]

British draw in all their outposts, from Kingstown and all outlying camps.

One hundred rounds of ammunition per man served out to the military.

Proportionate quantity of porter served out to the police.

Some swearing done before Mr Wall, Police Magistrate.

Government Proclamation issued forbidding the meeting on Sunday. Copies served on the Transvaal Committee: John O'Leary, Michael Davitt, Pat O'Brien, MP, Willie Redmond, MP[30] and James Connolly.

Meeting of Transvaal Committee. Willie Redmond, as chairman, advises the people to defy the police, and hold the meeting in Beresford Place.

Native runners out all night summoning the bludgeonmen of the Government.

December 17. – All the tactical positions in and about and streets debouching on Beresford Place occupied by masses of police. Military confined to barracks and in readiness to turn out. Thousands of people thronging to the place of meeting. Dublin wild with excitement.

Home Rulers Funk. Leave the people to face the police as they had advised them to, but take their own miserable carcasses to the seclusion of a back room.

Miss Maud Gonne, Mr Griffith of the *United Irishman*,[31] Mr Lyons of the Oliver Bond '98 Club, comrades Stewart and Connolly of the Irish Socialist Republican Party step into the breach and drive down to Beresford Place to hold the meeting.

Baton charges by police. Hired driver of brake seized by police, reins assumed by Connolly who had been moved to the chair by Griffith, procession organised through the principal streets, two meetings held, charges by mounted police, unsuccessful, but desperate, efforts of the mounted police – to keep their seats, triumphal conclusion of the procession, arrest of Connolly.

Fake meeting held by Home Rulers. Audience composed of five reporters and two ladies.

At the close of the meeting W. Redmond MP gets himself interviewed (?) and declares:

I have never seen anything like the enthusiasm manifested when I (I, I, Willie Redmond, to wit) stept out of the rooms of the Celtic Literary Society.

Saith Pat O'Brien: 'WE have demonstrated to England that she cannot go to war unless she has first conciliated Ireland.'
Quoth the man in the street: 'Rats.'

December 18. – Connolly fined £2, or one month imprisonment, and to find bail in the sum of £10 or go to prison for another month.

Fine paid, and security for bail found.

Socialist Republican meeting prohibited, the attempt at holding meeting frustrated by hundreds of policemen, vicious police charges upon the people.

Police raid on Socialist premises. One Red Flag, one Green Flag, two Boer Flags, and the Historic Black Flag which led the anti-Jubilee procession of 1897[32] captured by the police.

Several members maltreated. After a gallant struggle six stalwart policemen succeed in throwing one small boy, brother of one of the members, downstairs. Said policemen to be mentioned in despatches for 'distinguished conduct.'

After the retirement of the police meeting held in Socialist club-room, comrade Stewart in the chair. A resolution denouncing the Dublin Corporation, and protesting against the ruffianly conduct of the police, was put to the meeting, spoken to by Messrs Griffith and Quinn of the Transvaal Committee, and carried.

Chamberlain in his speech at Trinity apparently loses heart, for, instead of the expected war-whoop, he winds up by asking those present to believe 'he was not so black as he was painted.'

A 'Reconnaissance in force' of the Trinity College loyalists checked by an old woman in Dawson Street, and finally repulsed by a flying column of Catholic University boys. Loyalists retreat in two divisions, one towards Trinity, the other towards Mercer's Hospital – for surgical treatment.

Workers' Republic suspended for one week owing to disorganisation caused by above events.

December 19. – All quiet on the Potomac.

Moral

Although a body aiming primarily at economic change, at Social Revolution, yet wherever a blow is to be struck for freedom – national or social, political or economic – there you will find the Socialist Republicans, ready and willing to fight.

Our warfare against the domestic exploiter does not diminish our hatred of the foreign tyrant.

DIFFICULTIES OF SOCIALISM

[3 June 1900]

In every discussion on the aims and objects of a Socialist Party some one is sure to bring up the objection that even if the Socialist Party were to conquer their opponents, and make an effort to establish their ideal as a political and social edifice, the difficulties which would arise out of the inability of the common people to understand the complexity of the social system they were called upon to administer, would infallibly produce the downfall of the new order. This objection is, it seems to us, rather far fetched in view of the circumstance that the majority of those who at the present day are entrusted with the work of organizing and administering the capitalist system are completely ignorant of every development of the system outside of their own particular sphere of employment.

It is not at all necessary that everyone, or even a very large number, of those engaged in labour should be able to give an intelligent account of the multifarious processes of production, nor yet that they should be qualified even to trace the passage of the commodities upon which they are employed through all their stages from the crudity of the raw material up to the perfection of the finished product as it eventually reaches the hands of the purchaser. It is only necessary that each worker should perform with due skill and scrupulosity his own allotted task; to the few required as organisers of industry may be left the work of adjusting and interlocking the parts. Even this latter function – formidable as it may look when thus baldly stated – may be reduced to a mere automatic function to be executed as a part of the routine work of a clerical staff.

Any person reflecting upon the mechanism of the capitalist system can readily perceive how little its most important arteries of commerce are dependent upon international organization, and how much upon the reciprocal action of the economic interests involved at first hand. Where the international organization of Socialism will indeed come into play it will come to smooth over and simplify many of the difficulties which are constantly arising under capitalism as a result of the clashing of personal interests. Hence the Socialist organization of industry will preserve the effectiveness due to the development of capitalism whilst entirely obviating the friction and disputes capitalist competition entails.

It is well also to remember the multitude of things which in civilised society we are all compelled to take upon trust at the word of others. It is safe to say that what is called 'progress,' or civilisation, would be impossible were each individual in the community, or even a majority, to insist upon acquiring a complete theoretical and technical mastery of, say, each new application of Science to the needs of life before consenting to allow its use. There are few persons nowadays who would shrink from trusting themselves to railway trains, even although in all but complete ignorance of the mechanism of the steam engine, signal-boxes, points, and brakes; we have had gas in our houses, shops, and public buildings for several generations, but to this day the number of those who really understand the processes of gas production, storage, and distribution are extraordinarily few, yet that does not prevent us using it despite its well known poisonous and explosive nature. And so we might go on enumerating many things in daily use – the use of which involves risk to life – which are accepted and freely utilised by people at large without stopping to acquire a perfect knowledge of their active principle.

Much the same might be said of the pretended wonderful and mysterious results to be attained under Socialism – results too wonderful to be realised. In Socialism there is nothing so abnormal that its realization could exceed in strangeness things we see around us every day, and composedly accept with the greatest equanimity. In the proposition that the community can so arrange the work of production and distribution that plenty can be provided for every human being, there is nothing, in view of present day machinery, half so extraordinary as the fact that if a gentleman sitting down to dinner in Dublin sends a telegram to a friend in Australia that friend will have received said telegram before his Dublin correspondent could have finished the final course of his repast. The fact that people in Ireland were reading accounts of battles in South Africa, 7,000 miles off, while those battles were still in progress, is far more intrinsically wonderful than a system of society in which labour enjoys the product of its toil, and neither hereditary tyrants nor capitalist exploiters are tolerated.

If these stranger developments have been accepted whilst Socialism is still rejected, it is because the personal economic interests of the classes controlling the educative and governing forces of the world are in line with such developments, while the same personal economic interests of those classes are as directly opposed to Socialism. But the workers are in the majority, and their interests are in line with Socialism, which may, therefore, be realised as soon as they desire, and are resolute enough to put their desires into practice.

DIFFICULTIES OF CAPITALISM

[16 June 1900]

We wrote last week of the Difficulties of Socialism; this week we propose to treat of a few of the Difficulties of Capitalism. In this connection we would point out that the critics of

Socialism invariably devote their energies to demonstrating how far a Socialist system would fall short of ideal perfection, and, having so demonstrated to their own satisfaction, they affect to conclude that the last word has been said, and argument is at an end. It may perhaps surprise such critics to learn that such a line of argument leaves untouched the real contention of the Socialist Party which nowhere proposes that Socialism will escape the taint of fallibility due to all institutions of human origin, but only that the establishment of our social arrangements on a Socialist basis will ensure material prosperity to all men and women, and by so ensuring leave the race full freedom to seek for such expression of its faculties as is best suited to their varying characters. It does not assume that with the advent of Socialism all the evil of our nature will immediately disappear, that love, hate, ambition, lust, envy and all the forces which in our complex natures make for the stirring up of strife and discord, will be instantly eradicated, and the earth take on the aspect of Paradise. But it does contend that Poverty and the crimes born of poverty may be banished, and that with the elimination of the economic struggle from our life the intellectual forces which to-day expend themselves in striving for mastery will find expression in avenues of greater helpfulness, and individuals seek renown as benefactors instead of exploiters of their species.

Our sapient critics likewise forget that the line of argument which consists solely in discovering possible flaws in a future state of society is permissible only to those who defend a state of society in itself flawless. Such capitalist society obviously is not. Its glaring contradictions are so many and so apparent that many of its most zealous defenders rely for their success in maintaining its integrity intact upon their skill in impressing the ignorant multitude with the belief that reform is hopeless, and, therefore, politics a mere waste of time. The space at our disposal would not permit of the mention of a tithe of the problems and difficulties, the contradictions and absurdities, which abound in the very nature of capitalism, but a brief enumeration of a few of these may be of use in serving to convince the less obtuse of our critics that they are playing with a two edged sword when they speak of the difficulties Socialism may have before it.

Why is it necessary that human beings should work at all? In order that the world may be supplied with goods, of course. Do we therefore rejoice when the world is so supplied? Oh, no, that is the greatest disaster we can imagine, for then we would be thrown idle, owing to over-production. We must labour in order to supply the world, and when the world is supplied we must starve because there is plenty for all and our labour is not needed.

Science and invention by increasing the productivity of our labour lessens the period necessary to stock the world's markets, and thus, at one and the same time, lessens the period during which our labour is required and increases the duration of our compulsory idleness.

One difficulty – one insoluble difficulty – of capitalism is to devise a method whereby the march of science and inventive genius can assist industry without menacing the bread and butter of the working class.

Property of all kinds making for human comfort commands the respect of all men. Yet there are times when the unemployed building trades need not repine if a conflagration lays a street in ruins, or an earthquake wrecks some noble building; and we have known shipwrights to rejoice when some stately ship foundered in mid-ocean.

The world rejoices at the progress of medical science, yet the same healing art which withholds its victims from the grave robs the cemetery companies of their expected dividends, and the funeral undertakers of chances of earning a livelihood. Under capitalism matters of public calamity – war, pestilence, death – are often matters of private thanksgiving; the crepe on the widow's bonnet finds its counterpoise in the breakfast on the grave-digger's table.

When capitalism has made the private interest coincide with the common weal; when machinery becomes in reality 'labour-saving,' and not as at present, wage-saving; when an overstocked market means for the worker a well stocked larder, and not idleness and hunger, then it will be time for our enemies to tell us of our future difficulties.

But under Capitalism that time will never come.

PARLIAMENTARY DEMOCRACY

[22 September 1900]

Parliament is dissolved! By whom? By whom was Parliament elected? By the voters of Great Britain and Ireland. Was it then the voters of Great Britain and Ireland who called upon

Parliament to dissolve? No, it was the Prime Minister of England, Lord Salisbury to wit, whom nobody elected and who is incapable under the laws of his country of being a parliamentary representative;[33] it was this gentleman with whom lay the power of putting an end to the deliberations of Parliament and sending its members back to the ordeal of the hustings.

This ridiculous situation is highly illustrative of many anomalies and absurdities with which the English Constitution abounds. Eulogised by its supporters as the most perfect constitution yet evolved it is in reality so full of illogical and apparently impossible provisions and conditions that if presented to the reasoning mind as the basis of a workable constitution for a new country it would be laughed out of court as too ridiculous to consider.

Let us examine a few of its provisions in order that we may the more effectively contrast this parliamentary democracy with the democracy of the revolutionist. Parliament is elected by the voters of Great Britain and Ireland. When elected that party which counts the greatest number of followers is presumed to form the Cabinet as representing a majority of the electorate. But it by no means follows that a majority in the House represents a majority of the people. In many constituencies for instance where there are more than two candidates for a seat it frequently happens that although a candidate polls a larger vote than either of his opponents and so obtains the seat, yet he only represents a minority of the constituents as the vote cast for his two opponents if united would be much greater than his own. The cabinet formed out of the members of the party strongest numerically constitutes the government of the country and as such has full control of our destinies during its term of office. But the Cabinet is not elected by the Parliament, voted for by the people, nor chosen by its own party. The Cabinet is chosen by the gentleman chosen by the Sovereign as the leader of the strongest party. The gentleman so chosen after a consultation with the Queen (who perhaps detests both him and his party) selects certain of his own followers, and invests them with certain positions, and salaries, and so forms the Cabinet.

The Cabinet controls the government and practically dictates the laws, yet the Cabinet itself is unknown to the law and is not recognised by the Constitution. In fact the

Cabinet is entirely destitute of any legal right to existence. Yet although outside the law and unknown to the Constitution it possesses the most fearful powers, such as the declaration of war, and can not be prevented by the elected representatives of the people from committing the nation to the perpetration of any crime it chooses. After the crime has been perpetrated Parliament can repudiate when it meets the acts of the Cabinet, but in the meanwhile nations may have been invaded, governments overturned, and territories devastated with fire and sword.

The powers of Parliament are also somewhat arbitrary and ill-defined. Every general election is fought on one or two main issues, and on these alone. It may be the Franchise, it may be Temperance, it may be Home Rule, or any other question, but when Parliament has received from the electors its mandate on that one question it arrogates to itself the right to rule and decide on every other question without the slightest reference to the wishes of the electorate.

If Parliament, elected to carry out the wishes of the electors on one question, chooses to act in a manner contrary to the wishes of the electors in a dozen other questions, the electors have no redress except to wait for another general election to give them the opportunity to return other gentlemen under similar conditions and with similar opportunities of evil-doing.

The democracy of Parliament is in short the democracy of Capitalism. Capitalism gives to the worker the right to choose his master, but insists that the fact of mastership shall remain unquestioned; Parliamentary Democracy gives to the worker the right to a voice in the selection of his rulers but insists that he shall bend as a subject to be ruled. The fundamental feature of both in their relation to the worker is that they imply his continued subjection to a ruling class once his choice of the personnel of the rulers is made.

But the freedom of the revolutionist will change the choice of rulers which we have to-day into the choice of administrators of laws voted upon directly by the people; and will also substitute for the choice of masters (capitalists) the appointment of reliable public servants under direct public control. That will mean true democracy – the industrial democracy of the Socialist Republic.

HOME THRUSTS

[10 November 1900]

The Spiritual Inheritance of the Celt!

I suppose you have all heard that phrase. You may not understand what it means, but that, as the vulgar phraseology hath it, 'makes no matter.'

Nowadays the spiritual inheritance of the Celt is in evidence at almost every public meeting in the country: every public speaker who finds himself too densely destitute of the faintest traces of originality to evoke the applause of his audience, or is too ignorant of the question under discussion to speak even tolerably upon it, falls back as a last and never failing resort upon an appeal to the spiritual inheritance of the Celt.

That is always apropos. No matter what the subject of the meeting may be – Catholic University,[34] Financial Relations, Home Rule, or the location of the Pig Market, it can always be embellished and improved by a reference to the spiritual inheritance of the Celt.

What that spiritual inheritance is remains to me somewhat of a problem. I am a hard matter of fact individual and inclined I daresay to place too much stress occasionally upon material things as the first necessity, but I am open to conviction (no allusion Mr Mahony[35]) and hope some of my well informed readers will please enlighten me by answering this question.

The legends, romances, fairy tales, 'pisthrogs,'[36] and general folk-lore of this country deal largely in popular interpretations of the manifestation of the unknown forces of Nature; always giving, as is the wont of a half-educated people living in close contact with Nature, a personal form and intelligence to every natural phenomenon whose origin is unknown to them.

In other words, where the investigations of modern science have laid bare the working out of natural processes, our fore-fathers saw only the labours, or heard only the voices, of spirits – the roar of the tempest on the hilltops, the sighing of the wind through the valleys, the myriad undefinable noises of night, the phantasms across the minds of the insane, the weird phenomena of birth and death – all these were to the Celts of old the result of a perpetual war between superhuman intelligences, beneficent and diabolic.

Thus the Celt clothed the mechanism of the universe with form and colour; thus sprang into existence in his brain all the

spirits of good and bad, with which his fancy has invested every
hill and dale, river, loch, and island in Ireland: thus originated
the spiritual inheritance of the Celt – in an unprogressive desire
to escape the responsibility of investigating phenomena by placing their source beyond the reach of human activity.

But, I may be told, is not the fact that the Celt did show
himself prone to place a spiritual interpretation upon the
material manifestations of natural phenomena, proof in itself
of the spirituality of his mental bias, or inheritance?

It may be, but if it is, then the same proof holds good of
the Teuton, of the Russian, of the Indian; all of whom have
under the same conditions cherished similar beliefs, and all of
whom have in proportion as their material conditions were
modified and altered by the development of industry, and the
growth of towns and cities, abandoned such ideas in favour of
the scientific explanations.

The characteristic marks of Celtic spirituality are all to be
found parallelled in the Hindu and the Brahmin; the legends
of the Brocken and the Black Forest show the German mind
as fertile in weird conceptions as ever was Irish Seanchaí;[37] the
Russian moujik and baba still tell each other of the spirits of
forests and mountain steppes; and the peasantry of Somerset-
shire and other English rural counties credit such details of
occult happenings as sufficiently demonstrate the affinity of
their intellectual state to that of the spiritual Celt.

I do not war upon this quaint conceit of ours; I am only
tired of hearing it belauded and praised so much by superficial
thinkers and spouters.

You will hear a man or woman denouncing 'the gross
materialism' of England as contrasted with Celtic spirituality
one day, and the next you will find the same person
showing a most laudable (?) but 'grossly material' desire to
establish Irish manufactories where Irish wage slaves can be
robbed by Irish capitalists; or joining with rackrenting landlords and scheming company promoters to demand an abatement of taxation on their own precious incomes.

Now, I believe that the mental traits upon which our Celtic
enthusiasts base their claims, or should I say OUR claims, to
spirituality, are but the result of the impression left upon the
Celtic mind by the operations of the natural phenomena of his
material surroundings; that most, if not all, races have had
similar experience at similar periods of their history; and that
there was therefore nothing unique in the intellectual equip-

ment of the Celt, and nothing that he needs must cherish lest
he lose his individuality.

The influences which go to the destruction and debasement
of the Irish Celtic character are not racial in their character,
they are social and industrial; it is not Anglo-Saxonism but
Capitalism which pours its cheap filth into our news-agencies,
and deluges our homes with its gutter literature.

This fact is obvious to all who choose to open their eyes
and note that Paris, Berlin, and Vienna have each their gutter
literature, corresponding in all its vulgarity and inanity to the
Cheap Jack rubbish and filth which some people would have
us believe is Anglo-Saxon.

The debasing literature is common to all these cities
because its source is common to all; that source being, of
course, not the language but the capitalist system.

It is only a trifling degree worse in England because the
capitalist system is more developed in England than in the
countries named. As the people become brutalised by overwork
under capitalism they are incapable of appreciating healthy
literature, and require the strong meat of sensationalism and
suggestiveness – the stronger and more pungent the flavour the
easier it can be assimilated by the degraded wage slaves.

If you desire to pursue this line of thought further you can
do it by tracing the appetite for unhealthy literature in capitalist countries, such as England, America, and France; and the
corresponding absence of such literature in countries such as
Spain, Portugal, or Norway, where capitalism is in its undeveloped, infant, state.

As long as it was a question of Celt versus Saxon in Ireland
the Celt (considering the enormous odds against him) held his
own fairly well for six hundred years, without much deteriora-
tion in his national character – held his own so well that one
hundred years ago many districts were as un-English as at the
Norman Invasion.

But with the advent of capitalism all that was changed; the
cheapness of its wares opened a way for English capitalism into
districts where the political power of England had only excited
aversion; the use of the English product paved the way for the
use of the English speech, which in its turn made possible the
debasing floods of cheap literary garbage.

Thus capitalism has done more in one hundred years to
corrupt the Celt, and destroy his spirituality, than the previous
six hundred were able to accomplish.

Yet the 'Spiritual Inheritance' orators and writers are all in favour of capitalism, and opposed to Socialism.

Why? Because their belief in a spiritual inheritance does not weaken their determination to hold firmly on to the incomes derivable from their material inheritance of land and capital, – and the legal title it confers to a share in the plunder of the Irish worker.

I could mention one poet in this city who writes some most weirdly spiritual poems in the intervals of drawing rack rents from one of the most filthy slums of Dublin.

He is a patriot, a town councillor, a slum landlord, a publican, a poet, an heir to our spiritual inheritance – and other things.

A beautiful blending of the material and the spiritual – of both kinds.

Well, well! I have rambled a bit from my text, or rather the incident that suggested the text. That incident was a complimentary dinner given D. J. Cogan, MP for East Wicklow. Mr Cogan in thanking the friends who had feasted him gave this gem to the world. I quote from the *Evening Telegraph*:–

The sentimental was the spiritual side of man – it proceeded from the soul, and the man who was without sentiment would be without a soul (hear, hear). He therefore had no hesitation in admitting that the Irish character was highly sentimental, and he was proud of it. But why was it so? Because it is highly spiritual, and he thought it would be a sad day, indeed, for our country when the sentimental or spiritual side of it would become paralysed or lose any of its attributes (applause). In conclusion he would do what one individual could to further the interest of that branch of trade to which he had the honour to belong (hear, hear).

Now that is what I call 'lovely.' Mr Cogan is a provision dealer, and the beautiful and entirely ingenuous manner in which he promises to combine in his own person a solicitude for the spiritual side of the Irish character, and the interests of the provision trade is worthy of all praise.

But if an Irish workingman were to rhapsodise about our spiritual inheritance at the beginning of his speech, and at the end of it to denounce the tyranny of capital his audience would be shocked.

Perhaps that is the reason why the Socialist Republicans are not counted in, in the functions organised by the new cult. Perhaps! Yet I think we are favourable as need be, but we cannot work up any enthusiasm for things spiritual while lacking things material, and we cannot forget that there are thousands of our brother and sister Celts so poor to-day that if they could barter their spiritual inheritance for a loaf of bread and a 'rasher' it would be a profitable exchange.

But, gentlemen, before we part allow me to give you a toast. You will drink it, please, in water – the purest Vartry blend, with microbes of Irish manufacture only – and pledge me accordingly: 'Here's to the union of two mighty, epoch-making forces, "The Spiritual Inheritance of the Celt," and "The Interests of the Provision Trade"; these two, linked in indissoluble union, to go marching down the ages to immortality together.'

Sláinte![38]

SPAILPÍN.

HOME RULERS AND LABOUR
A Remonstrance

ADDRESSED TO ENGLISH SOCIALISTS

[October 1901]

A few months ago we called attention in the columns of the *Workers' Republic* to the extraordinary utterances of certain English Socialists concerning the Home Rule party and its attitude towards Labour and Socialism. We pointed out that this Home Rule party was essentially a capitalist party, inspired solely by a consideration for capitalist interests, and that the few 'Labour men' in that party were of the type of the Woods, Burts and Pickards of the English Liberal party – were baits to lure the workers on to the official party hook.[39] We also expressed the opinion that the action of English Socialists in giving such commendatory notices to the enemies of the Irish Socialists was nothing short of treason to the International Labour movement.[40] This remonstrance of ours has been as entirely disregarded as if it had been but the fulmination of a Liberal conference. That section of the English Socialists to whom we refer are apparently as ready to sacrifice the interests of the Irish Socialists to suit their party convenience as their English masters have always been to sacrifice Ireland to suit their class interests. The phrase 'International Solidarity of Labour' which they mouth so glibly does not take in Ireland in its scope.

Have we no remedy? We have, and if the present remonstrance is as little heeded as the first we shall take that remedy into our own hands with results that we have no doubt will be somewhat disastrous to the election prospects of future ILP[41] candidates in British constituencies where the Irish working class reside in any numbers. But first to explain the position. For some time past Mr Keir Hardie MP and his colleagues on the *Labour Leader* newspaper[42] have been assiduously instilling into the minds of the British Socialists the belief that Mr John Redmond's Home Rule party are burning with enthusiasm for labour and are favourably inclined towards Socialism. (We beg our readers in Ireland not to laugh at this; we are not exaggerating the case one whit.) Mr Keir Hardie has appeared on the platform with the Home Rule MPs at Irish gatherings, has given his most unqualified praise to them at gatherings of his own party – praise as staunch Labour men, please mark! – and in his paper, the aforesaid *Labour Leader*, he and another writer signing himself 'Marxian' have for the past few months left no stone unturned to imbue their readers with the belief that the Home Rule party are staunch democrats and socialistically inclined.

When Mr Keir Hardie was last in Parliament he on one occasion moved an amendment to an address to the throne – the amendment being in favour of finding work for the unemployed. The Home Rule members refused to support him. He moved an amendment to an address of congratulation on the birth of some royal baby, observing it should rather be a vote of condolence to the families of the Welsh miners who had just then been lost in a colliery disaster in Wales; the Home Rule members voted against him and in favour of royalty. The men who are leaders of the Home Rule party now, were the leaders of the party then also. This session they have voted in favour of several Labour measures, and Mr Hardie and his friends seek to make great capital of this fact. But, paradoxical as it may seem to say so, their vote is not cast in favour of these measures, but against the Unionist government which opposed them. Had a Home Rule government been in power in England and opposed these Labour measures, the Home Rule Irish party would have supported the government against Labour as they did in the past.

The present leader (?) of the Home Rule party, Mr John Redmond, is the gentleman who made himself notorious in

Ireland by denouncing (at Rathfarnham) the agricultural labourers for forming a trade union. He is the gentleman who, when the Irish Working Class first got the Municipal franchise granted them in 1898, stumped this country asking the workers to vote for landlords to represent them – in order, he said, to show the English people that we would not make a revolutionary use of our power.

The Irish working class answered him by forming independent Labour Electoral organisations, and sending landlords and middle class Home Rulers alike about their business. Mr Keir Hardie praised them in the *Labour Leader* for doing so; he now praises as the leader of the Irish democracy the very man whose insidious advice they rightfully scorned.

Mr Tim Harrington MP, and Lord Mayor of Dublin by the intrigues of the Home Rulers, is the gentleman who is notorious for having declared that sixteen shillings a week was enough wages for any working man. He is also the gentleman who ousted from the Mayoral chair another Home Ruler, Lord Mayor Pile, whom he declared to be a traitor, and then became treasurer of a committee organised to present this 'traitor' with a valuable testimonial for his services to the city.

One of the most highly placed men of the Executive of the United Irish League, the official Home Rule party, is Mr P. White, MP, who is well known to be the most detested employer of scab labour in the tailoring trade of the city of Dublin.

During last municipal election in Dublin the Home Rule party ran as candidate for the North City Ward one Alderman McCabe who had earned the detestation of every trade unionist by voting in favour of giving painting contracts to non union firms. Three Home Rule members of parliament, Messrs Tim Harrington, Pat O'Brien the Home Rule Whip, and Peter White were specially detailed to support this friend of blackleg labour against McLoughlin his Socialist opponent, although the latter had the unanimous endorsement of the Dublin Trades and Labour Council.[43]

But have not the Home Rulers declared in favour of Labour, has not Mr Redmond at Westport declared the fight against landlordism in Ireland to be a 'trade unionist fight'? The meaning of phrases can only be understood when you study the conditions out of which they arise. The Home Rule party in Ireland is today fighting for its very existence. The 'scenes' in Parliament are but the distant echo of the fight made by the Home Rulers to regain the support of the Irish Democracy. Despite all the puffing and booming of the press, despite the lavish expenditure of money on bands and faked up demonstrations, the United Irish League has not caught on in Ireland, and has not forty sound branches in all the country. The intelligent Irish Working Class despise the politicians. When after the first Local Government election in Ireland the professional politicians saw that the Irish workers had turned their backs upon them they took alarm, and in order to side-track the Labour movement in the next two elections they ran bogus labour candidates on their tickets in opposition to the independent candidates ran by genuine Labour organisations. This fact involved two sets of rallying cries. The Home Rule politician's election cry in such contests was, 'Nationality and Labour should go together;' that of the genuine Labour candidates was voiced by the then President of the Dublin Trades Council, Mr Leahy, when he said in reply that 'Labour should stand alone.' We need not insist upon asking which side English Socialists should agree with. Imagine then our surprise and amusement when we found such utterances as that of Mr Redmond at Westport, and the Home Rule rallying cry we have quoted, both in their essence piteous appeals to the Irish workers to return to the Home Rule fold to be shorn, reproduced in the *Labour Leader* and ILP speeches, as 'magnificent utterances in favour of Labour.' When an English Liberal says 'we are fighting the cause of Labour', the ILP laughs him to scorn, and when an Irish Home Ruler says the same thing it is accepted as gospel truth. But not in Ireland, we know our men.

But we are told the Home Rulers are at least staunch democrats. So was Mr John Morley,[44] yet Mr Keir Hardie made special efforts to defeat him at Newcastle because he was not sound enough on the Labour question. Staunch democrats! indeed, when they allowed an Irish National journal, the *United Irishman*, to be suppressed three times for its fight against the war, and refused to bring the matter up in the House of Commons, but made the world ring with denunciations when one of their own papers, the *Irish People*, was confiscated once.

We ask Mr Keir Hardie to consider these facts; we challenge any of his Home Rule friends to dispute either the statements of the inference drawn therefrom. We do not agree with Hardie's general policy, would most decidedly not adopt it as our own, but we believe in his honesty of purpose. We ask nothing from the English democracy but we do not wish to cross one another's path. We believe the Irish working class are strong enough and intelligent enough to fight their own battles and we would be the last to advise them to trust to outside help in the struggle that lies before them. We do not propose to criticise Hardie's voting alliance with the Home Rulers, but a voting alliance need not be accompanied by indiscriminate praise of your temporary allies.

Finally if this is not heeded we shall have to take other methods of enforcing attention to our protest.

We shall ask the editors of the various Socialist papers of Great Britain to publish the above, and we shall take their attitude towards that request as an indication of the strength of that international Solidarity of which we hear so much and see so little.

Signed

Executive Committee
Irish Socialist Republican Party,
138 Upper Abbey Street, Dublin

WOOD QUAY WARD
To the Electors

[December 1901]

FELLOW WORKERS,
Having been asked by the United Labourers of Dublin Trade Union to stand as Labour Candidate for this Ward, and as the majority of the members of that body live in this Ward, and their request has since been endorsed by a large number of other electors I have consented to allow my name to go forward for your suffrages.

As a member of the Irish Socialist Republican Party I endorse the national and municipal programme and policy of that body; that is to say I believe that in Ireland, as in the remainder of the world to-day, there are but two classes,

THE MASTER CLASS AND THE WORKING CLASS,

and that the Master Class live upon the labour of the Working Class, and use all the powers of government, nationally and municipally, in their own interest and against those who labour.

It is therefore, I believe, the duty of the workers to organise as a distinct party to put an end to this oppression by electing

men drawn from their own ranks, conscious of their own interests and determined to defend them, on all bodies having the
power either to make or to administer laws; the power of such
bodies to be used consistently towards putting an end to the
capitalist system of society, and making the Irish people really
and fully the owners of Ireland, which is what is meant by an

IRISH SOCIALIST REPUBLIC.

The United Irish Leaguers have supported the Socialist candidate at North East Lanark in Scotland, and are supporting the
Socialist candidate at Dewsbury, England; in opposing Socialist
candidates in Dublin they are only acting in the inconsistent
and treacherous manner that has marked their history from the
beginning.

If elected I will consider it my duty to act in the interest of
the class to which I belong – the Working Class; the interest
of the other classes are too well looked after already. The
Corporation of Dublin is at present ruled exclusively in the
interest of the middle class, and it is the rule of the middle
class in the towns, as of the aristocracy in the country, which
has made life so miserable for the Irish worker. The landed
aristocracy are the oppressors in the rural districts, and in the
towns the Middle Class take advantage of our necessities to
drive down wages and force up rents that they may profit
whilst the people starve. Labour, first, last and always shall
therefore be my especial care.

As a Republican in politics I consider that all bodies in the
elective power of the democracy should be used for the organising of the sentiment of the Irish people against all forms of
foreign rule – from the monarch to the capitalist.

I am a member of the Dublin Trades' and Labour Council,
and my candidature has received the hearty endorsement of the
most trusted representatives of Labour in the city.

I append herewith the programme of reforms for which I
shall agitate if returned.

Trusting to receive your hearty support at the polls on
January next,

I remain, Ladies and Gentlemen,
Yours in the cause of Labour,
JAMES CONNOLLY.

TAKEN ROOT!

[March 1902]

The Irish Socialist Republican Party was founded in Dublin in May, 1896. Six working men assisted at its birth. The founders were poor, like the remainder of their class, and had arrayed against them all those things that are supposed to be essential to success. They were without a press of any kind, their propaganda was generally supposed to be hostile to the religious views of the majority of the people, no great or well-known name allied itself to them, they had to count on the bitter opposition of all the organised parties which defend the interests of the propertied class, their opponents had more sovereigns to spare for political work than they had coppers, they were in a country undeveloped industrially, and a country in which political freedom was not fully realised, and where, therefore, the political mission of Liberalism or middle-class reformers was not yet exhausted – in short they were handicapped as no other party in this country ever yet were handicapped; hated by the government, held in distrust by the people, and in short generally regarded as Ishmaels in the political life of Ireland.

But that little band of pioneers stuck to their work manfully, and despite all discouragements and rebuffs continued sowing the seeds of Socialist working-class revolt in the furrows of discontent ploughed by the capitalist system of society. To-day they can look back on their work with pride. Nowhere, it is true, have they yet succeeded in getting on their side that majority necessary to place the nominee of their party, the SRP, on the seats of the elected ones – that triumph is indeed not yet vouchsafed to them – but he would indeed be a very ignorant or a very presumptuous person who would essay to review the possibilities of the political situation in Dublin, and would leave this little fighting party out of his calculations. In the elections just ended EIGHT HUNDRED VOTES WERE CAST FOR SOCIALISM in the only two wards of this city our finances allowed us to contest.[45] These votes were cast for no milk-and-water, ratepaying, ambiguous 'Labour' candidates, but for the candidates of a party which in the very stress and storm of the fight instructed its standard bearers to refuse to sign the pledge of the compromising Labour Electoral body, and to stand or fall by the full spirit and meaning of its revolutionary policy.

These 800 votes were cast for Socialism in spite of a campaign of calumny unequalled in its infamy, in spite of the fact that the solemn terrors of religion were invoked on behalf of the capitalist candidates, in spite of the most shameless violation by our opponents of the spirit of the Corrupt Practices' Act, and despite the boycott of the press. No other party ever had such a dead weight to lift ere they could appear as a recognised force in political life; no other party could have lifted such a weight so gallantly and so well. What is the secret of the wonderful progress of this party? The secret lies not in the personality of leaders, nor in the ability of propagandists; it lies in the fact that all the propaganda and teaching of this party was, from the outset, based upon the Class Struggle – upon a recognition of the fact that the struggle between the Haves and the Have Nots was the controlling factor in politics, and that this fight could only be ended by the working class seizing hold of political power and using this power to transfer the ownership of the means of life, viz, land and machinery of production, from the hands of private individuals to the community, from individual to social or public ownership.

This party had against it all the organised forces of society – of a society founded upon robbery, but it had on its side a latent force stronger than them all, the material interests of the Working Class. The awakened recognition of that material interest has carried us far; it will carry us in triumph to the end.

THE NEW DANGER

[April 1903]

The politics of France are so complicated that to the general public the task of comprehending them would require a closer study than most are able to give. Thus the fact that a leading French Socialist, M. Jaurès,[46] has been elected to the position of a Vice-President of the French Chamber was recorded in all our Irish papers as a great victory for the Socialist party, and has been accepted as such by the general reader. But few are aware of the true significance of the situation, viz, that his election is but a move of the French capitalist class to disorganise the Socialist forces by corrupting their leaders. M. Jaurès is one of the middle class element which, joining the Socialist party in search of a 'career,' were, by virtue of their

superior education, enabled to make of themselves leaders of
the working class movement.

Now, that working class movement having grown so formidable as to convince every one that the day of its triumph is
within measurable distance, the capitalist government seeks for
the weakest part of the Socialist armour that it might destroy
the dreaded force, and so seeking it finds that this weakest
part lies in the vanity and ambition of the middle class leaders.
First M. Millerand accepted the bait,[47] now M. Jaurès.

In other words the capitalist governments of the world are
now adopting and improving upon the policy of corrupting or
'nobbling' the leaders which has enabled the English governing
class to disorganise every serious attack upon their privileged
position. Here in Ireland we have seen our Home Rule leaders
most successfully pursuing the same game. In Dublin we have
Mr Nannetti taken into the ranks of the Parliamentary party in
order to confuse the working class who were beginning to
distrust the Home Rulers;[48] in Tipperary we had Kendal
O'Brien, and in Cork county Mr Sheehan, both of the Land
and Labour Association, the former a professed Socialist, and
the latter being a vehement critic of the enemies of the
labourer, now pliant followers of the men who antagonised
their Association from its inception. In England we see the
capitalist Liberals running a 'safe' Labour man for a Tory seat,
Woolwich; in the United States we see men like Mayor
Schmidt of San Francisco ran by a capitalist party as a Labour
Mayor, and boomed as such by the capitalist press throughout
the country, even whilst his police were breaking up meetings
of the Socialist Trade and Labour Alliance[49] in his own city,
and in the eastern states capitalist political parties placing upon
their electoral ticket members of a nominally Socialist party.

The universality of this capitalist dodge calls for an equally
universal move against it. Up to the present we regret to say
there is not much evidence that the Socialist parties of the
world are clear upon the course of action to be followed in
fighting this insidious scheme. If we except the Socialist Labour Party of the United States, and the Parti Ouvrier[50] of
France, there is no Socialist party which does not betray signs
of wobbling upon the matter. In Germany the Social Democratic Party has admitted into its ranks in the Reichstag the
High Priest of the men who accept such 'gifts from the
Greeks,' Bernstein;[51] and in many other Continental countries
the party is in a state of internal war over the matter. In

England no one as yet has been asked into the Cabinet from
the Socialist ranks, but there are scores fighting to get in a
position to be asked, and hungering to accept.

The Social Democratic Federation[52] has been drugged in
this matter in the most shameful fashion. At the Paris Congress[53] their representatives were induced to vote for Millerand
– the first of the intellectuals to sell out – chiefly by the
representations of Quelch and Hyndman, and against the
advice and indignant remonstrance of the pioneers and veteran
fighters of the Socialist movement in France. Now that all
Quelch and Hyndman, & Co, said in favour of the compromise
has been utterly falsified, and the most bitter denunciations of
Millerand most amply justified, Hyndman joins in the cry
against him, but even in doing so he shows no sign of shame
for having voted to condone the treachery he now condemns.

This carefully stimulated indignation only excites amaze-
ment. In an article in *Justice*, March 21, after recapitulating all
the acts of treachery of which Millerand has been guilty since
Hyndman voted against his condemnation the latter says: 'But
now comes the most serious part of the whole affair. Millerand
has just republished his speeches, with an introduction.' And
this is 'the most serious part of the whole affair,' in Hyndman's estimation. But to do our London comrade justice he
does not propose to leave us without a remedy. What is his
remedy? Consider! the Socialist movement is convulsed by this
capitalist move, and by the presence in the Socialist ranks of
weaklings and ambitious middle class elements ready to be
corrupted, and in this moment of international danger the man
who is the trusted leader of the Socialist movement in one of
the most important countries in Europe, England, proposes as
a means, nay, as the ONLY means of settling it all that HE
should debate the matter with Millerand at a public meeting.
This, he says, is the 'only way to bring the matter to an issue.'

As a piece of opera-bouffe that would be excellent; as a
piece of serious politics it is beneath contempt.

As an exponent of Socialist economics Hyndman has no
more ardent admirer than the writer of this article, but we
contend that as a political guide his whole career has been one
long series of blunders; a fact that explains, as nothing else can
explain, the wobbling state of the movement in England. The
key note of his character has been to preach revolution and to
practise compromise, and to do neither thoroughly.

But why should we criticise an English Socialist? Because

what injures the Socialist movement in one country injures it also in others, and because this country is unfortunately tied to England and therefore is influenced by her politics more than by any other. And the weakness of the real revolutionary movement in England is a constant danger to the hopes of freedom in Ireland.

As a matter of fact we would have criticised more often and more unreservedly than we have done the position of our SDF comrades were it not for the fact that they are English, and we had always an uncomfortable feeling that did we criticise them it would please the chauvinist Irishman, and we had no desire to flatter his narrow prejudices at the expense of Socialists, no matter how mistaken these latter were. But such considerations must yield to the greater gravity of the present circumstances.

It is necessary in Ireland as well as in England to emphasise the point that the policy of the capitalist at present throughout the world is the policy of pretended sympathy with working class aspirations – such sympathy taking the form of positions for our leaders – and the man who can not diagnose the motives directing that move BEFORE the harm is done, is a danger to the Socialist movement.

UNPATRIOTIC?

[May 1903]

In every country of the earth in which Socialism has taken root its advocates meet with the objection that their doctrines are 'unpatriotic,' that Socialism is a foreign idea. Whether it be in Ireland, Germany, France, America, England, Russia, Italy or any other country we find the enemies of Socialism harping upon this one theme, the unpatriotic character of the Socialist movement. It is fitting, therefore, that we should examine and analyse this theory in order that we may find out upon what it is founded, how it is that in countries so widely separated the Socialist movement meets with an almost identical objection – in conservative Ireland as in cosmopolitan America.

We need not go far in our analysis. It is an axiom accepted by all Socialists that the ruling class industrially will always be the ruling class politically, and will also dominate in all other walks of life and fields of thought.

That until the epoch of revolution arrives the interests of

the class who hold the dominant machinery of production will colour and mould the entire thought and institutions of society at large; making whatever serves such interests appear as 'patriotic,' 'native' and thoroughly 'Irish' or 'American' or whatever the nationality of the possessing class may be. And in like manner stamping as 'foreign,' 'unpatriotic,' 'un-Irish' or 'un-American' everything that savours of danger to that possessing class. In other words the possessing class always and everywhere arrogates to itself an exclusive right to be considered THE NATION, and basing itself upon that right to insist that the laws of the land should be in its hands to frame and administer in its own interests, which, it pleasantly informs us, are the highest interests of the nation.

This is a characteristic of the propertied classes everywhere, even where they are not a ruling class. The Land League agitation in Ireland, and in a lesser degree the present Land agitation,[54] exemplified this trait. The Land League agitation centred round the fight of the tenant farmers for better terms for their holdings. It was primarily a contest betwixt tenant and landlord.

The agricultural labourer had no concern in it, indeed he invariably got better terms from the landlord than the tenant farmer; the urban population had no interests directly at stake, town workers were not considered in Land Bills; all the mercantile, industrial and professional classes knew they would be left outside the scope of the settlement between landlord and tenant should one be arrived at, yet, the tenant farmers being organised politically and industrially, and above all being class-conscious, that is to say conscious of the identity of their class interests, succeeded in impressing the character of their movement upon the whole life of Ireland.

Every farmer's grievance became an Irish national grievance, every farmer refusing to pay rent was idealised as a patriot battling, not for his own purse, but for his country, every farmer evicted was acclaimed as a martyr for his country; if a man took an evicted farm he was not merely a landgrabber or scab on his class, he was a traitor to 'Ireland,' and every person who spoke to him, or helped to feed, clothe or shelter him was also an enemy to Ireland, a traitor to his native land, a Judas or a Diarmuid Mac Murchadha.[55] Thus the tenant farmers dominated the thought of the country and made the fight of their own class for its rights identical with the idea of Irish patriotism.

Now we are not pointing this fact out in order to denounce it. On the contrary we consider the farmers acted wisely in their own interests. But we do point it out in order to emphasise our contention that any particular act or political doctrine is patriotic or unpatriotic in the exact proportion in which it serves the interests of the class who for the time being hold political power. The Farmers of Ireland denounced as unpatriotic everything that failed to serve their class interests, – including even the labourer's demand for a cottage; let the Working Class of Ireland follow their lead and test the sincerity of every man's patriotism by his devotion to the interests of Labour. In the eyes of the farmer no wagging of green flags could make a landgrabber a patriot: let the Workers apply the same test and brand as enemies to Ireland all who believe in the subjection of Labour to Capital – brand as traitors to this country all who live by skinning Irish Labour.

For the working class of the world the lesson is also plain. In every country Socialism is foreign, is unpatriotic, and will continue so until the Working Class embracing it as their salvation make Socialism the dominant political force.

Then the interests of the Working Class will be in the ascendant and every man's patriotism will be gauged by his services and devotion to these interests, thus Socialism will be patriotic and native everywhere, and the advocates of Capitalistic property will be the unpatriotic ones.

By their aggressiveness and intolerance the possessing classes erect the principles of their capitalist supremacy into the dignity of national safeguards; according as the Working Class infuses into its political organisation the same aggressiveness and intolerance will it command the success it deserves, and make the Socialist the only good and loyal citizen.

Part Two

The Socialist 1902–1904

The Socialist was established in August 1902 by the revolutionary wing of the British socialist movement, concentrated mainly but not exclusively in Scotland. Chafing at the opportunism expressed by the leaderships of the Social Democratic Federation and the Independent Labour Party, they took their lead from the Socialist Labor Party of the US. The first five issues of the paper were printed on the ISRP's press in Dublin.

The *Socialist*'s editor was expelled from the SDF in 1903 for attacking its leaders, and the paper's followers responded by establishing the Socialist Labour Party of Great Britain. Connolly, as national organiser, wrote the new party's platform (included as an appendix to this Part).

As usual, much of his organising was with his pen. Connolly's articles in *The Socialist* are noticeable mainly for their views on the socialist movement internationally, as he preached the revolutionary gospel he'd brought back from the American SLP, and swept aside the timid reformists on both sides of the Atlantic.

When Connolly locked horns with Daniel de Leon soon after settling in America, his old comrades on *The Socialist* gave him use of their front page to put his case – until the word from the United States forced the British SLP to apologise to its American big sister. Connolly maintained links with the SLPers in Scotland, but the columns of *The Socialist* were closed to him.

THE SOCIALIST LABOUR PARTY OF AMERICA
and the London SDF

[June 1903]

> The prompt action of the SDF in dealing effectually with those
> malcontents who are bent upon following the lead of the German-
> Venezuelan Jew Loeb, or 'de Leon,' to the pit of infamy and disgrace,
> is regarded with much satisfaction on this side.

The above extract from our amusing contemporary, *Justice*,
may serve as an introduction to the following sketch of my
impressions of the Socialist movement in the United States.[1]
But first I would like to point out how accurately that paragraph photographs the mental conditions and methods of the
men in charge of that paper. Take the phrase applied to our
comrade Daniel de Leon – 'the German-Venezuelan-Jew.'
Here we see in a paper which a week or two previous had
been, in dealing with the First of May, complimenting the
international character of the Socialist movement, and vehemently asserting that our principles were superior to all conditions of race or nationality, in its evil-minded desire to
injure a Socialist editor[2] sneering at him as a 'German-
Venezuelan-Jew.' In other words, directly appealing to racial
antipathies and religious prejudices. But we who have been
studying *Justice*, not as an inspired emanation from the
brightest intellects of the age, but as a rare freak in the
political world, are well aware that this is no new trick of
its policy. We all remember how, when the late Boer war
was being launched upon this country, *Justice*, instead of
grasping at the opportunity to demonstrate the unscrupulous
and bloodthirsty methods of the capitalist *class*, strove to
divert the wrath of the advanced workers from the capitalists
to the *Jews*; how its readers were nauseated by denunciations
of 'Jewish millionaires,' 'Jewish plots,' 'Jew-controlled newspapers,' 'German Jews,' 'Israelitish schemes,' and all the stock
phrases of the lowest anti-Semitic papers, until the paper
became positively unreadable to any fair-minded man who
recognised the truth, viz, that the war was the child of
capitalist greed, and inspired by men with whom race or
religion were matters of no moment.

Now, comrade de Leon is a Venezuelan, and the descendant
of an old family, famous alike in the history of Spain and the

New World, but if he were all that the *Justice* phrase has him, what of it? Suppose he were a German-Venezuelan-Jew, or a Cockney-Irish-Scotsman, or even, horror of horrors, an Anglo-Saxon, what is it to us or to Socialists generally? Mr Hyndman always claims to be 'only a common Englishman,' although, as a matter of fact, he once stated to the writer that he was of Irish descent, and that one of his relatives was implicated in the insurrection of 1798, but as long as he claims England, no Irishman who knows him would seek to deprive England of the honour.

But Mr Hyndman assured us in the issue of *Justice* prepared for the last SDF Conference that de Leon killed his party. If this is so, and I would not dare to insinuate that Mr Hyndman was lying, then, from what I know of the SDF and of the American SLP, a dead party in the States must be a bigger political force than a live party in Great Britain.

First let us see what the SDF has not done, then look at what the SLP has done *and is still doing*.

The SDF is over twenty years in existence, yet it does not own or control a single newspaper or journal of any kind. At repeated Annual Conferences the delegates have been told by Mr Quelch that he would print in *Justice* any report of the Conference he pleased, and that they had no control over the matter. The Twentieth Century Press, as a matter of fact, was established upon shares sold all over the country at a time when Socialists, Anarchists, Fabians, Labourmen, Christian Socialists, and every kind of freak, were lumped together, and all of them were, and perhaps still are, represented among the shareholders. But the SDF as a party has no control over the shareholders or their property.

The SDF professes to be a political party independent of all others, and the only real exponent of Socialist principles, yet since the ILP came into existence the SDF has never had the courage to engage in a parliamentary candidature without soliciting the help of the ILP, and playing for the votes of the Radicals.

The SDF declares Trade-Unionism to be played out, yet denounces any attack upon the labour leaders who declare Trade-Unionism to be all-powerful.

The SDF declares the Workers' Representation Committee[3] to be worthless and a delusion since it will not pledge itself to a belief in the Class War, yet the SDF counsels its branches to refrain from criticising or opposing the candidates of this worthless and delusive committee.

Now what is the position of the SLP of the United States?

The Socialist Labour Party of the United States conducts a daily paper in the English language, a weekly paper, and a monthly paper in the same language. It also conducts a weekly paper in the German language, one in the Swedish language, and one in Yiddish. All these papers are owned and controlled entirely by the party membership. They are also set up and printed in a printing establishment which is the property of the party. In the offices of the *Weekly People*, New York, there are five linotype machines continually at work, an equal number of compositors setting from the case, and a Hoe printing machine capable of printing and folding 30,000 copies per hour.

There is also a paper in the Italian language affiliated to and supporting the party, but not owned by the membership.

At last election this party polled 53,000 votes in the United States. Every one of these votes were cast for its programme and policy, despite the fact that another (so-called) Socialist party was in the field against it. The 'Social Democrat,' or 'Socialist,' as this other party is called, is exactly analogous to the ILP of Great Britain. To exactly appreciate the value of the vote of the Socialist Labour Party as a criterion of its strength, you have to imagine what the vote of the SDF would be if it could muster up courage sufficient to run a candidate in an election in which the ILP had also a man in the field.

The SLP declares pure and simple trade-unionism to be played out, and acting on that belief, it attacks and exposes the treacheries and sophistries of the trade-union leaders.

The SLP declares itself to be the only genuine Socialist Party in the United States, and acting on that belief, it opposes every other party, and fights them at every election.

The SLP seeks to make Socialism a guiding principle in the daily life of the workers by organising trade-unions on Socialist lines, and by refusing membership to anyone who identifies himself with its antagonists by accepting office in a pure and simple trade-union.

In short, the SLP does everything the SDF has not heart enough to do; it therefore shows its belief in its own principles, and wins the respect of its enemies even whilst they hate it. On the other hand, the SDF recoils from the logical application of the principles it professes to believe in, and whilst continually criticising the ILP, as continually seeks to embrace it in unity, although as continually repelled with contempt. There was revolutionary activity and fight once in the SDF, but their leaders, Hyndman, Quelch, Burrows, etc, have led it indeed as a lightning conductor leads lightning – into the earth to dissipate its energy. Therefore the party which has been killed is stronger than the party which no one thinks worth killing.

JAMES CONNOLLY.

THE AMERICAN SDP
Its Origin, its Press, and its Policies

[July 1903]

In my article in the June issue of the *Socialist* I sought to place before our readers a correct picture of the position of the Socialist Labour Party of America, by contrasting it with the London SDF, and in doing so to expose the misrepresentations of Mr Hyndman and 'comrade *Justice.*' One point in the *Justice* American letter, however, I missed. It was the statement that the SLP had lost its place on the ballot in several states through corrupt practices. Of course no particulars were given, because none could be given as the statement was as destitute of any foundation in fact as the persons who made and retailed it were destitute of honour. Yet the persons who utter such slanders are they who whine about the 'outrageous language' of the writers in the *Socialist*. We would ask those honest men who still remain in the SDF to require from the organ of the Twentieth Century Press the particulars, state, and date where the SLP lost its place through corrupt practices, and the name of the correspondent who makes the charge.

In this article I propose to give some details about the Social Democratic, or Socialist Party, the pet protege in American politics of the SDF. This party was established by Eugene V. Debs,[4] and at its foundation was not a political, but a colonising party. That is to say, that it did not propose to realise Socialism through the conquest of the public powers of government by the working class marching to the ballot box in their respective localities. Oh, no! The bright brains of the leaders conceived a more brilliant plan than that. This plan was that all the Socialists in the United States should leave their then homes and move simultaneously into one State to be fixed upon by the party, and

so secure a majority in that State. Then that they should elect the
legislature of that State, appoint Socialists to administer the public powers, and so inaugurate the Socialist Republic. Then the
theory ran that all the other States in the Union would be lost in
admiration of the Socialist institutions in full working order, and
would signify their admiration by rushing into Socialism. This
plan was undoubtedly simple – so were the people who thought it
practicable.

But the Socialist Labour Party men began attending the
meetings of this SDP and asking irreverent questions. They
wanted to know why, if Debs was a Socialist, he supported
Bryan the Democrat in 1896. Considering there were already
many unemployed in each State, how the Socialists, who gave
up their situations in order to colonise, were going to find
employment in the new State while waiting for the majority.
Seeing that the United States Government was a capitalist government, and had already sent the Federal troops into Illinois
in order to put down a strike,[5] what would it do when the
Socialist governors or legislature of Mr Debs' colony-state
started in to socialise any capitalist property?

A few questions like these continually driven home and
supplemented by vigorous criticism soon punctured the colony
scheme, and eventually it was dropped by its promoters, thanks
entirely to the light let in on the subject by the SLP men. But
with the dropping of the colony scheme the SDP definitely
entered politics as a Socialist (?) party. In 1898 its ranks
received an accession of numbers from those who had either
been expelled from the SLP for treachery, or had incontinently
fled its councils to escape expulsion. These formed what was
styled the kangaroo party,[6] and the circumstances attending its
formation are worth recording.

The *People*, the organ of the Socialist Labour Party, was
at that time published in the office of a private printing
corporation, which was known as the Volkszeitung Corporation, from the fact that it had been established to print and
publish a Socialist paper in the German language – the
Volkszeitung. This paper accepted capitalist advertisements,
even the advertisements of capitalist politicians, and advocated all kinds of tax reform as Socialism. Eventually a
motion was sent round the SLP sections, to be voted upon
by the entire membership, in favour of placing the printing
and publishing of the SLP organs and literature generally in
the hands of the party itself. In passing, I may remark that

in the SLP general votes are taken by individual membership and not by sections or branches. In the case of the vote
under consideration, all those in favour of compromises, of
conciliating the Debsites, and truckling for the support of
pure and simple trade unionism, were in favour of leaving
the paper in the control of the Volkszeitung Corporation. But
as the vote came in gradually and was duly tabulated in the
columns of the *People*, it was seen that the straight and
uncompromising members were in the majority, and that the
private ownership of the party press was doomed.

Affrighted at this, the unclean section of the party strove
to avert disaster and keep the press in their hands by
making a midnight raid on the premises of the National
Executive, and by force to override the constitution of the
party and set at naught its vote. They failed, but as a last
measure formed another party and issued a rival paper, both
party and paper usurping the titles of the original until
compelled by law to abandon the fraudulent practice. Now
they are called in New York the Social Democratic Party,
and their organ is called the *Worker*, owned of course not by
the party, but by the aforementioned private corporation.

In the presidential election of 1900, this element sent a
deputation to the National Convention of the Debsite party
and succeeded in getting their nominee, Job Harriman, nomi-
nated as candidate for Vice-President of the United States.
This was to bring unity between the two sections of those
opposed to the SLP, but it did not succeed, for as soon as
the Convention was over Debs sent a letter to his press
vehemently denouncing what he termed the trickery and
treacherous methods of the Harriman party. As a result,
although the nomination held good for the election, the two
candidates, who were supposed to be running in harness and
harmony, never appeared on the same platform.

Some time ago a letter from that wonderful 'American
Correspondent' appeared in *Justice* announcing the consumma-
tion of unity among the socialists of the United States,
'except the De Leonite faction,' of course. This unity was
arrived at by means of a resolution at a convention in
Indianapolis, if I remember aright,[7] in which it was agreed
that all sections should unite on the following basis:–

> That each State should have full local autonomy in all matters,
> including policy and tactics.

That each State organisation should sail under whatever name it chose, or the laws of the State allowed.

That there should be no official organ of the party.

In other words, that everybody could join who chose, and could do what he blamed well pleased after joining. That each State should frame its own policy, even if that policy was in direct opposition to that of the party in the adjoining State, and that the party should have no official organ in case the members should get to know the muddled condition in which the party was. Thus was unity accomplished. What anarchist could desire more? The result of all this is made manifest in the present position of that united party. In some States it is named the 'Social Democratic,' in some the 'Socialist,' in some the 'Public Ownership,' in some the 'Union Labour' party. Its policies are as varied as its names. In the Eastern States where the example and record of the SLP is to be reckoned with, it gives a lip adhesion to the principle of the class struggle, and appeals to the working class. In the Middle West, where capital is not so highly developed and the petty middle class is still a force, it trades mainly in schemes of municipalisation for the benefit of the taxpayer. In the Western Agricultural States it declares that the hope of the Social Revolution is in the farming class, and in California it withdrew its candidates in favour of those of a Union Labour Party formed by the trade union, and supported Mayor Schmidt of San Francisco, a Republican trade-unionist and enemy of socialism.

Each faction of the party represented by those various policies has an organ in the press devoted to its interests, but always privately owned. The manner in which those various organs of the united party speak of their 'comrades' who belong to opposite factions makes the 'abusive language' of De Leon seem complimentary by comparison.

The following are the names and locations of the principal representatives in the press of the faction indicated:– The *Worker*, New York, the *Socialist*, Seattle, Wash., the *Chicago Socialist*, the *Social Democratic Herald*, Milwaukee, the *Los Angeles Socialist*, California. The body which acted as a National Executive of this hybrid organisation was situated at St Louis, Mo., and its official designation was the 'Local

Quorum.' Early in the present year its chief members made a furore by openly repudiating the principle that the wage worker and his interests should be the basis of the Socialist movement, and by insisting that the farmer was the real basis, and that our policy should be shaped accordingly. After a bitter and acrimonious discussion the members of Section St Louis met and suspended the chiefs of this local quorum for treason. Setting their suspension at defiance, the Local Quorum moved itself to Omaha, Nebraska, an agricultural State, and proceeded with their new propaganda. They were supported by the *Social Democratic Herald*, and denounced as traitors by the Seattle *Socialist*. The *Chicago Socialist* declared the seat of the Local Quorum as the party executive should neither be at St Louis nor at Omaha, but at Chicago, and the *Los Angeles Socialist* darkly hinted that both were wrong, that Salvation lay not in Socialist consolidation, but in Socialist support of trade union nominees.

This unity of purpose and principle is still further exemplified by the fact that in the Eastern States they support the American Federation of Labour, the head of which is Mr Samuel Gompers, and in the West they cater for the support of the Western Federation of Miners, whose official organ, the *Miner*, correctly stigmatises Mr Gompers as a 'traitor,' a 'fraud,' and a 'Judas.' Quite recently this latter organisation enacted a rule to the effect that none of its members could be allowed to accept nomination for office by any capitalist party. This seems to show that it is marching towards the light, and I have no doubt that when it realises that the SDP is busy all through the States in accepting those capitalist nominations the Western Federation of Miners will not allow its members to accept, then it will not hesitate to throw that bundle of inconsistencies overboard and cleave to the Socialist Labour Party with its clean record and uncompromising policy.

This brief sketch of the SDP of America will explain why *Justice* has such an enthusiastic love for that organisation, viz, it seeks its affinity.

Inconsistency and sacrifice of principle for the sake of votes mark both organisations, and 'Be all things to all men' might be the watchword of either.

JAMES CONNOLLY.

LOUBET – and other Things

[August 1903]

It is a matter of common occurrence in Ireland when a
perfervid orator works himself and his hearers into a fever of
enthusiasm to see some of the auditory spring to their feet
and exclaim, "Tis a great day for Ireland!' I fancy some
such sentiment must have been in the mind of the unemo-
tional Englishman on the day the French President, M.
Loubet,[8] visited London. A great day for England! Aye, and,
we are told, a portent of peace and goodwill amongst the
nations, as well as a proof of the growth of democratic feeling amongst all classes in this country. Certainly, looked at
from the standpoint of a superficial observer, such as the
writers on London *Justice, Reynolds' Newspaper, Labour Leader*,
as well as the other organs of the classes, it did seem to be
a proof of the spread of democracy when we saw the head of
a republican government feted and fawned upon by the representatives of the power which a little over a hundred years
ago financed every tyrant in Europe to make war upon the
republican principles then first espoused by his nation.[9]

But trite as the truth is it is best to recall to our minds the
fact it embodies – we are not living under the conditions of a
hundred years ago, and our friends who wrote such glowing
passages about the significance of the visit had better awaken
to that fact and to the necessity of discussing political happenings in the terms of to-day and not of a past epoch. Since the
era of the French Revolution the world has changed in many
things, and not the least in the economic conditions which
mould politics and diplomacy. When the governments of England and monarchical Europe made war upon France they
made war upon a country in the grasp of a *revolutionary* capitalist class; the development of a hundred years has transformed
that French capitalist class from being the rejuvenating agency
of revolution and a menace to established order, into a bulwark
of economic conservatism and an ally of the most brutal reaction. We have but to recall the history of the French Republic
since the overthrow of the Third Empire to realise that fact.
That history is but one long record of merciless repression of
the working-class, and of increasing intrigue against and war
upon labour. A republic which saved itself from the hands of
the Parisian workers by the aid of the soldiers of the German

Empire, and celebrated its baptismal rites with the blood of 30,000 butchered members of our class.[10] A republic which, within the past two years, under the rule of this 'messenger of peace,' M. Loubet, has broken nearly a score of strikes by military force; which at Martinique and Chalons has slaughtered French workmen for taking part in strike processions; and at Marseilles ordered the sailors of its navy to act the scab upon the merchant sailors on strike. It only required the visit to Russia last year and to London this to emphasise the fact that the revolutionary tradition has departed from France, and that her rulers have finally merged themselves in the ruck of European exploiters.

The visit is however not without its uses. It serves once more to illustrate the insincerity and hypocrisy of the leaders of the London SDF. When we remember that that body has for the past few months been endeavouring to cover up the tracks of their treachery in voting for M. Millerand, by denouncing his continued presence in the French Cabinet, and then see them shouting aloud to the people of England to welcome M. Loubet, the French President, we cannot but believe that the spectacle will compel the more honest of their following to inquire, Why all this denunciation of the servant, and such effusive praise of the master?

Our readers will know how to treat the sentimental slop of Belfort Bax[11] in *Reynolds' Newspaper*, and the inanities of Hyndman and the *Justice* writers when they understand what really is the purport of the visit so much eulogised. To the thinking mind the purport of that visit is clear. It was to ratify the formation of a new secret alliance between Russia, France and England. This is at once apparent when we remember what has happened in international politics within the past few months. We had the visit of M. Loubet to Russia, the visit of King Edward to Paris, the silence of both France and England over the question of the continued occupation of Manchuria by Russia in spite of all treaties to the contrary,[12] the open threat to Germany by Mr Chamberlain[13] when introducing his protectionist proposals, and the present visit of the President to King Edward. And now at the time of writing we have in all the press the statement that the Tsar intends visiting London, but has been advised by the diplomacy of this country to postpone his visit until the King first visits Russia, which visit would help to hide the real significance of his projected journey. This hastiness

of the Tsar was, in fact, nearly 'giving the game away,' as
his more lowly brothers in crime would phrase it.

It is really amusing to see how such a blatant Russopho-
bist as Mr Hyndman joins with the pack in halloaing in
favour of this latest move of the Muscovite; how Mr Belfort
Bax, who in his own felicitous phraseology, has wasted
'gallons of good ink' in demonstrating the utter imbecility of
the theories of the noble-minded political republicans of the
1848 period, now calls upon the democracy to worship at the
shrine of the head of a bastard republicanism; how, in short,
the truculent declamation of the 'Class War' has given way
to a shout of 'Vive l'entente cordiale' between the national
heads of capitalist society. The Tsar – whose Cossacks brutally murdered hundreds of working-class men, women and
children in the factory towns of Russia last year;[14] the
President – whose soldiery are hurled at every strike, whose
prefects, as at Carmaux, override the benificent proposals of
every Socialist city council; the King – whose class legislation has made trade-unionism a farce or a fraud, and whose
police at that very moment in Dublin were breaking the
heads of a peaceful procession,[15] yea, surely these are fit
objects for the reverential admiration of the SDF. When we
contemplate the antics of these men, our erstwhile 'leaders,'
the wonder is not that the Socialist movement in these
countries has made so little headway, but that it has made
any headway at all.

All this blundering on the part of the SDF leaders, to
whom political blundering has become a second nature (we all
remember how Hyndman blundered over the South African
war and patted Chamberlain on the back, until the restiveness
of the rank and file brought him to his senses), all this blundering will have a good effect if it is instrumental in causing
Socialists to revise their theories on France and the French
revolutionary tradition. Personally the writer believes that the
influence which that tradition exerts upon the minds of Socialists is disastrous to our movement. The theatrical splendour
and gorgeousness of that outburst has hypnotised the Socialist
mind, and even when theoretically clear upon its economic
character we find many of our writers and speakers still thinking and acting politically in terms of that past revolution. As a
result we find imported into our movement, and in too many
instances overlaying it, a whole host of theories of political
action, tactics, and strategy which are foreign to our principles

and destructive of our class spirit. This is not only the case in this country, it is so in the United States also, as well as in continental European countries. The sneaking fondness for any man who 'talks physical force,' even when he does it to cloak semi-reactionary principles, the concession of 'honesty of purpose' to every man who mouths radical phraseology, the idea (the fruitful mother of treason) of building a Socialist Party upon the working 'people,' instead of upon the working class, the vague but harmful belief that irreligion is necessarily linked with social revolution, and religious orthodoxy with capitalism, the tendency to rush off into all manner of speculations about the future, and the desire to exclude all who do not agree with the speculation upon the tendency resultant from the economic change, in short, all those wrong tendencies which spring from the habit of regarding revolution mainly from the standpoint of DESTRUCTION, instead of from the standpoint of BUILDING and CONSTRUCTION, are our baneful inheritance from the first French Revolution. It is because of that mental inheritance, those wrong tendencies, that we so often find in the socialist movement men whose whole conception of duty is that of the iconoclast – the image-breaker – and who, having such a conception, naturally tend to regard as socialistic everything which wages war upon present institutions. Such was perforce the nature of the French Revolution, which, being capitalist and therefore individualist, found the 'logical centre' of the universe in each man's brain, and worked outward to shape the world.

Such is not the nature of the impending Social Revolution which must seek the logical centre of society in the tool of industry, and is only concerned with those institutions or principles which are based upon its development. The capitalist French revolutionist had to fight to destroy the institution of his enemy; the social revolutionist has to fight in order to give the economic institutions of his enemy room to grow; the capitalist revolutionist of France dreaded the development of feudalism, the Socialist revolutionist hails with delight every fresh development of capitalism. This point of difference places our revolution at the very extremities of the poles of thought and tactics from that of the men of 1789 in France, yet the fact that these men killed a king and queen, ie, destroyed something, is often sufficient to blind men to-day to the utter inapplicability of their tactics to present day requirements.

We have to remember that the French Revolution was an uprising of the capitalist class, that their tactics may not be our tactics, and that their victory added another to the list of our enemies in power.

Then we will understand the visit of Loubet – and other things.

JAMES CONNOLLY.

Appendix

PLATFORM of the SOCIALIST LABOUR PARTY

The Socialist Labour Party is a political organisation seeking to establish political and social freedom for all, and seeing in the conquest by the Socialist Working Class of all the governmental and administrative powers of the nation the means to the attainment of that end.

It affirms its belief that political and social freedom are not two separate and unrelated ideas, but are two sides of the one great principle, each being incomplete without the other.

The course of society politically has been from warring but democratic tribes within each nation to a united government under an absolutely undemocratic monarchy. Within this monarchy again developed revolts against its power, revolts at first seeking to limit its prerogatives only, then demanding the inclusion of certain classes in the governing power, then demanding the right of the subject to criticise and control the power of the monarch, and finally, in the most advanced countries this movement culminated in the total abolition of the monarchical institution, and the transformation of the subject into the citizen.

In industry a corresponding development has taken place. The independent producer, owning his own tools and knowing no master, has given way before the more effective productive powers of huge capital, concentrated in the hands of the great capitalist. The latter, recognising no rights in his workers, ruled as an absolute monarch in his factory. But within the realm of capital developed a revolt against the power of the capitalist. This revolt, taking the form of trade unionism, has pursued in the industrial field the same line of development as the movement for political freedom has pursued in the sphere of national government. It first contented itself with protests against excessive exactions, against all undue stretchings of the power of the capitalist; then its efforts broadened out to demands for restrictions upon the absolute character of such power, ie, by claiming for trade unions the right to make rules for the workers in the workshop; then it sought to still further curb the capitalist's power by shortening the working day, and so limiting the period during which the labourer may be exploited. Finally, it seeks by Boards of Arbitration to establish an equivalent in the industrial world for that compromise in the political world by which, in constitutional countries, the monarch retains his position by granting a parliament to divide with him the duties of governing, and so hides while securing his power. And as in the political history of the race the logical development of progress was found in the abolition of the institution of monarchy, and not in its mere restriction, so in industrial history the culminating point to which all efforts must at last converge lies in the abolition of the capitalist class, and not in the mere restriction of its powers.

The Socialist Labour Party, recognising these two phases of human development, unites them in its programme, and seeks to give them a concrete embodiment by its demand for a Socialist Republic.

It recognises in all past history a preparation for this achievement, and in the industrial tendencies of to-day it hails the workings out of those laws of human progress which bring that object within our reach.

The concentration of capital in the form of trusts at the same time as it simplifies the operations of capital and increases the effectiveness of human labour, also simplifies the task we propose that society shall undertake, viz: the dispossession of the capitalist class, and the administration of all land and instruments of industry as social property, of which all shall be co-heirs and owners.

As to-day the organised power of the State theoretically guarantees to every individual his political rights, so in the Socialist Republic the power and productive forces of organised society will stand between every individual and want, guaranteeing that right to life without which all other rights are but mockery. Short of the complete dispossession of the capitalist class which this implies there is no hope for the workers, but in the hands of men who recognise that fact all proposals which maintain against the claims of capital the rights of the community, when coupled with the assertion of the interests of labour as the superior interests of the community, may serve as a good agitational basis for such preliminary skirmishing as will necessarily precede the final overthrow of the capitalist system.

Of such a character are the following proposals:–

THE CLASS WAR

1. The legal restriction of the hours of labour to eight per day or less, according to the development of labour-saving machinery.

2. The abolition of all child labour under seventeen years of age.

3. Graduated income-tax upon all income derived from capitalist property. Funds from same to be applied to
   (a) Old age pensions for all.
   (b) Free maintenance for all school children.

PUBLIC OWNERSHIP

1. Right of all national and municipal employees to elect their immediate superiors and to be represented upon all public departments directing their industry.

2. Nationalisation and municipalisation of all industries upon above basis.

POLITICAL

1. The abolition of all hereditary authority.

2. The degree of connection of any civilised people with our rule to be left to the vote of that people themselves, free from external pressure.

3. Extension of the franchise and full political rights to all adults, male and female; also to the military and naval forces.

But we must again warn the working class that all these measures are in themselves economically insufficient, and are but the temporary expedients of the passing moment. As the struggle between the workers and their exploiters develops all programmes will tend to become superfluous, and in the final issue the watchword of either side in the conflict will find expression in fidelity to a principle rather than in measures which are but details of administration.

Speed the Day

Part Three

The Harp 1908–1910

The Harp was the paper of the Irish Socialist Federation, edited by Connolly and appearing monthly from January 1908. Spailpín struck again after a five-year absence, this time to pluck the 'Harp Strings'. Connolly editorialised on the burning questions affecting American workers, and Irish American workers especially.

Connolly's writings in *The Harp* constitute almost a mental return to the old country, before the physical return that was soon to follow. Once again he felt at home, as an Irish socialist, applying socialist theory above all to Ireland and the Irish. Not that he turned his back on the fight in the United States – on the contrary, the paper is full of the struggles of the US working class, and Connolly was to the forefront in them, organising for the Industrial Workers of the World.

A shift in his politics is noticeable in *The Harp*. Connolly reacted to the sectarianism of the SLP by largely dismissing the need for a revolutionary party altogether, throwing out the baby with the bathwater. Industrial unionism, for all its fighting instinct, contributed by downplaying the role of politics in the fight for the socialist republic. In contrast to *The Workers' Republic*, Connolly was prone to blur the edges of political differences when writing for *The Harp*, rather than insisting on clarity.

The paper was transferred to Dublin in January 1910 under Jim Larkin's editorship, when Spailpín's contributions became 'Notes from America'. After six months, however, the threat of libel actions against the new editor closed the paper down. But Connolly was on his way home.

HARP STRINGS

[January 1908]

This is the *Harp*.

I am one of the favored few privileged to play upon the strings of the *Harp*.

Sometimes my notes will be gay, sometimes they will be sad; sometimes they will be lively, sometimes severe. As in Ireland the sun shines through the heaviest rainstorms, and the Irishman in the midst of his deepest woe will broaden out in a smile at a good joke, so the writer of these first columns of our paper will ever attune the strings of his harp to the music of the worldwide struggle between the oppressor and the oppressed.

And that struggle has its humorous aspects as well as its tragic. A grave demeanor does not always betoken a serious purpose, and a man offering up his life in martyrdom for a principle may yet march to the scaffold with a joke upon his lips.

Sir Thomas More, scholar and philosopher, executed by Henry VIII of England for refusing to admit the supremacy of that libertine king in religious matters, as he laid his head upon the headsman's block asked leave to brush his long-flowing beard out of the way of the executioner's axe. 'For,' he said, 'my beard at least has committed no treason.'

Yes, we are indeed fearfully and wonderfully constructed, as the near-sighted old gentleman said when he gazed at the skeleton of a donkey in the anatomical museum. Therefore let us laugh while we may, though there be bitterness in our laughter; let us laugh while we may, for capitalism has tears enough in store for all of us.

Fearfully constructed, indeed, and perhaps no race on earth more so, or has absorbed more heterogeneous elements into itself and at the same time given out more of the best of its blood to the upbuilding of foreign and alien races than the Irish.

All races are mixed more or less; a pure race does not exist. In all the world there cannot be found a territory of any size still inhabited exclusively by the autochthonous or original inhabitants, a territory whose records do not tell of a conquest and a settlement by alien invading hosts.

In Europe it is generally accepted that the Basques and the Finns are the only people of whose advent into their present location neither history nor tradition has aught to record, who are therefore possibly an autochthonous people.

But the Irish, to whom our capitalist politicians are forever preaching an aggressive insularity (as if a man could not love his own without hating his neighbor), can count as cousins and blood brothers practically all the nations of Europe. We have received and we have given the best and the worst.

The modern Irish race is a composite blending – on the original Celtic stock have been grafted shoots from all the adventurous races of the continent.

Let us glance for a moment at the tally of the races that have mingled and merged upon our island.

First in order we have the Celts, or Scots, or Milesians. Coming as invaders, they found a people of whose coming or origin no record exists. Settling in Ireland, the Celts colonized Scotland, Wales and the Isle of Man. Between those places and Ireland for hundreds of years there continued the closest friendly intercourse, commercial and social, marriage and inter-marriage. And down to our day the migration of the inhabit-ants of these places continues almost uninterruptedly, the sole distinction being that now it is the migrations of individuals as such and not of clans or communities.

Next we had the Danish, or, more properly speaking, the Scandinavian, invasion.[1] For hundreds of years Norway, Sweden and Denmark poured their best fighting men into Ireland, established cities and towns all around our coast – Dublin being their chief settlement – took our women and gave their own in marriage.

All around Dublin and the eastern coast the fair-haired Irish you meet are lineal descendants of the Vikings of the north who settled and married in Ireland, just as the dark-haired Scandinavians we often see in America are without a doubt the sons or daughters of the Irish maidens whom the northern pirates brought home from Ireland as the prizes of war to their homes in Scandinavia.

Then we had the Norman invasion – the fruitful source of all our evils to the present day. It also brought its mixture of foreign elements. Half Norsemen, half French, each in a gener-ation or two becoming imbued with the spirit of the island.

All during the centuries of struggle against England there have been continual eruptions into Ireland on one side or the other in the conflict of foreign soldiery, some of whom found their graves, some of whom found wives, most of whom settled in one way or another.

After the revocation of the Edict of Nantes in France,[2] Ireland was the refuge ground of thousands of French Protestant families, who established trades, founded new quarters of the cities and in a generation or two supplied the most determined recruits to the Irish struggle for liberty against the oppression of England.

In the Williamite war after the deposition of King James in England,[3] King William invaded Ireland at the head of an army composed of the adventurers of Europe, most of whom settled in the country when the war was over. Some became proprietors of the lands they had stolen from the Irish; most became tenants on the lands their swords had won for their leaders.

The common soldiers had helped to make serfs of the Irish, and in the course of only one generation their own descendants found the yoke of social and political serfdom upon their necks also.

Add to this record of the immigrations into Ireland, the fact that for hundreds of years the genial English Saxon had turned an honest penny by selling his womankind into slavery in Ireland – an old Gaelic writer calls them 'tall, fair-haired Saxon slaves, fit to weave wool in the mansions of a king' – and the further fact that hundreds of English Quakers at a more recent date fled from persecution in England to take refuge in Ireland, where their descendants multiplied exceedingly and waxed fat and prosperous, and you have a picture of a race dominated indeed by the Celtic, but as composite and varied in its make-up as any nation upon earth.

That is one side of the picture – the inflow upon our Irish shore, the record of the successive hosts of foreigners who came amongst us and, finding Ireland a green and pleasant land, chose to abide there and become bone of our bone and blood of our blood.

But there is another side, viz, the going forth of the Irish. Study the history of Ireland and you will find that, whether the compelling cause was love of adventure or stern necessity, this going forth of the Gael has been ever an abiding characteristic of the race.

'The chiefs of the Gael,' wails an old Gaelic poet, 'always went forth, but they never returned.'

Examine our earliest chronicles and you read of Irish

settlements in Scotland, Man and Mona, and all the British Isles. When Scandinavian hosts first conquered Iceland they found Irish books and evidence of Irish learning and Irish settlement; as the power of Rome declined Irish fleets and armies harried her legions retreating from the western sea-board, and an Irish king led a marauding army through France and Switzerland (Gaul and Helvetia) until at the head of his forces he was killed by an avalanche in the passes of the Alps.

When on the field of Bannockburn Robert the Bruce of Scotland overthrew the power of England,[4] one of his chief supports was an Irish auxiliary legion of the O'Neills. The district of Kincardine O'Neill, in Aberdeenshire, granted as a reward for their services, still perpetuates in its name the memory of the exploit.

Irish exiles served as soldiers in the armies of every sovereign in Europe for hundreds of years, lived and loved and married and left children speaking all the tongues of Europe. These soldiers, generally the best and bravest of their generation, left to Ireland nothing but their memory; to other countries they left the fruit of their loins and the heirs of their spirit and manhood.

In another column you will find some authentic figures of one Irish dispersion – the Cromwellian.[5] Here you find that in one generation alone no less than 34,000 soldiers in the prime of life went from Ireland to foreign countries. Irish soldiers, or Irishmen as a whole, have never been famous as celibates or as averse to the joys of matrimony, and there is no reason to believe that those in question were any exception to the rule. In all probability the greater number married in the countries to which they went, as the leisurely wars of the period gave them plenty of time to do, and left a numerous progeny behind them.

Consider, oh, my compatriots, what this implies! That Polack, whose advent into the workshop you are taught to view with such disfavor, if you could trace his ancestry back a few hundreds of years perhaps you would find for him an Irish ancestor who charged by the side of Hugh O'Neill on that fateful day when the English flag went down in disaster at the Yellow Ford.[6] That Dago, whose excited gestures win your disapproval so much; perhaps he has an Irish ancestor whose arms defended the colors of Queen Gráinne O'Malley when her ships swept the English pirates from our western

coasts.[7] And those Frenchmen – heavens, how many scores
of thousands of the best of our race have gone to build up
and recruit the armies and population of France!

But, you ask me, why this thusness? What has all this to
do with Socialism? My dear friend, this is a lecture on Internationalism. Didn't you notice it before? It is a lecture written
in characters of blood and fire in Irish history; a lecture on
the mingling and merging and therefore on the oneness and
unity of all the races of mankind.

Let no Irishman throw a stone at the foreigner; he may hit
his own clansman. Let no foreigner revile the Irish; he may be
vilifying his own stock.

Talking of France. What do you think of the comments
upon the recent proceedings of the International Socialist
Congress at Stuttgart, especially upon the militarist resolution? I mean the resolution of the French delegate, Hervé,
calling upon the soldiers to mutiny or desert in case of war
in order to prevent the capitalist class from again uselessly
shedding the blood of the workers in murderous wars.[8]

The comments of some American Socialists upon it have
been, to say the least, more interesting than instructive. I read
the other day where one leading American Socialist said that
the militarist question was one of those which we considered
settled in America, and could not come up for discussion in
our locals though it was a live question still in Europe, the
inference being that we were so much ahead of Europe on that
question. But are we?

Almost all the speakers and writers of the same party as he
whom I have quoted agree with the Hervé resolution, or think
they do. I think they only think they do. For I do not recall
that when the United States and Spain went to war[9] that any
organized body of Socialists in America called upon the United
States soldiers to mutiny or desert. The most they did was to
pass academic resolutions on the causes of the war; resolutions
such as the most reformist body of Socialists in Europe would
have passed without a dissenting voice.

And I am quite sure that if the United States and Japan
were to go to war next year there would not be the smallest
possibility of getting the National Conventions of either the
SP or SLP to pass a resolution in favor of an active
campaign to induce the United States soldiers to mutiny or
desert.

Why, then, talk of this as a settled question in America,

and inferentially condemn those who objected to the wording of the Hervé resolution? If that resolution was put not as a general proposition, but as a concrete one in the sense I have just spoken of (a war between the United States and Japan), we would soon find out whether it was or not a settled question.

The conflict between the French delegate and the Germans was not a conflict between revolution and reaction. The Germans, all criticisms to the contrary notwithstanding, are not reactionary. It was a conflict between the French method of doing things and the German method.

The German is cool, cautious, patient, given to analyze all the results of his words before uttering them, is determined and never recedes from a vantage ground once gained. And the German Socialist is the incarnation of the German spirit. He does not shrink from the idea of a fight, but he is resolved to fight in his own manner and, above all, in his own time. Hence he will adopt no resolution that might allow his enemies to fix the time and condition of the final struggle.

The French, on the other hand, are ardent, enthusiastic, optimistic, ready to sacrifice their all for a principle, recking little of consequences when a truth is at stake, and willing at all times to face a world in arms for a righteous cause.

As the Irish poet finely says:

Like the tigress of the Deluge as she heard the waters seethe,
And sprang onto the topmost peak, her cubs between her teeth;
So stood Red France, so stands Red France, her head bared to
    the sleet,
With Paris girdled to her heart and Freedom at her feet.

I consider that both French and German are earnestly and determinedly revolutionary. But they do things different ways. And one is needed as a check upon the other.

And American Socialists do not help the matter by adopting the Pharasaical attitude of thanking God we are not as these people.

SPAILPÍN.

OUR PURPOSE AND FUNCTION

[January 1908]

When the Irish Socialist Federation was first founded the action of its originators evoked a great deal of adverse criticism. We believe the launching of our journal will evoke still more. It is fitting, therefore, that we should devote some little space to explaining the central idea of this new venture in the fields of Socialist activity. We do so in no apologetic mood (our course is marked and mapped, and we shall resolutely pursue it), but in the belief that the more our purpose is understood the more will our methods be appreciated and endorsed.

The editor of this paper, the present writer, has been in the Socialist movement more years than he cares to enumerate, and in several countries as well as his own, and in each of the former he has noted with regret the adoption by Irishmen as soon as they became Socialists of a line of conduct fatal to the best interests of the Socialist cause amongst our people. To illustrate this, let us ask the reader to conjecture what should be the first result of the winning to Socialism of a worker of the Irish race. Obviously the first result should be that he should become a medium for, so to speak, translating Socialist ideas into terms of Irish thought, and a channel for conveying the Socialist message to others of his race.

But this he could only do as long as his Socialism did not cause him to raise barriers betwixt him and his fellow country-men and women, to renounce his connection with, or to abjure all the ties of kinship and tradition that throughout the world make the heart of one Celt go out to another, no matter how unknown. Yet this is precisely what their adoption of Socialism has caused in the great majority of cases amongst Irishmen. Led away by a foolishly sentimental misinterpretation of the Socialist doctrine of Universal Brotherhood, or International-ism, they generally began by dropping out of all Irish societies they were affiliated with, no matter how righteous their objects were, and ended by ceasing to mix in Irish gatherings or to maintain Irish connections. The result upon the minds of their fellow countrymen and women was as might be expected. At home and abroad the Irish Celt has had to keep up a perpetual watch and ward against insidious and relentless foes; for hun-dreds of years England has had the ear of the world, pouring into it calumnies and hatred of the Irish until the latter had become an Ishmael among the nations, and nowhere more so than in America. The bitter words of our poet –

> Aye, bitter hate and cold neglect,
>   Or lukewarm love at best,
> Is all we've had or can expect,
>   We aliens of the West.

simply chronicled truthfully the international status of our race.

Under such circumstances, and we repeat those were and are the normal conditions of our existence as Irish – under such circumstances the man or woman who broke away from and kept aloof from contact with things Irish and with an Irish environment became, in the eyes of their fellow country-men and women, deserters from the weaker side in a fight, and therefore objects of opprobrium and of hatred. In the case of those who became Socialists this was invariably the course of events; the dislike and hatred did not precede, but followed the breaking away from Irish associations. Had the convert to Socialism showed that his conversion did not operate to make him hold aloof from his fellow countrymen, or to decry their cause, he would have become a medium for attracting the Irish, instead of repelling them, and each fresh Irish recruit to our cause would have meant an added power of convincing the Irish worker that Socialism made its devotees better equipped mentally and morally to combat oppression than any scheme evolved by the invertebrate Irish middle class politicians; but this is just what the Federation and its organ proposes to do. We propose to show all the workers of our fighting race that Socialism will make them better fighters for freedom without being less Irish; we propose to advise the Irish who are Social-ists now to organize their forces as Irish and get again in touch with the organized bodies of literary, educational and revolutionary Irish; we propose to make a campaign amongst our countrymen, and to rely for our method mainly upon imparting to them a correct interpretation of the facts of Irish history, past and present; we propose to take the control of the Irish vote out of the hands of the slimy seoiníní[10] who use it to boost their political and business interests to the undoing of the Irish as well as the American toiler; we propose to chal-lenge all the other federations and nationalities in this country to a generous rivalry in the work of our common emancipa-tion; and we propose, finally, to show the world that after

seven hundred years battling against a mighty oppressor we are
still, as a race, lusty and vigorous for the fight, and that
abreast with the march of the intellect of the world we raise
the ideal of the legions of our unforgotten dead, 'Ireland for
the Irish,' on to the plane of the higher, nobler and all comprehending 'World for the workers.'

Thus all may see and learn that

Ireland has no leper sores
    Her eye is clear, her stature strong,
Still thro' her veins the life blood pours
    In mighty tides of speech and song.
She watches by eternal shores
    The birth of Right, the death of Wrong.

A POLITICAL PARTY OF THE WORKERS
[January 1908]

With the advent of an Irish Socialist paper in the labor
movement of America will come of necessity a host of questions and questioners upon the attitude of the proprietors of
that paper toward the political parties at present in the field
for Socialism. Such questions are unavoidable, and it is
therefore best that they be faced at once at the outset without delay or equivocation.

Let it be noted therefore that the *Harp* is the official organ
of the Irish Socialist Federation in America, and that that body
was founded with the intention, expressed and desired, of
spreading the light of Socialism amongst the working class
Irish in this country, and that, recognizing that the existence
of two political parties of Socialism has had in the past and
has now a confusing effect upon the minds of the American
working class, the founders of the Federation recognized that it
would be worse than folly to make allegiance to one or the
other of these political divisions a test of membership in the
newly founded camp of Irish Socialists in America. The Federation is not founded for political action, it is founded for
propaganda; it is not in existence to fashion a political machine, it is in existence to present Socialism as a historical
development from capitalism and as the only remedy for the
wage slavery of the workers. The task of presenting the Social-

ist side as against the side of the capitalists, with all their
powerful allies and weapons, is a big enough job for us without
also taking part in the campaigns of slander which form the
stock in trade of the American Socialists when they conde-
scend to refer to each other. In their mutual recriminations
many wrong things have been said, many right things have
been wrongly said, and we are convinced that if American
Socialists in general had been more solicitous in finding and
emphasizing the points they had in common, and less eager to
stretch the importance of the points on which they differed, a
great party – great in unity in essentials, great in numbers –
might long ere this have been built up in America. And until
that party does appear the ISF will confine its work to the
making of Socialists; let its recruits when made choose their
own political affiliations.

But, it may be said, since the Irish comrades deplore the
existing division, have they no suggestion to offer whereby it
may be ended? Is it not certain that as you make recruits to
Socialism, and those recruits choose their own political affiliations, that in course of time their differing choices will result
in bringing into the Federation the disputes which divide
Socialists outside? That is true, and therefore it is to our
interest as well as in conformity with our desires to find some
common ground upon which in our opinion earnest revolutionary Socialists could meet to combine their forces in battle with
the common enemy.

The common ground of action we favor is one for which a
strong sentiment already exists in the rank and file of both
existing parties. It has been adopted and endorsed by practically all the non-English using federations of Socialists in
America, and has therefore strong organized forces already
behind it, and it would, as a magnet, draw unto itself all the
true proletarian Socialists and weld them into an irresistible
force. A common ground of action to be effectual for its purpose cannot emanate from either SP or SLP; it cannot be
furnished by unity conferences, no matter how earnest the
conferees are; the ghost of all the hatreds and jealousies
aroused by the past years of strife will perpetually rise between
the most united unity conference and the realization of its
hopes, and, finally, it cannot be realized by an amalgamation of
the existing parties. There are too many leaders, save the
mark! Too many 'saviors of the working class' whose reputa-
tions have been built upon disunion; too many petty personal

ambitions which might be endangered did the rank and file have an opportunity to know and understand one another; and too much fear that a general reunion might mean a general housecleaning, and the consequent dumping upon the garbage heap of many great lights whose personal predominance is dearer to them than the power of the movement. Some men in the Socialist movement on both sides would rather have a party of ten men who unquestioningly accepted their dictum and called their blind faith 'democracy' than a party of half a million whose component elements dared to think and act for themselves. Unquestionably the realization of unity must have as its necessary concomitant the acceptance of the fact that the interests of the movement are greater than and superior to the prejudices or rivalries of its leaders.

What and where, then, is this common ground we have spoken of? As we have already stated, the ISF is pledged to no political party, but this neutrality on the political field is not extended to the economic. There, we believe, an assumption of neutrality would be a crime on our part. Between, on the one hand, the new economic organization, the Industrial Workers of the World, which prepares and organizes the administrative framework of society in the future, and at the same time furnishes the only effective method of resistance against present-day encroachments of the master class, and on the other hand the old-style pure and simple trade unionism of the AF of L[11] with its system of dividing the working class and its professed belief in the identity of interests between Capital and Labor, between these two economic organizations our choice is as plain and unmistakable as between Socialism and Capitalism; indeed, it is the same proposition presented in different terms. And as we believe that all working class Socialists must realize that their place is in the only real economic organization truly worthy of the name of union, the IWW, so we believe that the same body has it in its power to solve the problem of Socialist unity. On the day that the IWW launches its own political party it will put an end to all excuse for two Socialist parties and open the way for a real and effective unification of the revolutionary forces. To it will flock all the real proletarians, all the loyal-hearted working class whom distrust and suspicion have so long kept divided: it will be the real Political Party of the Workers – the weapon by which the working class will register the decrees which its economic army must and shall enforce.

We do not say this will end forever all fear of the existence of two parties calling themselves Socialists, but it will end all possibility of two revolutionary Socialist parties claiming the allegiance of the working class at the same moment. Compromisers and schemers will still erect parties to serve their personal ends and satiate their lust for being worshipped; intellectual mannikins will still perch themselves upon the shoulders of the workers and imagining their high altitude is the result of transcendent ability on their part will call the world to witness how great they are; but they will be deprived of their power to delude the real revolutionist by the simple fact of the existence of a political party of Socialists dominated by and resting upon the economic movement of the working class.

This is our hope, our proposed solution of the problem of divided forces, and on the day that that hope is consummated if anyone looks around for the class-conscious Irish workers he will, we believe, find them alert and determined at the head of the fighters.

Ollamh Fódhla.[12]

PS – We invite correspondence on this point. All letters must be limited to one column. – Editor.

IRISH SOCIALIST REPUBLIC
To the Irish People
(Issued 1896)[13]

[March 1908]

Fellow Countrymen:–

We are to-day face to face with a new crisis in Irish political history. The reactionary Tory Party – sworn supporters of every kind of royal, aristocratic, and capitalistic privilege – once more dominates the English Parliament;[14] the Liberal Party, long and blindly trusted by so many of our fellow countrymen, has proven itself to be to-day as treacherous and corrupt as it has ever been in the past, when it succeeded in obtruding its slimy influence across the field of Irish politics; the Home Rule Party, split up into a dozen intriguing sections, seek by senseless vilification of each other's character to hide their own worthlessness and incapacity; in the country the tenantry seek in vain for relief from the economic pressure, born of landlord robbery; and in the towns the employing class strive by every means in their power to still further reduce the wages and deepen the misery of their unfortunate employees. On all sides personal vanity, personal ambition, and overmastering greed are seen to be the controlling factors in public life, and Truth, Freedom, and Justice are forgotten, or remembered only to round off a period or give a finish to a peroration in a speech of some huckstering politician. Such is the state of Irish politics to-day. Fellow workers – the struggle for Irish freedom has two aspects: it is national and it is social. Its national ideal can never be realized until Ireland stands forth before the world, a nation free and independent. It is social and economic; because no matter what the form of government may be, as long as one class own as their private property the land and instruments of labor, from which all mankind derive their subsistence, that class will always have it in their power to plunder and enslave the remainder of their fellow creatures. Its social ideal, therefore, requires the public ownership by the Irish people of the land and instruments of production, distribution, and exchange to be held and controlled by a democratic state in the interests of the entire community. But every Irish movement of the last 200 years has neglected one or the other of these equally necessary aspects of the national struggle. They have either been agrarian and social, and in the hunt after some temporary abatement of agricultural distress have been juggled into forgetfulness of the vital principles which lie at the base of the claim for National Independence, or else they have been national and under the guidance of middle-class and aristocratic leaders, who either did not understand the economic basis of oppression, and so neglected the strongest weapon in their armory, or, understanding it, were selfish enough to see in the national movement little else than a means whereby, if successful, they might intercept and divert into the pockets of the Irish middle-class a greater share of that plunder of the Irish worker which at present flows across the channel. The failure of our so-called 'leaders' to grasp the grave significance of this two-fold character of the 'Irish Question' is the real explanation of that paralysis which at constantly recurring periods falls like a blight upon Irish politics. The party which would aspire to lead the Irish people from bondage to freedom must then recognize both aspects of the long-continued struggle of the Irish Nation. Such a party is the newly-formed Irish Socialist Republican Party. In its resolve to win complete separation from all connection with the British Empire, and the establishment of an Irish Socialist Republic, it embodies to the full the true Irish ideal – an independent nation with a social-democratic organization of society, thus adapting to the altered environment of the nineteenth century the vital principle of common ownership of the means of life which inspired the Brehon laws of our ancient forefathers.[15] In its program of immediately practical reforms will be found the only feasible proposals yet formulated, either for averting from Irish farming the ruin with which it is threatened by the competition of the mammoth farms and scientifically equipped agriculture of America and Australia, for lessening the tide of emigration or for using the political power of the Irish people with potent effect in paving the way for the realization of a revolutionary ideal. We ask you then to join our ranks; to spread our ideas; to work for our success, which means your emancipation; to help us to blend the twin streams of National and Industrial Freedom into one irresistible torrent, sweeping all obstacles before it, and bearing grandly onward on its bosom the toiling millions of the Irish race, proudly enthusiastic in their desire to join the mighty ocean of lovers of Humanity who in every clime under the sun are working and hoping for the time when oppression and privilege will be no more; when 'every man will be a Kaiser, every woman be a queen.'

Youth of Ireland, stand prepared,
   Revolution's red abyss,
Burns beneath us, all but bared;
   And on high the fire-charged cloud,
Blackens in the firmament,
   And afar we list the loud
Sea voice of the unknown event.
   Youth of Ireland, stand prepared,
For all woes the meek have dreed,
   For all risks the brave have dared
As for suffering so for deed
   Stand prepared!

– James Clarence Mangan

TO IRISH WAGE WORKERS IN AMERICA
[May 1908]

Fellow-Workers:

As all the political forces of the United States are busily engaged to-day in lining up for the great conflict of the Presidential election of 1908, as on every hand there is a measuring of strength, a scanning of 'issues,' and a searching of souls we desire on our part to approach you for the purpose of obtaining your earnest consideration of our principles before determining where to cast your support in the campaign. Let us reason quietly together! We speak to you as fellow workers and as fellow countrymen, and we ask where do you stand in politics to-day? Hitherto the Irish in the United States have almost entirely supported the Democratic Party, but the time has come when the majority of thoughtful Irishmen are beginning to realise that as the causes that originally led to that affiliation are no longer existent, the affiliation itself must be reconsidered. Political parties must thrive or fail according to the present development of the class in society they represent, and cannot be kept alive by a mere tradition of their attitude in past emergencies. The antagonism of the Democratic party towards the Know Nothing movement in the past[16] won for it the support of the Irish Workers, but Know Nothingism is not an issue to-day, and as the Democratic party is going down to an unhonored grave because of its inability to grasp the problems of our own time shall we Irish Workers suffer ourselves to be dragged to social perdition with it?

No; fellow countrymen, political parties are the expression of economic interests, and in the last analysis are carried to victory or defeat by the development or retardation of economic classes. Examine the history of America for the last decade in the light of this analysis of the springs of political action, and the truth of that contention will be at once apparent. The Republican Party is the political weapon of advanced capital, of great trusts and mammoth combination of wealth. Hence as during the last decade the whole trend of industry has been toward greater concentration of capital we find that the Republican Party has grown stronger and stronger and its hold upon the political institutions of the country has proportionately tightened. To-day the governmental machinery of the United States is completely in the hands of the servants of

capital, and Senate and Congress are but instruments for regis-
tering the decrees of the trust magnates of the United States.
On the other hand the Democratic Party is the party of the
small business man, and of those narrow ideas upon economics
and politics which correspond to the narrow business lines and
restricted economic action of the middle class in general.
Hence as the last decade has witnessed the continual absorption by the trusts of the business of its petty competitors so it
has also witnessed the absorption by the Republican Party of
the one time adherents of the Democracy; as it has witnessed
the downfall of the middle class as a social factor so it is
witnessing the downfall of the political party of the middle
class and its elimination as a political factor. And just as the
petty business man may hang on to a meagre existence in
business whilst no longer seriously considering himself as a
competitive factor in industry, so the political party of the
Democracy may hang on to a sordid existence in local affairs
by means of its control of graft whilst entirely eliminated as a
serious aspirant to national power.

We Irish Workers are then not under the necessity of considering ourselves as bound by tradition to the Democratic
Party; political parties are not formed by traditions, but by
interests. Where then do our interests lie? Certainly not in the
Republican Party – that is the party of our employers, and as
our employers we know do not allow their actions to be governed by our interests we are certainly not under any moral
obligation to shape our political activity to suit the interests of
our employers. Where then? To answer that question properly
we must ask ourselves why are we Irish here at all in this
country, instead of in Ireland. Certainly we have no complaint
to make against our native land, and we for the most part did
not come here for pleasure. We came here because we found
that Ireland was private property, that a small class had taken
possession of its resources – its land, its lakes, its rivers, its
mountains, its bogs, its towns and its cities, its railways, its
factories, and its fisheries. In short, that a small class owned
Ireland and that the remainder of the population were the
bond slaves of these proprietors. We came here because we
found that the government of the country was in the hands of
those proprietors and their friends, and that army and navy
and police were the agents of the government in executing the
will of those proprietors, and for driving us back to our chains
whenever we rose in revolt against oppression. And as we

learned that since that government was backed and maintained by the might of a nation other than our own, and more numerous than us, we could not hope to overthrow that government and free our means of living from the grasp of those proprietors, we fled from that land of ours and came to the United States.

In the United States we find that every day the condition of matters for the working class drifts more and more in the direction of the conditions we left behind. Here the resources of the country are also in the hands of a small class – the land, the rivers, the lakes, the forests, the fisheries, the towns, the cities, the factories, the railroads, the entire means of life of eighty millions of people are in the hands of a class which every day grows smaller and whose rapacity and greed and lust for power grows as its numbers diminish. Here also we find that government is but the weapon of the master class, that the military and police forces of the nation are continually at the service of the proprietors in all disputes just as in Ireland, and that the 'rifle diet' is served out to workers in America oftener than to peasants in the old country. But here the analogy stops. In Ireland the government was a foreign government. It was outside our control and beyond our reach, and hence no political action of ours could completely master the situation or achieve our freedom from the oppression of the master class. That class sheltered behind the British Government, and our vote for freedom was answered by a foreign army shaking thirty thousand bayonets in our faces. But, in the United States, although the master class – the proprietors – rests upon the Government, and although that government rests upon armed forces to maintain and enforce its will, yet all alike, being native and not foreign, are within the reach of the political and economic action of the American workers, and can at any moment be mastered by them. Hence the hopelessness which at one time seized upon the popular mind in Ireland need never paralyze the action of the wage-slaves here. Freedom lies within the grasp of the American wage slave, he needs but the mind and knowledge to seize it.

What then is the lesson for the Irish Workers in America? We are not trust magnates, nor little business men, and the interests which bind us to those who work beside us and suffer with us are infinitely stronger than the traditions which draw us towards those of our race whose interests are those of our despoilers. Hence our duty is plain. We must fight against in

America that which plundered and hunted us in Ireland. Here as there, and here greater than there, the enemy of our race is private property in the means of life. In Ireland it was fundamentally private property in land that was the original and abiding cause of all our woes; in America it is again private property in land and in machinery that recreates in the United States the division of classes into slavers and enslaved. In Ireland it was private property, immature but bloodthirsty, in America it is private property, grown mature from the sucking of human blood. In both it is the enemy of the human race. To quote the words of Ernest Jones, the Chartist leader of '48, friend of Ireland and fellow worker of John Mitchel in whose defense he spent one year in prison,

> The monopoly of land drives him (the worker) from the farm into the factory, and the monopoly of machinery drives him from the factory into the street, and thus crucified between the two thieves of land and capital, the Christ of Labor hangs in silent agony.

We appeal to you then, fellow countrymen, to rally around the only banner that symbolises hope for you in America as in Ireland – the banner of Socialism. Cast off all your old political affiliations, and organize and vote to reconquer society in the interests of its only useful class – the workers. Let your slogan be, the common ownership of the means of life, your weapons the Industrial and Political Organization of the Wage Slaves to conquer their own emancipation.

HARP STRINGS

[June 1908]

This month I wish to say a few words about signs of progress. As Socialists we have to spend so much time and energy pointing out the decrepitude and imbecility of capitalist society, so much time and energy in rousing our fellow slaves to a proper hatred of the degrading conditions under which we live and suffer, that we are apt to overlook the thousand and one factors that are making for the regeneration of the social order.

It is well to be discontented; it is well to have a heart hot with passionate hatred of injustice; it is well to be a rebel against a social system that makes for iniquity; it is well to be ceaseless in your denunciations of the wrong that sitteth in the seats of the mighty, but it is also well to have a hopeful spirit, and an eye to note and appreciate all those manifestations of social activity, organized and unorganized, that indicate the stirring of the human conscience, the restlessness of the human intellect under capitalist conditions.

Let the 'canting fed classes' purr their approval of the preachers of contentment and resignation, I at least wish to reserve my tribute of praise to the men and women who succeed in arousing in their fellows a divine discontent with a system 'conceived in sin and begotten in iniquity.'

Discontent, my friends, is the fulcrum on which the lever of thought has ever moved the world to action. Therefore blessed be discontent: Let no man repress within himself the stirrings of hatred of injustice, of discontent; they are the manifestations of the divine impulse towards better things, the workings of the leaven that shall transform the soulless slave into the perfect freeman.

Discontent! Let us see: Have we anything to be discontented with. I quote from a report in the Chicago *Daily Socialist* the following description of conditions in the South, as they were told by a delegate from that territory:[17]

'Little children five years old have to go out and hoe cotton in May, June and July,' he said. 'In August and part of September they go to school.'

'In September the cotton picking begins and the parents of these little children drive them like so many little ponies back to the cotton fields and drive the little tots to work. It takes constant driving and watching to make them work.

'Later the weather begins to get quite chilly and fires are built where these little workers stop now and then to warm their little toes and fingers. They don't seem to understand why they have to be driven away from these warm fires back to the frosty fields.

'Finally these people reach the starvation point and are no longer able to work. Then they begin to borrow, beg and finally steal. They lose all moral sense and the landlords drive the families away from the farms.

'The cotton field paupers then become slaves in the factories of the large cities of the South and sink to the lowest depths.'

That is bad, and so some workers are foolish enough to be discontented. But the officials of the capitalist republic of the

United States are also discontented. Thus I see that Admiral Robley D. Evans (Fighting Bob), realising that there is a weakness somewhere, rises and in his bluff, sailor like manner demands a remedy. And what is his remedy?

'We need 48 more battleships.'

I am not sure that he meant this as a remedy for the oppression of little children by the capitalist class of the United States, but I am sure that he imagined the need, real or imaginary, of more battleships to be the only thing worth talking about.

And I am also sure that the capitalist press of the United States acquiesced in his point of view, for his remarks were heralded far and wide whilst the awful conditions pictured in the report I have just quoted are scarcely deemed worthy of an occasional paragraph.

Such is the capitalist conception of statesmanship. Untold fruits of the perverted ingenuity of men to be devoted to the task of destroying human life, but at best cold neglect or a passive indifference to every suggestion for the preservation and ennobling of the lives of the workers.

Nevertheless how the heart of the patriotic American must have throbbed within him as he read of the splendid reception given to the US fleet upon the Pacific coast, how he must have felt honored when he reflected that those noble vessels, so ably manned by such a gallant crew, were American, and that he, as an American citizen, was honored also in the honors so lavishly heaped upon 'his' sailors and 'his' fleet.

Of course those poor oppressed little tots of children working in the cotton fields are American also, and by analogy every cruelty and every outrage inflicted upon them are also inflicted upon the 'honor' and 'patriotism' of the whole American citizenship that tolerate such a state of affairs, but then as the great American press does not draw that moral of course the great American public does not allow it to impair its digestion.

As a once favorite writer of mine has said: 'Such is modern civilization: brilliant and beautiful where it rises into the sunlight, but within it is full of dead men's bones – the bones of the poor who built it.'

But what about those signs of progress. Dear, oh, dear, my imagination has led me away from my subject, as it always does when I stop to reflect upon the anomalies of this social system we are living under. My thoughts run 'a seachrán,'[18] as my father used to say when he would set me to do ten minutes' work and find me an hour after sitting, dreaming with the job not yet commenced.

The first sign of progress I wish to note is the formation of the new organization in Ireland whose program will be found on another page – The Irish National Union of Workers. I have as yet no definite information about the persons who drafted that program as I have seen none of their names except that of their secretary, Councillor P. T. Daly, therefore I am judging only from my knowledge of the labor situation in Ireland when I hail that movement with pleasure.

I know P. T. Daly personally. He is a young man, a compositor by trade, and with an absolutely clean record. His first participation in public life was as a speaker at meetings in connection with the Old Guard Benevolent Union, an organization of veterans of the Fenian movement, and of those who subscribed to the principles of that movement.

Most of the members of this body were earnest whole-souled enthusiasts, but quite a few, especially those who joined during the Centenary Celebrations of the Rebellion of 1798, were wire-pullers who desired to use the Old Guard for personal purposes. I have always classed Daly among the former number.

Fortunately for him he had read most of the literature sold by the Irish Socialist Republican Party, and all of the literature published under the authority of, and by that body. In fact as a compositor he had helped to set it up, as it was printed to a great extent in the shop where he was employed. Such reading helped, no doubt, to steady him at a time when much foolish matter about the 'union of classes' was being preached in Ireland.

Since then he has become a Sinn Féiner,[19] been elected to the Dublin City Council, and has always, so far as we know, lined up on the right side.

Hence whilst it is more than possible that we do not see eye to eye with the new movement in all things we hail it with delight for two reasons: First, Whilst unmistakably Socialist it is unquestionably Irish; Second, It is in honest hands.

A bit of Irish history is apropos. The Irish Local Government Act of 1899[20] first gave the Irish workers the right to vote in municipal affairs. Immediately upon the passage of this act the Trade and Labor Associations all over Ireland formed bodies for the purpose of contesting municipal elections in the interests of labor. When the elections came these bodies under the name of Labor Electoral Associations contested everywhere against the nominees of the Home Rule and Conservative parties.

The result was surprising. The success of the Labor Electoral Associations was only limited by their own lack of courage. Everywhere the Irish working-class had rallied to the standard of labor and elected their men with surprising majorities. Conservatives and Home Rulers alike went down in defeat not only in the large cities, but in small urban constituencies as well.

In most places practically the whole ticket was elected, and in the city of Limerick the labor men obtained a majority in the City Council, electing the mayor.

It was a moment full of promise for the Irish Labor movement. Had the men elected been men with a true understanding of the situation, had they understood their class position in society, or even been as responsive to the class spirit as the men and women who elected them (for even the women had votes), or had they even grasped the fact that as they were elected in defiance of the opposition of the Irish capitalist politicians they should respond to the will of their supporters by remaining an independent party, the whole history of Ireland during those few years would have been altered for the better.

But they were for the most part weaklings like Alderman Fleming of the North Dock Ward in Dublin, or ignorant spouters like Alderman Kelleher of Cork, and knew no better than to form alliances with the old time politicians. As a result they disgusted their own supporters, and their actions on the City Councils stemmed the tide of Labor instead of clearing the way for its progress.

In the midst of this upheaval the Irish Socialist Republican Party, the only organised body of Socialists in the country who stood for the Marxist doctrines as understood by International Socialism, could not remain passive if it would be true to its mission. It was however in the position where a false step would have done incalculable harm to the revolutionary cause.

It made no false steps. On the launching of the Labor Electoral Association it recognized that although that body was by no means Socialistic it was a spontaneous manifestation of the class spirit on the part of the Irish workers, and therefore worthy of encouragement and support. Accordingly its speakers and its paper, the *Workers' Republic*, vehemently urged the election of the candidates of the Labor Electoral Association.

When, after election, the representatives of that body proved unworthy of their trust the Irish Socialists regretfully, but firmly opposed them. And when in following elections the same body abandoning their former independent attitude formed alliances with capitalist parties of Home Rulers and Unionists the Socialists were unsparing and effective in their denunciation.

This was not inconsistency. It was in conformity with the duty of the Socialist as laid down in the Communist Manifesto, that we must not be a sect standing apart from the general labor movement, but be instead a part of the movement, that part which comprehends the whole line of march, in the midst of the interests of the moment takes care of the interests of the whole, and pushes on all other sections of the working class.

This requires encouragement where encouragement is desired, and opposition and censure where opposition and censure are deserved.

I have no authority to speak for Socialists in Ireland to-day, but I believe that they will meet the new movement in the same spirit. Unlike the Labor Electoral Association this new movement is organized in harmony with the central principle of Socialism – the achievement of common ownership in the means of life by and through the organized working class; unlike the mere political Socialist it recognizes seemingly the absolute necessity of combining the economic and political organizations of labor, and in a true spirit of constructive revolution it depends upon the development of the class feeling amongst its members to clarify any obscurity or rectify any omission in its present program.[21]

That is one good sign of progress.

Here is another. As you all know by this time Spailpín is unequivocally a proletarian Socialist, and would rather depend upon the class instincts of the man in the workshop than upon the knowledge of those estimable Socialist men and women who belong to the classes who live upon our labor. Indeed the wisest of these 'intellectuals' are of a similar mind upon that matter.

When Marx had to choose between throwing in his lot with the intellectuals of the Socialist sects of his time, or with the rough men and women with whom he formed the International[22] he unhesitatingly chose the latter. He did so even although the intellectuals at least understood the workings of capitalist society and were able to analyse it, and the working class Internationalists were not.

He knew that once their feet were set upon the right track all the instincts of the working class would lead them aright, and that their material interests would co-operate in the good work. Time has proven his wisdom on this point.

But much as I insist upon the working class as the prime factor, even although a correspondent recently called me an intellectual, yet I hope I will never make the mistake of over-looking or slighting the value of the co-operation of the really educated classes in the work of Socialism.

I want all the intellectual Socialists whom we can get but I have little use for the Socialist intellectual. Now that is a cryptic saying you can ponder over while I am trying to work in the next paragraphs.

Read carefully this chunk of wisdom. If you found it as hard to read as I did to formulate you would either value it highly or – not read it at all.

The decadence of capitalist society is evidenced on every field in which human thought expresses itself; it is seen in the trend of science, in the uprooting of all old beliefs, customs and orthodoxies, in the shakings and readjustments of religious doctrines to suit the new conditions, as is illustrated in the Christian Socialism of Protestantism and the Modernism of Catholicism, it is evidenced in literature, art, and the drama, and in each and every case in which such manifestation comes within the ken of a Socialist it is his duty to recognize the good work that may be in it without abandoning his own view point.

Capitalist society is like an old barrel which has been packed to the rim with unfermented yeast; as soon as the yeast begins to ferment and swell it will burst the old barrel and come streaming out in every direction between the hoops. He is a fool who hails the yeast running to waste as Socialism, he is a greater fool who denounces the activity of the yeast as a capitalist trick; the wise man is he who hails it as a sign of the new life stirring within and breaking through the old environment. The new life will take care of itself obedient to the laws of its creation.

Well, why this thusness? This is apropos of many things. More particularly is it apropos of and an introduction to the following speech of Mr W. B. Yeats in Dublin. Mr Yeats about

4 years ago made a tour of the colleges and intellectual centers
of the United States on behalf of the Irish Literary Revival
and was everywhere honored and feted. He is an intellectual
Irishman, poet, author of many plays, and a son of the Yeats
whose fulsome flattery of our race aroused my ire some months
ago.[23] Here is what he says of the Irish bourgeoisie – the
capitalist class of Ireland:

'Ireland at the moment,' he said, 'is running the danger of surrender-
ing her soul to the bourgeoisie, and to a worse bourgeoisie than ever
fought in France – to an ignorant, undisciplined bourgeoisie. The
bourgeoisie of France was disciplined, and it had great qualities. If
they were to make the people great, the first to be fought was the
bourgeoisie, so that the latter might get disciplined. They, artists,
stood not for some pleasure, but for the laborious, disciplined soul,
because all fine art – everywhere in which there was a personal
quality – was the result of long labor. Art for art's sake was an
intolerable toil. Any man could make himself popular if he took a
few moral sayings, a few conventional moral platitudes, and put them
into pictures, verses or stories. But such a man would be forgotten in
ten years, although during that ten years he would be popular and
would gain wealth. In art and literature the unconventional always
seemed the immoral, because it was not the accustomed. It was easy
for a man with his mouth full of commonplaces to sail to popularity.
The bourgeoisie of Ireland, being undisciplined and untrained, were,
therefore, essentially immoral. At this moment this bourgeoisie were
attacking every artist who was sincere, or who was doing unconventional work, and in doing that it was merely doing what everyone
said it would do, and what every bourgeoisie had done in this world
for the last 200 years.'

My hand goes out to W. B. Yeats. Also my memory goes
back to a certain quiet but earnest discussion in which Miss
Maud Gonne, Mr W. B. Yeats and your humble servant were
the sole participants in the lady's reception room in a hotel in
Nassau Street, Dublin, when Mr Yeats was urging the necessity
of a union of classes, even to the extent of inviting loyalists to
join the 98 Executive Committee, and, remembering all that, it
seems to me that the speech just quoted shows progress and a
better appreciation of the forces that make for or against the
uplifting of the human race.

Certainly the intellectuals of Ireland are beginning to see a
great light. It is not so long since it would have been impos-

sible to find an Irish Scholar who would admit the essential bond between the language and industry of a people, or rather the dependence of the former upon the latter. In the *Workers' Republic* I once pointed out to some of my Gaelic friends that capitalism was their real enemy, that for 600 years Irish had withstood every attempt of England to uproot it by force of arms from its place as a spoken tongue, and that it was only when English goods invaded the Irish market that the Irish tongue gave way. As I said, 'the cheapness of English products paved the way for the introduction of English speech.'[24]

This is or was the application to Irish history of the Socialist position that the economic conditions of society – the social system – are the determining factor in shaping history. Now here comes one of our greatest Gaelic scholars, Eoin Mac Néill, and in an article in the Gaelic monthly magazine, *Irisleabhar na Gaedhilge*, attacks his fellow Gaels for their neglect of this point, and for their dependence upon tradition to restore Gaelic to its place in Irish life, instead of applying themselves to show it to be adaptable to the needs of modern industrial life.

I remember that some years ago a Cork priest urged in favor of Gaelic that it was full of reverent phrases, and was suitable and moulded to holy expressions whereas English was the language of unbelief. The poor sagart[25] did not seem to realise that he was really arguing that Irish was unfit to express certain forms of thought. If this were true it would have been an argument against Irish not for it.

I quote a part of Eoin Mac Néill's article and wonder if he realises that his appreciation of the essential truths of Socialism has enabled him to see this deduction from Socialist premises. It is a long article, but you can tell your good lady that you are better employing your time reading this than trying to drink a brewery out of business.

> About 300 years ago, when printing became general, the languages of modern civilization woke up. Till then they had been content with folklore, or with forms of literature that were closely akin to folklore. The literature of the working mind was monopolised by Latinists. One by one the different languages began to break the monopoly. Intellects were keen in those days, and it was clearly perceived that the new art of printing made it not only possible but imperative to write for the multitudes whom Latin could not reach. The vernacular languages set themselves to conquer the entire world of literature and thought.

Even Irish began. This was particularly the great achievement of Seathrún Céitinn (Geoffrey Keating), the clearest and most inseeing Irish mind of his time.[26] Céitinn realised that the Middle Ages were come to an end, that the literary forms of the annals and the uraiceacht[27] were, as the Yankees say, back numbers, that a literature that was to hold its own must seize on the inheritance of Latin and conquer the whole domain of the expression of the working mind. Accordingly, he essayed for the first time to reduce the whole history of Ireland, annalistic and legendary, to straightforward literary form. He also applied the same straightforward literary form to the subjects that were then foremost in all men's thoughts, the great questions of Christian doctrine. He introduced logical and philosophical exposition of difficult matters directly from Latin into Irish, exactly what was being done in the other languages of civilization.

The Latinity of his Irish has been censured. To some extent the censure may be just, but one would like to hear or read the trenchant terms that Céitinn would have applied to the doctrine, implied if not asserted, that the conversational forms of our grandparents or the narrative forms of the traditional storyteller, forms quite familiar to him, were adequate for a theological treatise or for a scientific defence of the sources of Irish history.

Hardly had the victory of the modern languages over Latin been secured, when the whole situation began to take on a new phase. The world's industry had heretofore been based mainly on tradition and experience. The whole knowledge necessary to every craft had passed directly from the journeyman to the apprentice. Gradually the developments of physical science as well as of technical mechanics wrought a great revolution. I need not describe the change. It is enough to point out that 200 years ago industry was practically independent of written thought. Its basis was purely empirical and traditional. At the present day, every form of industry except that of the most primitive peoples has become intimately dependent on physical science. The quill that Céitinn held may have been shaped by himself from a feather plucked from a neighbour's goose. The pen in my hand has been manufactured by Galvani and Isaac Watt, by Kelly the steelfounder and Lord Kelvin, and by a host of other men, theoretical and practical, whose sole contact, however, with this pen itself has been through vernacular literature.[28] No language that cannot make that sort of contact can ever hope to thrive in the world we live in. Man must earn his bread in the sweat of his brow, and since it has come to this, that literature has an essential function in the earning of every man's bread, people will throw away a language by whose literature they cannot live.

All these things are signs of progress. They show that Socialist philosophy is conquering the mind of the world.

In my notes last month I challenged the *Gaelic American* to give an account of the suppression of the *Peasant* by Cardinal Logue,[29] apropos of the visit of His Eminence to this country. The day after the publication of the *Harp* I received a marked copy of the *Gaelic American* of the issue of January 19, 1907, in which a full account of the matter appeared. The person who so kindly sent me the paper misunderstood me if he believed that I doubted the willingness of the *Gaelic American* to expose such a matter 3000 miles away from the scene of action. What I did mean to convey was that, as the Cardinal had honored us with a visit, an exposure of his dictatorial action in the past, if made now, would do more to make him and his like realise that clerical oppression was a two edged weapon to use than would any amount of newspaper exposure which did not interfere with his plans.

'The price of liberty is eternal vigilance,' and the liberty of the press can best be safeguarded by making its enemies realize that they are apt to be struck at and punished in the moment that they least expect or desire it.

Now that Cardinal Logue is here a concerted press campaign against him for his action against the *Irish Peasant* would be a lesson his cloth would take seriously to heart, and never forget.

Well, well, my notes this month have covered a wide range! It is another proof of the wide spread range of Socialist influence. Perhaps also it will serve to convince you that there are more things in Socialist philosophy than you dreamed of before. If it does it will help to satisfy

SPAILPÍN.

Part Four

The Irish Worker 1911–1914

Jim Larkin launched *The Irish Worker and People's Advocate* in June 1911, the organ of the burgeoning Irish Transport and General Workers' Union. His editorship was even more libellous than his short-lived term at *The Harp*, but this time he had the support of 20,000 regular readers to protect him: *The Irish Worker* established a foothold in the Dublin working class firmer than any other paper before or since.

The life of *The Irish Worker* coincided with what was certainly the most turbulent period in Connolly's political development. His organising activity both for the Socialist Party of Ireland, and for the ITGWU in Belfast appear in the speeches and articles of his in the paper. The lockout of 1913 brought Connolly to Dublin, occasionally to edit *The Irish Worker* when Larkin was in prison. The paper contained Connolly's responses to the outbreak of the world war, and he took over as editor when Larkin went to the United States in October 1914.

The paper reflects the optimism Connolly felt in his early years back in Ireland, with high hopes for a fighting labour movement making steady gains in a Home Rule Ireland. The bitterly fought battle of 1913 led to a hardening of Connolly's vision, and the workers' defeat, followed by the threat of partition, and then the war, left Connolly severely isolated. *The Irish Worker* shows his attempts to hold his ground following the collapse of the socialist movement at home and abroad, get allies wherever he could, and get what could be got during the war.

The paper went, not with a whimper, but with a bang. The British army prevented the printing of 'Courtsmartial and

Revolution' – Connolly's editorial for 5 December, a blistering defiance of government attacks on freedom of speech – and then dismantled the press. *The Irish Worker* was no more.

BELFAST DOCKERS
Their Miseries and their Triumphs

[26 August 1911]

Probably the readers of *The Irish Worker* will be glad to learn something of the condition of affairs in the port of Belfast. In the stress and storm of building a Union during and immediately after a strike there is not much time left to an organiser to do much descriptive writing, and hence I have not been able to keep in as close touch with the journal of the Union as I would have wished to, but will in the future. But this battle of the working class should be recorded, and the tale of its martyrdom preserved – the first as an inspiration and the second as a warning. Belfast has had its battles of Labour, and the record of Labour in the port of Belfast for the past five years has every right to be recorded as a record of martyrdom.

Never have I seen the evil results of want of organisation better exemplified than in the Low Docks of Belfast prior to our recent strike.

With the usual fiendish ingenuity of the capitalist class, every device was employed to spur on the dockers to increased activity, and to promote discord and strife. With the disruption of the Union the men were left dispirited and powerless, and stevedores, shipowners, and foremen wrought their sweet will upon them. In order to extract the last ounce of energy out of their bodies a system of bonuses was introduced among the grain labourers. Every gang turning over more than 120 tons of grain received as a bonus the magnificent sum of 6d per man. This, taking 100 tons as an average day's work, meant that for one-fifth of a day's work extra crowded in the ten hours they received one-tenth of a day's pay. This in itself was bad enough, but in actual practice it worked out even more mischievously. By tips to winchmen, firemen, and others, the pace was kept up upon the unfortunate fillers and carriers – curses, obscene epithets, and even physical violence were freely used to supplement the usual fear of dismissal, while the tally-men and checkers were forbidden to reveal the actual tonnages being done until the end of the day's toil. As a result of this systematic slave-driving the average day's work was driven higher and higher, until 160, 180, and 200 tons as a day's work ceased to excite any comment or be considered anyway remarkable. If the reader unacquainted with the technical details of dock labouring at grain vessels will try and realise that this means that one man of each gang, the man carrying to the ship's rail from the ship's hatch, has to carry over his own back all this immense weight, he will begin to understand the depths of slavery to which these men were reduced, as well as the cold-blooded cruelty and avarice of their employers. All day long in the suffering heat of a ship's hold the men toil barefooted and half naked, choked with dust; while the tubs rushed up and down over their heads with such rapidity as to strain every muscle to the breaking point in the endeavour to keep them going, and with such insane recklessness as to be a perpetual menace to life and limb. Add to this inferno of industrial slavery that the men could not even retire to attend to the wants of nature unless they paid a substitute to take their place, that a visit to a WC or a drinking fountain often entailed dismissal, and that every slave-driving foreman or lickspittle 'master's man' had a free hand to apply the spur, and the reader will have some conception of the depths of degradation to which our unfortunate Belfast brothers were reduced. Accidents were common, as is always the case when men are rushed to the breaking point, and physical break down was so prevalent that it was but rarely that men were able to finish three days' work in succession, the inevitable consequences of their exhausting labours compelling men to remain idle in order to recruit their strength, followed in the complete demoralisation of the workers.

Dockers are as a rule not famed for steadiness and sobriety, but when the nature of their casual labour is taken into account the fact cannot be wondered at. Were some of their 'cultured' critics subject to the same conditions perhaps their genteel varnish would not survive the strain very well. Labour carried to such an excess that men must rest on alternate days to recuperate naturally produces demoralisation and evil habits; hence the organiser and agitator who preaches rebellion against exhausting, ill-paid labour is doing more to uplift and regenerate humanity than they who preach righteousness, but tolerate and encourage slavish conditions and the slavishness begotten of them. The men engaged in timber carrying, in general cargo, and in the coal boats all suffered, in varying degrees, such abominable conditions as these I have but faintly described. In general it may be said that since the general exodus from the Union after our friend, Jim Larkin, left this city[1] the exploiters of labour had piled outrage upon outrage and iniquity upon iniquity until every man in the port with a spark of manhood left was ripe for rebellion. It but required a spark to ignite the magazine; that spark came in the fullness of time.

I had been agitating all up and down the docks, and at every available street corner since the inception of the seamen's strike, urging the men to seize the golden opportunity to strike a blow for their brothers, the seamen, and incidentally for themselves, and found the stream of recruits slowly, if surely, gathering in volume, when I learned that the proprietors of the Head Line, the Ulster SS Co, had refused to pay the Belfast seamen and firemen on the *Innishowen Head* the rate of wages the same firm was paying in the British Channel. Seizing the opportunity along with Mr Bennett, the Secretary of the Seamen and Firemen's Union, we called upon the dockers at that boat, and all their mates around the docks to come out at once, strike a blow for the sailors, and end their own slavery. Before night we had 600 men on our hands – the battle had begun. How this battle was won I need not remind you.[2] That it was won was largely due to the noble help so generously given by the Dublin men we are not likely to forget. We had not a penny in our funds when we struck. We paid 4s strike pay on the tenth day of our strike, and 4s 6d on the second week. Of this sum more than half came from Dublin, the remainder came from street collections among the loyal-hearted workers of Belfast.

What has been the result of this battle – the fruits of this victory? To tell it in detail would involve the printing of many technicalities, the meaning of which would be lost on many of our readers. But in general it might be said that in wages the grain labourers have gained an increase of at least 3s per week, while their gain in improvement of conditions and increased self-respect cannot be overestimated. On returning to work I announced as organiser that the Union would insist upon the day's work being restricted to 100 tons per gang, and that any gang exceeding that amount would be treated as scabs. It is a great pleasure to record that in enforcing this restriction the Union has been able to count with certainty upon the loyal support of its members. Despite the fact that the employers renewed their offer of a bonus for increased output, no gang have yet consented to earn it. Indeed, in order to make it more attractive the employers offered a bonus of 6d per every 25 tons 'or practical part thereof' over 100 tons. Thus a gang turning over 100 tons and one cwt would be entitled to claim this bonus, but it lies yet unclaimed. The awful memory of their recent slavery has made our members watchful. Also, all the slave-driving, curses, obscenity and physical violence on the part of the bosses is a thing of the past. All have been warned that any attempt at a renewal of it will be met with a strike for the dismissal of the offender. Similar conditions have been gained for the timber labourers, and for the men on general cargo. Increase of wages all round, abolition of slave-driving, full and complete unionising of all labour on foreign-going vessels, and spread of the union all around the Coal Quay, is our present record. We have enforced union conditions for the Seamen and Firemen on all ships coming into the Low Dock, downing tools on about a dozen occasions in order to do so; and we stopped work on railway waggons ten minutes after receiving word from our General Secretary and the Executive of ASRS in Dublin. The Belfast branch of the Railway Servants were still considering the matter for days after they received word from their Executive, but the Belfast Branch of the Irish Transport Workers' Union acted in the Railwaymen's interest ten minutes after we got the joint mandate from Dublin. The timber labourers in the employ of Messrs Dixon were locked out in Dublin; we immediately withdrew our men from Messrs Dixon's yards in Belfast. As a result of this promptitude our Dublin brethren were reinstated with pay for the last day. A boat belonging to Messrs G. & R. Burns (*Lord Inverclyde*) was sent down to the Low Docks for 500 tons of grain. It had on board Messrs Burns' own 'constant hands,' men who would not join the union, and cheerfully scabbed all during the recent strike. We told them we would give them to breakfast time to join the union; they said that according to the newspapers there was to be no discriminations; we told them that we would give them an experience that would lead them to have less faith in newspapers. They did not join, and much to their surprise our members refused to give their boat another pound weight, and after lying all day it had to be taken out of the dock, and down to Larne.

The Branch has rented extensive premises at 122 Corporation Street, and intend having a smoking and reading room in

connection therewith; we are considering the organisation of a
band, and have in contemplation also the launching of many
other schemes for the moral, social, and financial uplifting of
the members.

We are proud of taking part in the recent wonderful revolution in the World of Labour, and look forward, with pleasure,
to future activities in the same cause, and to future successes
under the banner of the Irish branch of that great onward
moving, conquering army of toil, which is destined, I believe
in our own time, to conquer and to own the world.

The Irish Transport and General Workers' Union is in the
vanguard of that Irish branch of the Army of Labour, and we
are honoured when we carry its banner. – Yours,

CONNOLLY.

WALTER CARPENTER FREE
Public Congratulations
SUNDAY'S MEETING IN BERESFORD PLACE
[2 September 1911]

A public meeting under the auspices of the Socialist Party of
Ireland was held last Sunday at Beresford Place to congratulate
Mr Walter Carpenter on his discharge from Mountjoy Prison,
where he had been confined for a term on a charge of having
used language alleged to be derogatory to King George of England.[3] There was a considerable attendance, which included
numbers of the National Boy Scouts[4] in their uniform. Unlike
previous meetings in Beresford Place, which were attended by
a considerable force of the DMP,[5] there was NOT A SINGLE
COSSACK at Sunday's gathering.

MR JAMES CONNOLLY, Organiser Irish Transport Workers' Union, Belfast, presided. In the course of his address opening the proceedings Mr Connolly said he was glad to see such
a large meeting despite the rain and other adverse circumstances. They had their comrade, Carpenter, again with them,
and next to him, but perhaps higher in the degree of criminality, they had Miss Molony[6] (applause). It is, continued Mr
Connolly, perfectly shocking to hear you cheer such criminals.
I take it that in expressing my own sentiments in this matter I
am expressing the sentiments of every man around me – that
is to say, that in welcoming Carpenter on his release from
prison, we take that opportunity, not only of associating our-

selves with him in the crime that he committed, but of declaring our fullest sympathy, and not only our fullest sympathy, but our COMPLETELY UNQUALIFIED ENDORSEMENT OF THE WORDS FOR WHICH HE WAS SENT TO PRISON (cheers). We are to-day living in times of change – in times of what it is no exaggeration to describe as a revolution. On such an occasion it is but fitting that the party to which our friend Carpenter and Miss Molony belong – the Socialist Party of Ireland – should come forward and take their position with the people in the great crisis with which we have been face to face. It is a pleasure to me as one of the oldest pioneers of trades unionism in Dublin to say how glad I am to be able to call your attention to the fact that in the two great crises – the national crisis and the industrial crisis – in both of which the people of Dublin were met with all kinds of temptations and bribery and with all kinds of poison in order, if possible, to lead them astray and destroy their national spirit – in both these crises the Socialist Party of Ireland were ready with the people to recognise that the national cause and the industrial cause were at stake, and that their place was in the firing line in front of the people (cheers). I am glad to recognise that during these crises you and they acted up to the fullest sense of your responsibilities as men and women. In the first of these crises they had to encounter A PERFECT ORGY OF FLUNKEYISM. According to the English newspapers Dublin was the most loyal place in all the dominions of the king of England, and the people were supposed to be like bellowing slaves going down on their knees and protesting their loyalty and selfless adulation and worship to a king who rules, we are told, according to the grace of God, but with forty thousand bayonets[7] at the back of him (cheers and laughter). Despite all this attempt to represent Dublin as enthusiastically loyal about a month ago, no sooner had his Gracious (?) Majesty taken his departure from their shores than they saw Dublin a seething mass of discontent – seething with rebellion and ready to go to any extreme in the attempt to gain freedom. I cannot tell you how this old heart of mine rose with gladness when in the North I heard that the people of Dublin – the workers of Dublin – had taken the measure of their responsibilities and HAD UNFURLED THE BANNER OF FREEDOM – of national and industrial freedom – not only for themselves, but for their struggling brothers across the water. Those men and women who were most enthusiastically national in the first of these crises were at the

same time most enthusiastic in support of the industrial uprising during the last few days and weeks;[8] and whether in the
workshop or outside it were amongst the first to support their
brothers who took active steps to uphold the dignity and the
rights of the working classes (cheers). Let us draw the lesson
of this great struggle of the last few days and weeks. The
newspapers told them that England was one mass of rebellion.
Fifty thousand troops were concentrated in London, four warships were in the Mersey, and the guns of these warships and
the bayonets of the soldiers were pointed, not against Germany,
not against Russia, but against the working classes in the cities
of England, just as they were presented against the working
classes here in Dublin. All the newspapers had been full of
this great upheaval in England, in Dublin, and in Belfast and
elsewhere. They had been telling you in great headlines of the
terrible news of the great strike in England, Ireland, and Scotland – everything was powerless, works had been suspended
and railway communication cut off, and the nation had been
threatened with bankruptcy. AS MR MAHONY DECLARED in the
Dublin Police Court, if this went on society would be dissolved. Why? Because the workers had stopped work – the
poor ill-considered, badly-paid, ill-requited, slave-driven and
degraded workers had stopped working; and mark you, my
friends, the moment you stopped working society went to
chaos, to everlasting smash. Does not that teach you a great
lesson – the power of the people; the power of the working
classes? We are living in a new age – the age of solidarity of
labour. You must recognise that you are living not only in an
age of progress, but in an age of revolution. We in Ireland did
our part in that struggle, and we have shown that we are
determined to win for the workers complete industrial freedom,
and the right to live in the country in which they were born.
They had but one thing to serve in this struggle, and that was
to maintain and uphold the dignity of labour, and they would
do that by acting their part as men and as women. In conclusion Mr Connolly read for the meeting the following resolution, which would be proposed for adoption:– 'That this
meeting of Dublin workers tenders a cordial welcome to Mr
Walter Carpenter on his release from prison, and heartily con-
gratulates him on his timely and effective protest against the
recent outburst of flunkeyism in the city' (cheers). ... [9]

DIRECT ACTION IN BELFAST

[16 September 1911]

We have just had, and taken, the opportunity in Belfast to put into practice a little of what is known on the Continent of Europe as 'Direct Action.'

Direct Action consists in ignoring all the legal and parliamentary ways of obtaining redress for the grievances of Labour, and proceeding to rectify these grievances by direct action upon the employer's most susceptible part – his purse. This is very effective at times, and saves much needless worry, and much needless waste of union funds.

Direct Action is not liked by lawyers, politicians, or employers. It keeps the two former out of a job, and often leaves the latter out of pocket. But it is useful to Labour, and if not relied upon too exclusively, or used too recklessly, it may yet be made a potent weapon in the armoury of the working class.

The circumstances under which we came to put in practice the newest adaptation of it in Belfast were as follows:–

A dock labourer named Keenan was killed at the unloading of a ship owing to a bag being released by one of the carriers a moment too soon. Flying down the chute it struck Keenan, knocking him to the ground and killing him. The accident happened owing to the practice of the stevedores of backing in a team of horses about ten minutes before the meal hour, and demanding that the men rush the work in order to load the vans before quitting for their meals. It was in this perfectly needless rush the sad affair happened.

What was our surprise to read in the report of the inquest that the solicitor for the merchant insinuated that the man was killed because he was a non-union man – that in short he was murdered by the union members! As a matter of fact he had promised to join, and being an old dock labourer had been given a few days grace in which to come up to our offices and make good.

All the papers of Belfast gave prominence to this 'Extraordinary Allegation,' as one journal called it, and the matter was commented upon freely throughout the city.

After due deliberation, thinking over all the possible means of redress for *this foul libel* we resolved to take the matter into our own hands, and put a little pressure upon the purse of the man who employed this libeller to slander the Union.

Accordingly at dinner time we told the men employed on

the ship in question – the *Nile* – not to resume work until the merchant repudiated the libel or disclaimed all responsibility therefor. The men stood by loyally, and immediately all the forces of capital and law and order were on the alert. The news spread around the docks as on a wireless telegraph, and both sides were tense with expectancy.

While we were thus waiting and watching the stevedore of the *Nile* sent for the merchant, and asked me through one of his foremen to wait on the spot for him. I waited, but whilst I waited one very officious Harbour official ordered me off the Harbour Estate. The Harbour of Belfast, unlike Dublin or Liverpool, is practically enclosed property. I informed Mr Constable that there was no meeting in progress, and that I was only waiting an answer to our request for a disclaimer from the merchant. He then became rude and domineering, and eventually began to use force. I then told him that if I, as a union official, could not speak to the men individually on the Harbour Estate we would take the men off where we could talk to them.

So we gave the word and called off every man in the Low Docks. In ten minutes 600 men responded and left the docks empty.

In ten minutes more a District Superintendent, merchants, managers, detectives, and Harbour underlings generally were rushing frantically up to the Union rooms begging for the men to go back and 'everything would be arranged.'

Well, everything was arranged within an hour. The offending solicitor, after many hoity-toity protests that 'he would not be dictated to by the dockers,' climbed gracefully down and dictated a letter to the Press disclaiming any intention to impute evil actions to the Union members, and the letter accordingly appeared in all the Belfast papers.

In addition the Harbour Master assured us that he regretted the action of the constable, which would not be allowed to happen again, and that we would be given full liberty to go anywhere in the docks or ships at all times.

It was all a great object lesson, and has had its full effect on the minds of the Belfast workers. It has taught them that there are other ways than by means of expensive law-suits to vindicate the character and rights of the toilers; and as a result it has given dignity and self-respect to the members of the Union.

We have found it necessary, in order to cope with the needs of our increasing membership, to open new offices for the

Ballymacarret side of the city. These offices are at 6 Dalton
Street, and will be in charge of a Union official between the
hours of 4 and 7 pm during the week, and from 12 to 5 pm on
Saturdays. They will be a great convenience to the local Quay
and to our new members from the Chemical Works.

Our campaign against the sweating conditions in the Rope
Works is now in full swing. Breakfast and dinner hour meetings are being held when the gospel of discontent and wise
organisation is preached to the sweated employees of this huge
capitalist concern. We expect good results to the workers from
this campaign.

On Tuesday, September 11th, we held a most successful
joint demonstration with the seamen and firemen, with Father
Hopkins[10] as our chief speaker. The magnitude of the meeting
surprised and delighted our comrade, and his speech surprised
and delighted the vast audience.

Mr D. R. Campbell, President Belfast Trades Council, was
in the chair, and the following resolution was moved by James
Connolly, seconded by James Flanagan, supported by Father
Hopkins, and passed amid great enthusiasm:–

Resolved – 'That in the opinion of this meeting of Belfast workers,
the action of Wexford employers in discharging men for joining the
Irish Transport Workers' Union was an outrageous attack upon the
liberty of the workers; and that we call upon our Wexford brothers to
stand firm, and also call upon all trade unionists in Ireland to answer
this outrage by boycotting all the bicycles and other products manufactured by the firm in question.'[11]

The meeting closed with ringing cheers for Father Hopkins,
singing of 'He's a jolly good fellow,' and cheers for the Transport Workers' Union. – Yours,

CONNOLLY.

SOME RAMBLING REMARKS
BY JAMES CONNOLLY

[Christmas number 1912]

No one at all acquainted with Ireland at the present can
doubt that the country is feeling the throbs accompanying
the birth of great movements. Everywhere there are stirrings
of new life – intellectual, artistic, industrial, political, racial,

social stirrings are to be seen and felt on every hand, and the nation is moved from end to end by the yeast-like pulsations of new influences. Amid such a renascence it would, indeed, be a strange phenomenon if Labour remained passive; if Labour alone moved in the old ruts and failed to respond to the call for a new adventuring of the spirit. Such a lack of response would argue a lifelessness of attitude, a blindness of mental outlook in the part of the toilers which would go far to neutralise and discount the value of the higher aspirations of the rest of the nation. Considering the state of slavery in which the masses of the Irish workers are to-day, some few aspects of which we have already noted in these columns, a state of restlessness, of 'divine discontent,' on the part of Labour in Ireland is an absolutely essential pre-requisite for the realisation of any spiritual uplifting of the nation at large. With a people degraded, and so degraded as to be unconscious of their degradation, no upward march of Ireland is possible; with a people restless under injustice, conscious of their degradation, and resolved, if need be, to peril life itself in order to end such degradation, though thrones and empires fall as a result – with such a people all things are possible – to such a people all things must bend and flow. A large nation may become great by the sheer pressure of its magnitude – the greatness of its numbers, as Russia to-day. A small nation, such as Ireland, can only become great by reason of the greatness of soul of its individual citizens.

It is, therefore, a matter of sincere congratulation to every lover of the race that the workers of Ireland are to-day profoundly discontented, and, so far from being apathetic in their slavery, are, instead, rebellious, even to the point of rashness. Discontent is the fulcrum upon which the lever of thought has ever moved the world to action. A discontented Working Class! What a glorious promise for the future! Ireland has to-day within her bosom two things that must make the blood run with riotous exultation in the veins of every lover of the Irish race – a discontented working class, and the nucleus of a rebellious womanhood. I cannot separate these two things in my mind; to me they are parts of the one great whole; different regiments of the one great army of progress. To neither will it be possible to realise its ideals without first trampling under foot, riding roughshod over, all the false conventions, soul-shrivelling prejudices, and subtle hypocrisies with which a tyrannical society has poisoned the souls and warped the intellect of mankind. Apart from the material, political and industrial forms in which the Labourer or the Woman may clothe their respective struggles, there is, in the fact of the struggle itself, in both cases, an emancipating influence which cannot be expressed in words, much less formulated in programmes.

The Struggle Emancipates, let who will claim the immediate petty triumph.

We of the Working Class have much to be thankful for in the fact that in the upward march in which we are engaged, we are permitted to reap advantages of a material nature at each stage of our journey. If our wages are not increased, our toil lightened, our hours lessened, our conditions improved as a result of the daily conflict in which we are engaged, we know that it is because of some faltering on the part of ourselves or our fellow-workers, some defalcation on the part of some being of our army, and not a necessary or unavoidable part of the conflict itself. The Modern Labour Movement knows that a victory of any kind for the Working Class is better for the Cause, more potent for Ultimate Victory than a correct understanding of Economic Theory by a beaten Labour Army. The Modern Labour Movement is suspicious of theorising that shirks conflict, and seeks to build up the revolutionary army of social reconstruction by means of an army that fights and wins concessions for the fighters while it is fighting. Every victory won by Labour for Labour helps to strengthen the bent back, and enlarge the cramped soul of the labourer; every time the labourer, be it man or woman, secures a triumph in the battle for juster conditions, the mind of the labourer receives that impulse towards higher things that comes from the knowledge of power. Here and there, to some degraded individuals, the victories of Labour mean only increased opportunities for drink and degeneracy, but on the whole it remains true that the fruits of the victories of the organised Working Class are as capable of being stated in terms of spiritual uplifting as in the material terms of cash.

Let us then, with glad eyes, face the future! Ireland salutes the rising sun, and within Ireland Labour moves with the promise and potency of growing life and consciousness, a life and consciousness destined to grow and expand until the glad day when he who in this Green Isle says 'Labour' must say 'Ireland,' and he who says 'Ireland' must necessarily be planning for the glorification and ennobling of Labour.

IRISH REBELS AND ENGLISH MOBS

[22 November 1913]

Sunday, November 23rd, will be the forty-sixth anniversary of the execution in Manchester of Allen, Larkin and O'Brien.[12]

On the night before these, our brothers, were hanged, a howling mob of the scum of that English city held orgy around the prison walls and made right hideous, as well as profaned, the last hours of The Three by the singing of indecent songs and the shouting of blasphemous insults at the faith of the Irish rebels who had dared to outrage the majesty of England. To that English mob the words 'Irish Rebel' summed up everything hateful and odious. At these words their worst passions were aroused, and in their fury they behaved as only savages can behave when a gallant foe is stricken down. To work their passions up to that point the English Press exhausted every effort, and tapped every reservoir of vitriolic denunciation and callous slander. The English public responded to the call of the prostitutes of the Press with but few exceptions; one of these few, Ernest Jones, the great Chartist, took up the thankless task of defending the Irishmen, and thus completed a round of devotion to the cause of Ireland begun in the stormy days of the Young Irelanders.

But to the vast multitude – as to that howling mob desecrating the last hours of brave men by their ribald insults and loudmouthed indecency – the name of Irish rebel was like a red rag to a bull. *Forty-six years ago!*

Forty-six years after that outrage a gathering of the democracy of Manchester met together a few hundred yards away from the spot on which stood Salford Jail. This gathering was at least three times as large as that other mob of historic ill-fame. It was composed, not of the degraded slum population, but of intelligent, educated, self-respecting men and women – the flower of the Manchester working class.

Again, the centre of attraction was the presence of Irish rebels. But this gathering of the Manchester democracy roared out to these Irish rebels of our day a welcome and a promise – a welcome to them because they had dared and suffered for democracy; a promise to do likewise if the word was only given. To this latter-day gathering to be an Irish working class rebel – standing for all and more that the immortal three had stood for – was to possess a passport to their admiration and esteem. So much had education accomplished – so much and so far had the toilers of England progressed towards a realisation of their true position – realising at last that they are not citizens, but helots and slaves of an Empire.

Are we saying too much when we say that this welcome accorded last Sunday to Larkin and to Connolly at these magnificent gatherings of over 25,000 people[13] went far to wipe out the bad memories of the past, and to make it more possible for the two democracies to understand each other – and understanding, to co-operate together in the march of their own class emancipation?

On Sunday there will be a procession through the streets of Dublin to commemorate that martyrdom. We trust that every member of the Transport Union and its sister organisation, the Irish Women Workers' Union, will be in their allotted place in that procession. No excuse can be taken for absence. There are bodies allotted places in that procession whose every public act is a negation of what the Fenians stood for, but no murmur should be allowed against the desecration of their presence. At other times and other places, that question must be raised. But upon that day let our reproach be the reproach of our silence in their presence.

It is our duty to show the world that neither the friendship of the English nor their hatred can turn the Irish democracy from their resolve to win for their country her right to be a free and independent Nation enjoying a true Republican freedom.

The architects of that freedom will and must be the Irish working class. Ours is the task to prepare them. While that preparation is going forward we must take our place in every good and wise movement for the upholding of the highest ideals born of the age-long struggle of our people.

JAMES CONNOLLY.

HOME THRUSTS
BY SPAILPÍN

[13 December 1913]

The event of this week was, of course, the great Labour Conference at London. It was also the great failure of the week, if not of the century.

For the first time in the history of the Labour movement in these countries an effort was made to gather together the

forces of Labour for a definite purpose – a fact that was in
itself of sufficient importance to mark an epoch in the
forward movement of Labour. There were to be representatives of the political movement and of the industrial movement. Delegates were to be there from the Federation of
Trade Unions,[14] from the Transport Workers' Federation, and
from the Trade Union Congress, and all the joint energy and
combined power of these great bodies were to be directed
with a single mindedness of purpose towards the one great
end of raising the siege of Dublin.

There was also to be a special attempt to lend impressive-
ness to this Conference by arranging for a special vote of all
the Trade Unions affected, in order that the voice of the
rank and file might be heard. To do this properly a delay of
three weeks was enforced between the date of the resolution
to summon a Conference and the Conference itself.

Thus conceived, the idea of the conference spread all over
the civilised world, and all eyes from Johannesburg to
Shanghai, and from Rio de la Plate to the Pottle River were
strained with burning anxiety upon London on the fateful
day of December 9th, 1913, and it was a thought noble in
its conception and immensely fruitful in its possibilities. In
the hands of men gifted with imagination or blessed with
the vision of the pioneers of progress the chance to gather
together into our fold all the manifold activities of labour
would have been seized upon and used to its fullest extent,
in order that the step thus gained might open the way to
greater action upon similarly concerted lines in the future.

The employers saw this, the capitalist press saw this, all the
watchful eyes of the capitalist world were tremblingly watching
for the result of this, and as anxiously and tremblingly as it
was watched for by the capitalist enemy so it was watched for
eagerly and hopefully by the aspiring souls of the armies of
labour.

But neither the enemy, nor the friend calculated upon the
colossal stupidity, or criminal vanity of a few men being able
to wreck all the hopes of labour upon a mere question of
personality, as was done in the Conference which resulted
from the plans so elaborately presented for our enlightenment
before the day of meeting.

With a stupidity almost unthinkable, as a criminality
positively Machiavellian in its cynical deliberation the
proposal dealing with the original purpose of the meeting

was put last upon the agenda, and the resolution best calculated to stir up fratricidal conflicts, rouse embittered feelings, and poison the atmosphere of debate was given priority.[15] Amongst intelligent and honest people the purpose for which a meeting was called is always first to be considered; on Tuesday it was put last and received the scanty consideration usually given a subject when a Conference is about to break up.

And the voice of the members, in order to consult whom the Conference had been postponed for three weeks, what of them? Was the voice of the Conference their voice?

Well, Mr Bob Smillie, the honest and veteran Miners' leader, confessed in open Conference that his Union, one of the largest, had not given its members any opportunity to vote on the matter or to elect delegates. The following is a copy of a letter sent out by the President of the National Union of Railwaymen, and explains how solicitous it was that its members should not be 'anxious' over the Conference about Dublin:–

Unity House,
Dec 6, 1913.

DEAR SIR,

Special Conference of TUC on Dublin Dispute.

Two or three of the delegates have written me asking if they would have to attend the Conference which is to be held on Tuesday next. I have, therefore, to inform you that the EC have decided to send thirteen of their own members to this Conference, and it will not be necessary for you to attend. I send this intimation to you in case you are in any way anxious.

Yours faithfully,

J. E. WILLIAMS.

And the writer of the following letter from Scotland seems to think that the voice of the members has not been very zealously inquired after in his Union either:–

Boilermakers' and Iron and Steel Ship Builders' Society,
Leith Branch

2 Kinghorn Place,
Edinburgh,
10th December, 1913.

Mr M. McKeown,[16]
Irish Transport Workers' Union.

DEAR COMRADE,

I enclose Money Order for £25 payable to Mr John O'Neill[17] to help you to carry on the fight. This is the best proof we can give of our sympathy. The special Trades Congress seems to have been a farce, as it was composed of permanent officials of the various Unions. This Union, I know, did not elect or instruct anyone to represent them, and I am making enquiries to know who attended and who authorised them, etc.

Kind regards and best wishes.

Yours,

J. M. AIRLIE.

So this great historic meeting of the united forces of Labour was, it appears, carefully rigged in advance, and when it did meet it turned itself into a great laundry for the public washing of very dirty linen, and the officials smiled, whilst the enemy laughed in joyful scorn at the futility of the thing he had feared.

We think, with all due respect to those who think other-wise, that those who framed that agenda, and decided the order of the questions to be discussed, committed a crime, not only against the Dublin workers, but against the future of the Labour movement in these islands; and we think this quite irrespective of the voting upon the questions involved in the amendment proposing the isolation of Dublin.[18]

The decision of the National Union of Railwaymen to re-open the London and North-Western boats from Dublin to Holyhead put their Dublin members in the position that they had either to be disloyal to their Union or to their class. So the Transport Union officials, in view of the long and heroic fight those men had made, told them that for the present, and pending negotiations, the latter Union would not demand from the men the payment of such a heavy penalty as refusal to obey their Union would involve. They could go back to work, but we were not filled with admiration for the Union which, with millions at its back, threatened its men with forfeiture of Union benefit unless they consented to betray their brothers. To compel men to scab at the eleventh hour is a poor job for the officials of a great Union, and the Transport Union officials did right to save the men from being placed upon the horns of such a dilemma. They have shown the mettle they were made of, and we can bide our time.

We were glad to see that in last week's *Sinn Féin*[19] Mr Griffith had a few scathing words to say about the manner in which the police of this city are preparing themselves to secure convictions against all and sundry connected with the strike. It was time somebody outside ourselves came out openly in denunciation of this iniquity. The police in Dublin have proven themselves to be cold and callous perjurors of the most degraded type – swearing away the lives, liberties and honours of men, women, boys and girls in a manner to make Harvey Duff blush to be named in their company.

And the promised Government enquiry on the lines published, with a Commission so constituted, is simply a whitewashing job. No responsible representative of labour will be on it, and no opportunity will be given to bring home to the police the responsibility for the crime they have committed.[20] The Government, in fact, dare not press the matter against these perjurors. We have it on good authority that the police informed the Government that if any attempt was made to proceed against them with a really fair enquiry made by responsible men they would go on strike.

They would down tools, or down batons. They often do so. Down batons on the heads of the poor people, but this idea of 'down batons' if the Government dares to investigate the police is a new idea, and as it is a government of treachery and pusillanimity the threat was effectual.

By the way, will the enquiry investigate the Police Magistrates as well? or is that too dangerous? The man who issued a 'proclamation' prohibiting a public meeting,[21] and remains on the bench after the Crown Prosecutor admitted that his 'proclamation' was not a proclamation, and that the meeting was perfectly legal, that man surely needs investigation. But what a smell it would cause.

ADDRESS TO THE DELEGATES [22]
BY JAMES CONNOLLY

[30 May 1914]

No body of workers that ever met in Ireland have ever had
before them a more important and delicate function to fulfil
than you have. You are meeting in the capital city of Ireland
in a year that the millions of the Irish race the world over
have been looking eagerly forward to as the year of the political resurrection of the Irish Nation. And you are also meeting
in a year whose opening months saw the close of the greatest
general engagement between the forces of Capital and Labour
that Ireland ever witnessed.[23] To the thoughtful delegate both
these considerations will operate to make him or her approach
the Irish Trade Union Congress of 1914 with feelings of disappointment. There must be disappointment upon the political
field because not only is the political Ireland of our hopes but
miserably caricatured in the Ireland offered to us in the Home
Rule Bill, but even that Bill lies under the menace of still
further dismemberment and emasculation.[24] Still over our head
hangs the threat that the political charlatans who control our
national destinies will commit the unparalleled outrage of dis-
membering this country in order to please the unnatural hatred
of their own country which a section of Irishmen and women
have had instilled into them by the foul brood of aristocracy
which for so long fattened upon the vitals and drank the life-
blood of Ireland. The Exclusion of Ulster, or any part of
Ulster, is the fearful price we are asked to pay for our weakness as a nation – a price so dishonourable that rather than
consent to submit such a question to the arbitrament of a vote
all patriotic Irish men and women had better far consent to
accept the destiny of being rebel slaves of England in an
undivided Ireland, as preferable to contented accomplices of
English statesmen in the partition of Ireland. That there are in
Ireland to-day accepted leaders of the Irish Race who feel that
they can receive from an English minister a proposal to dis-
member their country without being compelled to instantly
avenge that insult by throwing such a minister out of office is
bad enough, but that such leaders can come back to Ireland
and still secure the confidence and be sure of the plaudits of
the Irish people is worse, as greater proof of the degeneracy of
national life in Ireland.

Disappointed as we may well be at the fact that such a suggested abandonment of the high national ideals of the past could be met in the sordid huckstering spirit we see around us on this question, so also must we feel disappointed that the Labour Movement in Ireland did not emerge from its recent ordeal with more substantial spoils of [success?].[25]

But in this case our disappointment is tempered by the reflection that never did men and women better deserve success than did the heroes and heroines of the Dublin Labour Struggle of 1913–1914. As the souls of the politicians descended to the mire of national betrayal the souls of the workers ascended to greater heights of comradeship and solidarity. By all that makes for the greatness of a people, by heroic refusal to surrender principle, by comprehension of all the true essentials of liberty, by devotion to the common cause, by undaunted facing of all the powers of government and by scorn of its batonings and its jailings, by its patient martyrdom of hunger and its blood atonement of deaths by violence by uniformed bullies, the working class of Dublin have redeemed the honour of their race in an age saturated by the spirit of the huckster and the worshippers of mammon. Never did Ireland in her most heroic moments rise to higher altitudes in the estimation of all lovers of progress than she was raised to by the fact that her working class – although surrounded by the most unclean pack of wolves that ever yelped at the heels of honour, and threatened by the most unscrupulous coalition of tyrants known to industrial and political history – by their own strength had forced forward to the front the question of the moral responsibilty of all for the sufferings and degradations of each. That responsibility which the teachers and rulers of all the ages have been engaged in evading or denying was at last raised by the Dublin Working Class into its true position, and forced upon the consciousness of an unwilling public compelled by the events of a great dramatic industrial war to consider its portent. To the Dublin Working Class belongs the honour of making the sentiment of AN INJURY TO ONE IS THE CONCERN OF ALL one that all Labour Organisations and all political parties must henceforth be measured by.

That the Irish people as a whole did not realise the great moral issues involved in this struggle was to be expected and deplored. We are cursed in this country with the most unscrupulous, and where not unscrupulous the most evil minded set of journalists that ever consented to prostitute their talents in the service of a purchaser, and when a naturally open minded people have to depend upon a Press served by such creatures it is but natural that the interpretation of public events which that people receive should be of the distorted and filthy nature such a Press must furnish. It was not so reasonable to expect that even a small section of the Labour world should fail to rise to the same height as the Labour Movement of Dublin as a whole did rise. But a stream cannot rise higher than its source, and when Trade Unionists take their inspiration from the columns of the Capitalist Press, and accept the praises of that press as evidences of wisdom instead of regarding such praises as proofs of foolishness or worse, then it is but natural that their Trade Unions will fail their brothers in the hour of trial.

We are not mentioning these disappointments in order to carp at or belittle your and our Congress and the movement it represents. Rather do we mention them in order to stimulate you to still further exertions by pointing out the real underlying causes of our present unsatisfactory position, socially and politically. That underlying cause is to be found in the industrial divisions amongst the Working Class. WE HAVE TOO MANY UNIONS IN IRELAND, too many Executives with separate Balance Sheets to nurse; too much temptation to nurse these separate Balance Sheets at the expense of Solidarity. We need to set our face resolutely towards the task of joining all the workers of each industry into one Industrial Union; all General Workers into one General Workers' Union; all such Unions into One Big Union, able to launch the powers of all in the instant service of each. We need to realise that the Master Class has definitely decided to make war upon the Working Class; that for the purposes of that war they have co-ordinated and disciplined all their forces, and hold them ready to use at a moment's notice whenever the further subjection of Labour seems possible of achievement. We need to feel in every fibre of our consciousness that all the offices and positions through which civilization performs its every function are manned, equipped and sentinelled by alert and implacable enemies of our class, and so feeling we must labour to create a public opinion of our own – a Working Class public opinion that shall eventually supersede and destroy the public opinion of the master class as the standard by which our patriotism and the value and efficiency of our institutions are to be judged. At present the slave spirit is, so to speak, dominant in our souls, and as a result we unconsciously and instinctively accept inferior position and inferior treatment in all things as being right and proper for our class. Hence as we are subjected socially we are ignored politically, and forced to be content with the merest of husks educationally. This slave spirit arises from the fact that the disorganised, or badly organised, position of our class renders us impotent upon the industrial field, and any industrial impotence finds its accompaniment in our political outlawry and national helplessness in this hour of our national danger.

From all this the moral is plain. The true path of salvation for our class is along the line of a closer organisation of our forces: let us regard the industries of this country as our own; let us organise our Trade Unions as we would organise them were it our purpose to conduct industry and to have the operatives regimented and brigaded for the task. Let us in short proceed upon the principle that if the employer needs a man or woman in an industry we need him or her in the Union of that industry.

As we reach the completion of that task we will feel the result in the increasing self-respect of the worker, and in the increasing determination to exert upon the political field that working class independence such unity will give upon the industrial. Political power must wait upon economic or industrial power; you must be strong on the dock, ship, railway or workshop before you can be strong in the halls of legislation. But if political POWER will only come as the ripened fruit of economic power political AGITATION need not wait. Nor yet need wait political organisation. Let them march abreast – the army of organised Labour the director of the campaign on both fields.

Had we such an organisation of Labour to-day there would be no fear of the Exclusion of Ulster, nor any other betrayal of our national hopes.

The Ulster Volunteers[26] may be able to frighten a Liberal Government willing to be frightened, but were a Labour Movement able to call out the Textile Operatives of Belfast, or even its spinners, and to keep them out until Ulster threw in her lot with Ireland, the paralysis of industry and loss of profit to Belfast capitalists would frighten the guns out of the hands of the Carsonite army without the shedding of a single drop of blood.

In conclusion we say to our fellow delegates with all

solemnity that we believe that there are no real Nationalists
in Ireland outside of the Irish Labour movement. All others
merely reject one part or another of the British Conquest,
the Labour movement alone rejects it in its entirety, and
sets itself the Re-conquest of Ireland as its aim.

Let that be the end and aim of all our deliberations. –
Yours fraternally,

JAMES CONNOLLY.

THE NATIONAL DANGER
BY JAMES CONNOLLY

[15 August 1914]

In my article last week I said that only from the working-class
democracy could a real lead be expected in this crisis.[27] I am
happy to be able to state that we are not so isolated in this
matter as I at first feared. In many other quarters the fact that
keeping the foodstuffs in Ireland is the first duty of every true
Irishman and woman had already been realised before my
article appeared. We of the Irish Transport Workers' Union are
so often Ishmaels in public life, with every man's hand against
us and our hand against every man, that it is a rare treat to be
able to acknowledge that on a question of supreme importance
such as this we are but one among many agreeing voices. The
editor of *Sinn Féin* strikes a perfectly correct and sane note
upon the crisis, we are glad to say, as does also *Claidheamh
Soluis*, the Gaelic League weekly.[28] Other newspapers and journals make tentative and truly fearful suggestions along the
same lines; in many Dublin companies of Volunteers[29] the
members have discussed the matter and came to agreement on
the right side, and despite the fearful wave of pro-English filth
now spread over the country signs are multiplying that in
actions upon these lines there will be found the possibility of
making a stand for Ireland that will win the adhesion of all
that is best in the land.

Meanwhile the daily Press continually reports news that
confirms the attitude of the *Irish Worker* towards all the sections of the enemy upon whom it makes war. The Carsonites
remain as obdurate and anti-Irish as ever. It is noticeable that
all the talk about a 'union of North and South in defence of
Ireland,' about 'blending the Orange and Green,' about 'marching united as Irishmen against the common foe' and all the

other clap-trap has been strictly confined to the Nationalist side. No response has come from the Ulster Volunteers; no Carsonite official has made the smallest overture towards peace; there has not been the slightest melting of the sour bigotry of the Orangeman. The following extract from the columns of a Belfast evening paper of last week is a valuable index of the present frame of mind of these people –

> The verdict of the Dublin coroner's jury on the victims of the Bachelor's Walk shooting[30] is not so extreme as was expected. Counsel sought to have a verdict of wilful murder brought in against persons by name, but the jury wisely did not go that length. A great deal of vindictiveness was displayed during the inquiry by some of the counsel against the soldiers. These men, it is clear, did not fire till they were in deadly peril from a mob of Dublin hooligans, who are the greatest cowards on earth. The testimony of the witnesses who sought to show that nothing more harmful than banana skins were thrown at the military was disproved by abundant testimony. It is to be hoped that no more will be heard of the affair now the country has sterner things to do than squabble about this incident.

One cannot but admire in this connection the tact and skill with which Sir Edward Carson has conducted, and still continues to conduct, his campaign against any extension of liberty to the Irish people. It has been marked by one long series of success. Despite sneers and jeers and laughter, despite reason and justice, despite threats and against seemingly overwhelming odds, he has kept serenely on his way pursuing the policy he had marked out for himself and his followers. For him there was no compromise, no conciliation. He met each fresh concession with studied insult; at each fresh offer of peace he shook fresh rifles in the face of the Government; when the Home Rule Party basely consented to put the question of the integrity of their country at the mercy of a local majority of bigoted traitors of Ireland, he put machine guns upon the streets of Belfast and Lisburn. Mr John Redmond now blatantly declares in the House of Commons that the National Volunteers will defend Ireland for the Government. Sir Edward Carson says grimly that nothing is yet altered in Ireland, and the Belfast Orange Press warns the Ulster Volunteers against being sent out of Ireland and leaving Ulster to the mercy of a Government that they cannot trust. Like the Irish after the Battle of the Boyne, the National Volunteers should offer to 'swop leaders' with the Orangemen.[31] It would be to Ireland's advantage if Sir Edward would fight for Ireland as skilfully and as courageously as he has fought against her.

Contrast with such leadership the attitude of Mr Redmond and his Party towards the Volunteers. First he slights and secretly opposes them. Then when they get strong he demands the power to control them.[32] Granting that he is honest, here was a great blunder. His former leader – Charles Stewart Parnell[33] – always believed in a physical-force party, but would never join it. This gave him always the power to say to the English Government that if it did not grant his moderate demands then the physical-force party would take control of Irish affairs out of his hands. 'And,' he would assure Mr Gladstone,[34] 'you know I have no control over that extreme party.' Had Mr Redmond pursued a similar policy and kept clear of the Irish Volunteers he could always have met every move of the Government towards the Carsonites, every proposal to mutilate Ireland's rights, with the quiet statement that the Volunteers over whom he had no control would scarcely allow it. 'You know, Mr Asquith,'[35] he could have said, 'I would be willing to do what you ask, but I have no control over the Irish National Volunteers, and I am afraid that they would cause trouble if I gave in to Carson.' Thus, like Parnell, he would have had the power of an organisation of armed men behind him whilst he had no responsibility for their actions. This he threw away when he set out to obtain control of the Volunteer forces.

Why did he throw it away? What did he get in exchange that was good for Ireland? Would it be too much to suggest that he was compelled by the Government to try and get the Volunteers into his hands, and that the Government so compelled him because they knew that this European war was coming.

With a European war on and Ireland organised with Volunteer regiments, such regiments, even without arms, could have made the adhesion of Ireland to either side, or even the real neutrality of Ireland, of so much importance that great and substantial national advantages would have been offered her to secure such adhesion or neutrality. With a European war on and the Volunteers in the control of Redmond and Party, the active co-operation of the Volunteers in the defence of the empire was given to the Government without a single concession of any kind being obtained; nay, even whilst the menace of an amending Bill to mutilate Ireland was still part of the Government plan. Now we are assured by the Home Rule Press that as a consequence of the happy union of Ulster and National Volunteers (which exists only in their imagination) still more generous concessions are to be given to Ulster.

Alas that I should live to see it! North, South, East and West the Irish Volunteers are marching and parading with the Union Jack in front of them, their bands playing 'God Save the King' and their aristocratic officers making loyalist speeches.

North, South, East and West the anti-Irish landlord classes are now hurrying in to officer the Irish Volunteers, and brave true-hearted men who have given their lives in earnest, unobtrusive service to their motherland are thrust contemptuously aside that positions may be given to those aristocratic jackanapes. The fools who are in control hail this as a sign of national unity. The wise who know the history of their country ask how can we expect swift and prompt action for Ireland in any emergency when the officers in command will thus be men whose whole life, opinions, instincts, class bias, and prejudices have been coloured with hatred of all that the Irish National Movement ever stood for. Remember the words of the greatest Irish Revolutionist, Wolfe Tone:–

> When the aristocracy come forward the people fall backward; when the people come forward the aristocracy, fearful of being left behind, insinuate themselves into our ranks and *rise into timid leaders or treacherous auxiliaries.*

The fatal policy of the Irish Volunteers is producing and pushing these timid leaders and treacherous auxiliaries into every position where their timidity or treachery will work the most havoc in any emergency.

It is a humiliating thought that Mr Redmond's declaration on this war has completely changed the status of this country. Before it we were a 'subject province of England,' now we are 'an English province' in the eyes of the world. And there are more enemies of the Empire in a small corner of Toulon than there are in the whole of Ireland.

We have reached the very lowest depths as a race, and the greatest part of the responsibility lies with those who in their cowardly fear of an ignorant, newspaper-rigged public opinion surrendered the control of the Volunteers to the Redmondite wirepullers. Henceforth Irish discontent will not be regarded abroad as symptoms of an aspiration after distinct nationality, it will only and rightly be interpreted as the discontent of leisure in the game of imperial politics.

I have had few more unpleasant experiences in my life than I underwent when listening to the pitiful attempts of some members of the Provisional Committee to explain and justify their votes upon their surrender. To hear them telling of their great diplomacy, and their wonderful wirepulling was a revelation. It showed at once that they were attempting to do the work of a revolutionary movement by the methods of a ward-canvasser in a Municipal election; that they were approaching a supreme crisis in a nation's history in the temper and spirit of a political registration agent out for votes for his party. The kindest thing that can happen to them now is that their names may be forgotten; at present it seems an equal chance between oblivion and malediction.

The time is now ripe, nay, the imperious necessities of the hour call loudly for, demand, the formation of a Committee of all the earnest elements, outside as well as inside the Volunteers, to consider means to take and hold Ireland and the food of Ireland for the people of Ireland.

We of the Transport Union, we of the Citizen Army are ready for any such co-operation. We can bring to it the aid of drilled and trained men, we can bring to it the heartiest efforts of men and women who in thousands have shown that they know how to face prison and death, and we can bring to it the services of thinkers and organisers who know that different occasions require different policies, that you cannot legalise revolutionary actions, and that audacity alone can command success in a national crisis like this.

Freedom, we believe, cannot flourish, or even awaken into life in the miasmatic atmosphere of wirepulling and intrigue, but as St Just[36] said:–

> Liberty is born in storm and tears as the Earth arose out of chaos, and as man comes wailing into the world.

We who have faced the storm for industrial liberty, and wept the tears for the sufferings of our own class will not shrink from either for the sake of our country.

Try us!

NORTHERN NOTES [37]

[22 August 1914]

In numbers, Sunday night's meeting at Library Street was the greatest held on that pitch this summer. James Connolly spoke on the war and its effects industrially. Like all other parties his own was divided in opinion. For that reason he made it clear that his opinions were personal and did not necessarily bind others who spoke from that platform. The war was the greatest crime of modern times. The nations and peoples involved in it were plunged into it by a dozen men about whose doings and intrigues nobody was allowed to know anything. All the misery, murder and suffering were brought about by those few men in spite of the wishes and desires of the people. The workers of all countries were the sufferers, and it was they who were paying for the war in both blood and money. Already its evil effects were felt in the prevailing unemployment and the rapid rise in the cost of living, and they were only at the beginning of it.

Thousands upon thousands of workers in France, Germany, Austria, Belgium, Britain and Russia were being sent straight to death in a war in which they had no interest, fighting for a cause they neither knew nor understood. Homes were broken up, wives and children left behind to starve and suffer, and blood spilt like water to satisfy rulers and exploiters who never as much as consulted their peoples before going to war. He had worked with men from all these countries. He knew the German workers to be a kindly people and he could never forget or fail to admire the sacrifices and fights made by the French for liberty and freedom all over Europe. But Britain's was a criminally disgraceful part in the war. Everybody knew that her pretence of defending Belgian independence and integrity was a sham and hypocrisy. Even the English people were not consulted about the war, and with none of the peoples had Ireland any quarrel. Every soldier or sailor killed in that war was in reality murdered. Even should he stand alone he would always protest against wars of aggression. One thing he would not sacrifice at any cost and that was honour and principle. ... [38]

IRELAND AND THE WAR
The Position of the Nation

[17 October 1914]

On Monday evening in the Antient Concert Rooms a mass meeting was held under the auspices of the Irish Neutrality League. The demonstration was principally intended to act as a set off to Mr John Redmond's recent recruiting meeting in the Mansion House, and to define the position of Ireland in relation to the present European War. When the proceedings opened the building was filled to overflowing by an enthusiastic gathering. Mr James Connolly took the chair amidst applause, and was accompanied on the platform by Mr Arthur Griffith (Editor *Sinn Féin*), Mr William O'Brien (President Dublin Trades Council), Mr John T. Kelly, TC; Mr J. J. Scollan (AOH, IAA), Major John MacBride, Mr Seán Milroy, ex-Alderman Macken, and the Countess Markievicz.[39]

Mr Connolly, in his opening address, explained that they were met together to launch a campaign which he thought would prove historic in the annals of this country. He had with him on the platform men drawn from all classes. There were labour men there, and men who by no stretch of the imagination could be called labour men. They had Home Rulers and Republicans, Socialists and Sinn Féiners (applause). They had members of the sane section of the Volunteers, members of the Citizen Army (applause), and representatives of Cumann na mBan, Inghinidhe na hÉireann, and the various Franchise Leagues in Ireland.[40] All of these represented ideals that were strangely different and ideas of the future that were strangely hostile. They represented many diverse ideas that for the time being were relinquished, so that they could come together on a common platform. But having mentioned the things they disagreed on, he would now turn to the one thing upon which they all agreed, namely, that the interests of Ireland were more dear to them than the interests of the British Empire (loud applause). They wanted to emphasise the fact that the enemies of England were not necessarily the enemies of Ireland. It was their duty to gather together the forces in Ireland so that they might place their country in the position it ought to occupy – a position of neutrality (applause). Having acquired the force, it was their duty to arrive at a conception of this question, and that conception was not likely to be of concern for the British Empire. They were now gathered together to emphasise the fact that their duty was to Ireland and to Ireland only (cheers). In doing so they would, of course, be accused of all sorts of motives. Mr Redmond (groans) told them that it was their duty as Irishmen to support England in the present crisis, because she had closed for ever the record of her past in this country, but he (Mr Connolly) held that they could never map out their plans for the future unless they were able to understand the past (applause). When he (the speaker) was told of the promises made by England he remembered the promises made by England in the past and the result of those promises – which were never kept – he would tell them they ought not to heed her promises now unless they had the power in their hands to see that they were kept (applause). If Mr Redmond, instead of pledging the support of the Irish people in the British House of Commons had told Mr Asquith that he proposed going home to Ireland to consult the voice of Ireland, then, had he made such a statement, the Irish nation would be born again (cheers). But that opportunity had been lost. The English people were now crying out about the woes of Belgium, but when Belgium was devastated with fire and sword there were no British there to help her. Even when Belgium was in the throes of agony England sent her expeditionary force to France. This, of course, was done for 'strategic reasons,' but she knew that her army was safer beside the big French force than with the smaller army of Belgium. Germany was fighting for the commerce of the seas and for the means of building up a sane civilisation in Europe (cheers). This was no rigged meeting – they had no RIC[41] force to protect it. Irishmen wanted to see their country emerge from the present crisis with her dignity preserved (loud applause). ... [42]

LABOUR MANS THE BREACH

[21 November 1914]

As we announced in our Stop Press issue last week the British Government through its military commandant in Dublin has gone one step further in the direction of the suppression of the liberties of the Irish people. Captain Monteith, of the Irish Volunteers, was summarily ordered to leave the Dublin Metro-

politan District within twenty-four hours, and also to report to
the military authorities wherever he took up his future residence. Mr Walsh, of Cork, and Messrs Hegarty, of the same
city, have also had the same sample of British zeal for civilised
government meted out to them. Numbers of Civil Servants in
the Post Office, as well as in the Custom House, have been
interviewed by their superiors and told plainly to cease their
activities in the Irish Volunteers or take the consequences in
dismissal from their position, and all over the country this
inquisition into the political opinions of every educated man is
manifesting itself as a part of the settled policy of the Government. A cowardly Press is calling out for the suppression of all
newspapers and journals refusing to take their orders from the
Government, employers are commenting adversely upon the
refusal of workers to wear loyalist badges, and gradually a
White Terror is spreading itself over the lives of the people.

One of the victims, Jack Hegarty, of Cork, writes to us
protesting that he does not complain of the action of the
Government in striking him down, scorns to whine. We
quite well believe you, Jack! But we complain when any man
or woman who stands for Freedom is struck down, and our
complaint is not based so much upon a sense of injury to
the man, as upon the fact that through him Freedom is
struck at. To remain dumb in front of the assassin's blow is
to encourage the assassin. We will not be dumb, we will not
be silent, 'we will speak though all earth's systems crack.'
And we do not hesitate to offer our lives or our personal
liberties as the earnest of our speech.

For this reason and in this spirit the Irish Citizen Army,
and the members of this Union gathered together on last Sunday in a drenching downpour of rain, and in face of the threat
of military suppression, to voice our protest against the outrage
upon Captain Monteith. He is not of our counsel, he is not of
our Union, he is not of our Army, but as he was struck at by
our enemy because he had the same high ideal of National
Rights as we had, we sprang to offer our all for his aid. That
was the true spirit of militant Irish Labour – the fearless spirit
which teaches the working class to guard what rights it has
whilst reaching out to win greater rights for the future.

There are certain elements in Ireland to-day, and notably
in important offices in Dublin, which, under the guise of
caution, are disguising a timorous shrinking from the ugly
realities of their position and are attempting to masquerade

as astute diplomatists in the endeavour to hide from their followers their own reluctance to advance. Whilst their fate and the fate of the potential liberties of their country hangs upon the swing of the balance, these leaders who will not lead idly speculate upon the possible plans of the enemy, hatch schemes it would take a generation to mature, and pray for the coming of opportunities that are already worn weary with standing unrecognised at their elbows.

With them or without them the Irish working class goes forward to the conquest of the future. In this attack upon Germany it sees an attack upon the nation whose working class had advanced nearest to the capture of the citadels of capitalism; in this enthusiasm for Russia it sees exultation at the domination of a power rightly feared by every friend of freedom on the Continent of Europe; in this carnival of English jingoism in Ireland it sees the abandonment of all the high hopes and holy aspirations that sanctified Irish history and made the sacrifices of the past the foundation of noble achievements in the future; in this gospel of hatred preached by the capitalist press it sees the denial of human brotherhood.

Recognising in this awful hour the fearful forces arrayed against us, Labour in Ireland sees in this war a fiendish plan of the British capitalist class – the most astute ruling class in the world – to plant the Iron Heel upon the heart of peacefully progressing peoples, and so recognising stands ready to draw the sword, to die if need be that Freedom might live. None have suffered more than the Irish workers, none will do and dare more. Truly can it be said of them that

> The sufferings of the people have been but an initiation in the worship of liberty; their sorrows were blessed, they learned a truth with every tear.

TELL THE TRUTH
A Challenge to Mr Birrell

[28 November 1914]

Every day it is becoming more evident that the slaughter of men in this war exceeds anything known in human history. The vast numbers of men engaged and the deadly character of the weapons employed have combined to make of the scene of conflict one vast slaughterhouse. No longer is it the case of the comparatively small numbers of a professional army, but rather of the contending forces of the entire manhood of nations. Along the battle fronts of France and Belgium, as along the battle fronts of Austria and Poland, it is nations that are marching out to slaughter, and along those battle fronts each day sees the destruction of as many human lives as were lost in a month's warring on the old scale and in the old manner. France and Belgium, Poland and Austria are becoming vast graveyards in which are being buried the flower of the manhood of the warring nations, in which are also being buried the hopes and brightness of life for countless thousands of women, and millions of children left fatherless to face a heartless world. On the sea the same toll is being taken by this horrible war. In the full bloom of health and strength one moment, in the next hurled into eternity before being able to realise that even a blow is being struck; the manhood and courage, and love, and capacity of the sailors whelmed in oblivion at one fell stroke.

The hospitals of every city in the three kingdoms are crammed with the mangled, twisted, and maimed bodies of the wounded; more than half-a-million soldiers we are told by eminent authorities lie groaning in the hospitals of France, and lying under the sod of France and Belgium or under the heaving billows of the oceans are many thousands whose names are still appearing in the lists of missing, and whose relatives still hopefully believe they are alive and safe as prisoners of war.

We are told that the truth must be kept back lest it give comfort to the enemy. If a town is taken by the Germans or the Boers the fact is concealed for weeks, and we only learn that it was in their hands when the war correspondents are able to tell us that it was re-taken by the Allies. It cannot be that the truth is withheld for fear the enemy should know; if the enemy takes a town, he surely knows that he has taken it. It is not he, but the peoples of these countries that are being deceived. Similarly, if a Dreadnought is sunk by the enemy, or a cruiser sent to the bottom, the news is withheld on the same alleged lying excuse.

We assert that the truth about the loss of human lives in this war is being kept back because it is too awful to be told, because the hopes of the human race are being slaughtered; because if the truth were known people would realise that no victory would compensate any of the warring nations for the loss of the flower of their male population; because the governing class believe that it is necessary that the peoples of the world shall never learn the fearful price mankind has to pay as a punishment for allowing such a criminal class with such murderous instincts to be a governing class. For this reason the Government has issued orders to the Press to keep back all news of disasters, forbade the Press to issue posters telling of British defeats, instructed the Press to avoid keeping track of the totals in the casualty lists, and in general insisted that nothing must be sent out that would be 'calculated to depress the public.' The punishment for refusing to obey these orders would be a suspension of telegraphic service.

We on our part have a duty to perform. A duty to our class and our country. That duty compels us to do what in us lies to avert the slaughter of any more of our people in the shambles of the Continent. Our duty to our people is greater than any supposed allegiance to the British Empire. The value to Ireland – aye, the value to humanity of any breadwinner of a working class Irish family is immeasurably superior to the value of all the crowned and coroneted murderers and exploiters that ever gibbered in glee over the number of corpses on a battlefield.

Let the truth be known! Count every corpse that the Empire requires us to pay for its victory; add up the total of the wrecked human lives of the wounded soldiers, let us know the sum of the tears that the women and children must shed in oceans that Britannia might rule the waves and browbeat the nations.

We challenge Mr Birrell[43] to the issue. Let he and his fellow conspirators take us into court, not into a secret military tribunal, but before an open court of our fellow subjects. Let them tell the truth about what this war has cost day by day in human lives, and we will guarantee to prove that it is a crime against humanity, and that every person who in this crisis urges the nation to continue the conflict is a traitor to the highest interests of the human race, that every man or woman who does not raise his or her voice in protest, or who pretends that because we are in a murderous conflict we must continue murdering and being murdered – that every such person is a coward and dastard.

Let Mr Birrell test the matter in open tribunal, find out what are the 'sentiments of the vast majority of Irishmen,' and then – bring on his gaolers.

Part Five

The Worker 1914–1915

Connolly wasn't long finding a successor to the suppressed *Irish Worker*. He crossed to Scotland, where the SLPers agreed to print a paper and smuggle it across to Dublin between sheets of glass. *The Worker*'s illegal status was obvious from its first number (26 December) onwards: there were no names, no pack drills. Even pseudonyms were considered too risky, and Jim Larkin was down as nominal editor – partly for the sake of continuity with the paper's predecessor, and partly because he was away in the US, out of reach of the British.

A large part of Connolly's concern in *The Worker* was to illustrate the existence of opposition to the war: many of his articles consist largely of quotations showing the reality of the war, and the stand that some were taking against it. His own words rammed home the need for the working class to hold firm against the odds, defending what they had and fighting for more.

The clandestine paper had a short life. The 20 February issue was seized by the authorities, and *The Worker*'s jig was up. Connolly was a man without a paper.

'IN THIS SUPREME HOUR
OF OUR NATIONAL DANGER'

[9 January 1915]

> The report is a terrible indictment of the social conditions and civic
> administration of Dublin. Most of us have supposed ourselves to be
> familiar with the melancholy statistics of the Dublin slums. ... We did
> not know that nearly 28,000 of our fellow-citizens live in dwellings
> which even the Corporation admits to be unfit for human habitation.
> We had suspected the difficulty of decent living in the slums; the report
> proves the impossibility of it. Nearly a third of our population so lives
> that from dawn to dark and from dark to dawn it is without cleanliness,
> privacy or self-respect; the sanitary conditions are revolting. Even the
> ordinary standard of savage morality can hardly be maintained. To
> condemn the young child to an upbringing in the Dublin slums is to
> condemn it to physical degradation and an appalling precocity in vice.

The above quotation is from the *Irish Times'* comment upon
the report of the *Inquiry into Housing Conditions in Dublin*
issued during the last days of the great dispute of 1913–14. We
reproduce it to-day because there is a danger that amid the
clash of arms, and the spectacular magnificence of international
war, the working class voters of Dublin may be dazzled or
chloroformed into forgetfulness of the horrors, and the responsibility for the horrors, that lie around them and degrade and
destroy many thousands of their lives. It is our duty to our
own class, to our country, and to ourselves to see that the
voters do not so forget, but that on the contrary they seize the
opportunity given them by the elections to strike as hard a
blow as they can at the system responsible for such atrocities,
and at the political parties which uphold that system.

Of course, we will be told that 'now in this supreme hour
of our national danger,' etc, all ideas of war between classes
should be laid aside and we all should co-operate harmoniously
together. In answer we would ask – Has any capitalist or landlord shown any forbearance towards the workers more than
they have been compelled to by the force of law, or by the
power of labour unions? Is it not the fact that 'in this supreme
hour of our national danger' the employers are seizing eagerly
upon every pretext to reduce wages and victimise the workers?
The great loyalist firm of Switzer and Co. have enforced a
severe cut in the wages of the employees in their drapery

establishment, and their example has been followed all over the city and country. The firm of S. N. Robinson, coal importers, have cut down the carting rates for all government contracts, so that their drivers now receive from 2d to 6d per ton less for coal carted to government establishments than they are entitled to receive. The law says that all government contractors must pay the standard rate paid in their district, but this firm laughs at the law and steals their employees' wages. 'In this supreme hour of our national danger' rents are going up, prices are steadily mounting to the sky, more and more men, women and girls are disemployed; more and more we see few workers compelled to do the work usually done by a greater number, and persistently as all the necessaries of life go up the wages of the labourer are relentlessly hammered down. 'In this supreme hour of our national danger.'

Nay, let the truth be told though the heavens fall! The greatest danger that we see at the present moment is that the whole brood of parasites and spongers upon Labour whom our past agitations have dragged into light, the vile crew who have waxed fat and wealthy by the robbery of Dublin's poor, the slum landlords of the vile and disease-laden Dublin tenements condemned alike by the laws of God and man, the sweaters whose speciality is the grinding down of women and girls, and all the unclean politicians, ward heelers and personators who have fastened upon the vitals of the working class – the greatest danger is that these enemies of their kind should succeed in escaping the public wrath under cover of the excitement and confusion of the war.

Therefore we cry aloud that all might hear: War or no war those slums must be swept out of existence; war or no war those slum landlords are greater enemies than all the 'Huns' of Europe; war or no war our children must have decent homes to grow up in, decently equipped schools to attend, decent food whilst at school; streets, courts and hallways decently lighted at nights; war or no war the workers of Dublin should exert themselves first for the conquest of Dublin by those whose toil makes Dublin possible; war or no war the most sacred duty of the working class of Ireland is to seize every available opportunity to free itself from the ravenous maw of the capitalist system and to lay the foundations for the Co-operative Commonwealth – the Working Class Republic.

'In this supreme hour of our national danger,' we call upon the Working Class of Ireland to remember that the only enemy it actually knows of is the enemy that lives upon its labour, that steals its wages, that rackrents its members, that oppresses its women and girl workers, that constantly seeks to encompass its social degradation. All the fleets and armies of the 'alien enemy' are not as hurtful to our lives, as poisonous to our moral development, as destructive to our social well-being as any one street of tenement houses in the slums of Dublin.

The Municipal Elections are the most important things for the moment in the interest of our class. That the flag of the Dublin Labour Party should float victoriously over each of the seven wards it is contesting is more essential for the better interests of civilisation in this island than the planting of the flag of a robber empire upon the ramparts of some alien capital in Continental Europe.

Our call then is for Volunteers for this great fight to redeem Dublin from the hands of the capitalist barbarians.

Will Magnificent Dublin of the Workers magnificently respond?[1]

JOTTINGS

[16 January 1915]

The Socialist press of the world continues to make every effort possible to arouse the conscience of the working class against the iniquity of war. Taking advantage of the stand made in the German Reichstag by Dr Liebknecht[2] against the jingo sentiment now aroused in Germany, several French Labour leaders sent articles to a French newspaper, *La Bataille Syndicaliste*, dealing with the declaration of their German comrade. We quote the translation from the *New York Call*:–

> The first, L. Jouhaux, secretary of the French Federation of Labor (CGT), does so in an article entitled 'Hope and Comfort!' He thinks the declaration comes somewhat late, but, he continues, 'it comes at its own time. And if we cannot yet say that the whole of the working class of Germany shares the point of view of heroic Liebknecht, we can at least assert that these words have been the clarion call which bids us hope. We who do not wage a war of conquest, who do not wish the extermination of the German nation, we are also determined that the end of these horrible sufferings shall be the alliance of the peoples.

'That conception of ours is also that of the working class of England, Belgium, Italy, the United States; from one end of the world to the other it represents the hope of the working class, because it is the only basis for a lasting peace, and can assure the uninterrupted development of democracy on the globe ... Liebknecht, you have been our comforter, we shall be your supporters,' Jouhaux concludes his article.

The second French labor leader, who is scarcely less well known than Jouhaux, is A. Merrheim, the secretary of the important French Metal Workers' Union. Merrheim has been very reticent during the war. He and his friend Lenoir have not found themselves in agreement with the general sentiment prevailing at present in the French labor movement, where nationalism – to use no worse term – is very rampant, as it is indeed in the whole of Europe. Merrheim explains that for the second time he will break his self-imposed silence. His article has the heading, 'For the International Entirely and Before Everything.' About Liebknecht Merrheim writes:

'And I doubly applaud the courageous declaration of Karl Liebknecht supporting the view which I, together with my friend Lenoir, have never ceased to affirm wherever it was possible for me to do so since the beginning of the war. And I repeat here that of which I am profoundly convinced, viz, that this war will not mean the end of militarism, which is, on the contrary, as necessary to capitalism as the sea is indispensable to men-of-war and trading vessels.

'The present war will not kill, will not abolish, capitalism; that is incontestable. And, with Karl Liebknecht, I cry with all the power of my conscience and conviction to the French workers:

'Only the peace which has germinated in the soil of the international solidarity of the laboring class can be a lasting peace. It is for this reason that it is the duty of the proletariat of all countries to continue also in this war mutual socialistic labor in behalf of peace. It has been an imperishable honor for the CGT (French Federation of Labor) to have affirmed it clearly and loudly with Karl Liebknecht.'

From America, along with the demand of the American Socialists, which we publish in another column,[3] we gladly reprint the following quotation from the *Leader* of Milwaukee as typical of the efforts to arouse the peoples to the fact that this war, like all such wars, is, in the striking American phrase –

A Rich Man's War, but a Poor Man's Fight

Occasionally the horror of the present is lifted from the mind long enough to glimpse the greater horror of the future. At first there seems to be nothing but horror heaped upon horror in the vision.

Financiers and professional statisticians have made many guesses as to the public debt that the war will leave behind. Most of these guesses fall close to $50,000,000,000 as the load that will be piled up at the end of the first year. This will be added to a debt that was already commonly designated as crushing.

This debt, if present property relations continue, will erect an idle bond-holding plutocracy to which the remainder of the earth will be bound in perpetual servitude. The interest on such a debt at 5 per cent, and none of these nations will borrow for less, rises to the incomprehensible sum of $2,500,000,000 annually. These bonds will bind the entire laboring population of the nations involved to a small capitalist class with fetters of gold stronger than ever held the serf to his master.

The remnants of the miserable wretches that are freezing in the trenches in Flanders, along the Aisne, in East Prussia, Poland, and a hundred corners of the four continents where mechanical mayhem is being practised on a wholesale scale will crawl back to their homes to find themselves bound out for life and the lives of their descendants to the class of money lenders who send dollars instead of bodies to the front.

Bearing the stupendous weight of this monstrous debt upon their mangled bodies, these poor devils will be required to drag wealth from a land shattered back almost to savagery by the explosions of military blood lust.

All this sounds impossible. The one hope of the race is that it will be made impossible. The one bright spot in this black vision is the strong probability that the hypnotism of patriotism may be shocked away in the clash of battle, and that, when the warriors once more become workers, they will have retained their intelligence to such an extent that they will war upon their real enemies, the capitalists, the money lenders who are now seeking to fasten themselves leech-like to the class that must furnish the great mass of the fighters and all of the producers of wealth.

This war is teaching some big lessons as to the ease with which property relations can be changed when they conflict with the interests of rulers. The ruled are certain to learn some of these lessons, and the first of these should be that public debts can be repudiated when they become instruments to the enslavement of half the world.

Dr Liebknecht himself writes upon the subject in last week's *Labour Leader*:–

> As a German Socialist I am pleased to be able to write a message of brotherhood to British Socialists at a time when the ruling classes of Germany and Britain are trying by all means in their power to incite bloodthirsty hatred between the two peoples. But it is painful for me to write these lines at a time when our radiant hope of previous days, the Socialist International, lies smashed on the ground with a thousand expectations, when even many Socialists in the belligerent countries – for Germany is not an exception – have in this most rapacious of all wars of robbery willingly put on the yoke of the chariot of Imperialism just when the evils of capitalism were becoming more apparent than ever. I am, however, particularly proud to send my greetings to you, to the British Independent Labour Party, who, with our Russian and Servian comrades,[4] have saved the honour of Socialism amidst the madness of national slaughter.
>
> Confusion reigns amongst the rank and file of the Socialist army, and many blame Socialist principles for our present failure. It is not our principles which have failed, however, but the representatives of those principles. It is not a question of changing our principles; it is a question of applying them to life, of carrying them into action.
>
> All the phrases of 'national defence' and 'the liberation of the people' with which Imperialism decorates its instruments of murder are but deceiving tinsel. Each Socialist Party has its enemy, the common enemy of the International, in its own country. There it has to fight it. The liberation of each nation must be its own work. ...
>
> Only in the co-operation of the working masses of all countries, in times of war as in times of peace, does the salvation of humanity lie. Nowhere have the masses desired this war. Nowhere do they desire it. Why should they, then, with a loathing for war in their hearts, murder each other to the finish? It would be a sign of weakness, it is said, for any one people to suggest peace; well, let all the peoples suggest it together. The nation which speaks first will not show weakness but strength. It will win the glory and gratitude of posterity.

The *Labour Leader*, we may say, has covered itself with imperishable glory owing to the stand it has taken against the war. It should never be forgotten also that to take such a attitude in England requires more insight and moral courage than in Ireland. All the national history and traditions of this country move influences against our participation in this war on

England's side. To those Irish men and women who opposed the
war, the act was thus easier, and required less clearness of vision
than was required from the English workers who refused to bow
before the war god erected for their worship by the jingo press
and the secret diplomacy of their country. It was hard for them
as it was easy for us. We know, of course, that military rule and
Government persecutions will get a freer hand in Ireland than in
England, that jailing, and deportations from certain districts, will
occur more frequently here than there; that stealing printing
machinery in Ireland will not cause so much trouble to the
Government as it would in England. But that does not alter our
argument. Irish people, as a rule, would rather a thousand times
face the worst a Government can do than face an adverse Irish
public opinion. Therefore, we can the better appreciate what the
English opponents of the war have had to face.

On the same subject, the following letter appeared last week
in the columns of our Glasgow contemporary, *Forward*:–

(To the Editor of *Forward*.)
Dear Sir,

It is questionable whether any appreciation of the good work done
by *Forward* since this war began would be helpful to *Forward* if that
appreciation comes from one who, like myself, had the misfortune to
edit the only paper in the United Kingdom to suffer an invasion of a
military party with fixed bayonets, and to have the essential parts of
its printing machine stolen in defence of freedom and civilisation!
But as the Editor of *Forward* has declared that the action of Jim
Larkin in New York[5] makes it impossible to arouse feelings against
the forcible suppression of the *Irish Worker* in Ireland, it becomes at
least probable that *Forward*, after that disclaimer, will not suffer even
if I do write a word or two in its praise.

I wish I could express myself freely in this matter. If I could I
would tell how proud I was to have been associated ever so slightly
with the little paper that held so close to the idea of Internationalism
when so many who had given that principle lip services had so basely
deserted it. The moral and physical courage required to take up and
maintain such a position is, in my humble opinion, a hundredfold
grander than anything on exhibition in the trenches from end to end
of the far-flung battle line of the warring nations.

Yours fraternally,

JAMES CONNOLLY.

OUR RULERS AS A STUDY

[16 January 1915]

The most interesting study for an intelligent worker to take up
and make his own is, in our opinion, the study of the natural
history of the ruling class. It is not only interesting in itself,
but leads to and makes necessary excursions into all sorts of
allied fields of study, so that once you have begun to take it
up seriously you are led on almost unconsciously to a broaden-
ing of your field of vision, and a deepening of your insight
into the heart of things. Also, as you grasp more firmly the
lines on which the ruling class proceed, and the policy which
enables them to retain their place in the saddle, you receive a
higher opinion of the worth to the world of the mere toilers
and humble ones whose place is among the ruled, whose backs
itch with the gall sores of the saddle these gentry bestride.

Some such thoughts as these must surely be arising in the
minds of many Irish workers in Dublin and throughout Ireland
to-day. They must see around them continually accumulating
evidences of the unscrupulous methods by which the ruling class
strive to ensure a continuance of their ruling. They must see how
in times of security the ruling class bully, brow-beat and tyran-
nise over the people, and how in times of insecurity these same
rulers come around whining and crawling, and protesting their
common interest with those whom but yesterday they denounced
as dogs and rabble.

Do we need to particularise, to bring evidence of the truth
of our assertion? Is not the truth striking us in the face at
every fresh development of our public life?

When there is a strike on in any industry, when some body
of workers, unable to bear any longer the miseries of their lot,
strive to secure a little betterment by withdrawing their labour,
what is the attitude of the master class to any poor wretches
who betray their brothers or sisters by scabbing. They may be
the most degraded wretches, the off-scouring of the jails and
workhouses; they may be, and generally are, the most inefficient as workers; they may be sunk in crime and bestiality;
they may be in their vile bodies carriers of disease and pestilence; but the master class will hug them to its bosom, will
pay them better wages than ever was paid for self-respecting
labour, and its press will laud them as heroes, benefactors, and
souls of honour, the word of any one of whom is worth more

in a Court of Law than the oath of ten thousand strikers of unblemished character.

Or is it perhaps a war that rivets the attention of the world – a war that endangers the interests of the particular nation whose life blood that section of the capitalist class is sucking. Marvellous again is the change! In times of peace that ruling class may have ruled with a rod of iron, may have sent its uniformed police into the homes of the poor to baton and murder and destroy, to beat their women and club their children and destroy their poor furniture; may have ordered the same callous brutes to charge and cripple and murder hundreds of unarmed passers-by until the streets of the city looked like a battlefield, and the blood of murdered men and women ran along its pavements. Or it may have orde[red its soldiers armed][6] with ball cartridges to [fire upon an un]armed crowd of men and [women and] children, and as the corpses of [the victims] were carried to their last resting pl[ace] may have set up its chief spokesman [in] the place of government to say with a sardonic grin upon his sneering face that it would be found that no reflection could be cast upon the soldiery. But once the bugles sang for war that grin of defiance would disappear, that soldiery would be hastily smuggled out of sight; those policemen would be instructed to be as tolerant as they had been brutal; those pressmen would be instructed to praise the people whom they had vilified, to coax and caress and seduce the workers whom they had slandered; the haughty and noble and honourable lords and ladies and gentlemen to whom the poor had been as cattle, as scarcely human, as contemptible hewers of wood and drawers of water for their betters – those ultra-refined rulers and lords of the earth would come down to beg and cringe, and praise and flatter and fawn upon the poor that these latter might furnish soldiers as cannon-fodder, to fight in the armies that the same set of employers may continue to rob them, the same set of policemen to club, murder and imprison them on perjured evidence, that the same set of pressmen may continue to vilify them as they vilify the nation with whom they are at war, and that finally the same set of rulers may continue to rule and ride them in the same saddle and flog them with the same whips as before, if not with worse.

Or perhaps it is a municipal election that calls for the attention of the rulers. Again weird and wonderful is the change. It may be that the workers have stewed for a twelve-month in the filthiest tenement houses in Europe; that the cleanliest woman finds it impossible to keep clean the miserable buildings in which her rooms are situated; that dark and dismal streets and hallways drive men and women to drink and boys and girls to destruction of soul and happiness; that disease rages around the families and rising from fetid yards and badly kept drains strikes down young and old in a never-ceasing slaughter; that the slums of the city are the byword and horror of civilization, and the city representatives the emblem for municipal incapacity and scorn of the electors. But let the working class electors so scorned resolve to take the matter in their own hands, and to elect one of their own number to save the honour of the city, the lives of the poor, and the dignity of their class; in the moment that decision is known all the harpies who feed upon municipal incompetence and social misery will flock to the ward like vultures to a feast. Every poor woman will be visited, and smiled upon, and petted and coaxed by suave and oily gentlemen from whose path her children would ordinarily be kicked like diseased reptiles; every poor man will be sure of a handshake from well-fed, well-clad business men who at other times encourage the police to club him to death as a 'ruffianly striker,' each court and alley and slum will be haunted for days by the municipal representatives who have forgotten its very existence since the day they were elected, and cabs and cars and motors will be at the service of the poorest of the poor to bring them to the polling booth to vote for the men who during the rest of the year would, if they were hurt in their employment, make them pay for the car that took them to the hospital.

O, yes! The ruling class are worthy of study. The natural history of the ruling class is of fascinating interest. You begin with interest, you proceed with awe and admiration, you deepen into hatred, and you wind up with contempt for the nature of the beast. You realise that – **The Capitalist Class is the Meanest Class that ever grasped the Reins of Power.**

Part Six

The Workers' Republic 1915–1916

To a man who always understood the importance of a paper as a revolutionary weapon, the lack of one – especially during the crisis atmosphere of the war – irritated Connolly greatly. After drawing a blank in Liverpool, he managed to dig out an old printing machine in Dublin. He brought it into the basement of Liberty Hall, and after defeating an attempt by more cautious counsels within the ITGWU to keep such seditious matter away from the union, the second *Workers' Republic* made its first appearance on 29 May 1915.

The theoretical and practical experience of Connolly's last year, therefore, stand out in the paper. The collapse of the socialist movement when war broke out left him severely alone: he faced the dilemma of wanting to fight back, but lacking the resources. Fighting together with the republicans might give him a chance to strike a blow, but it would have to be on their terms – socialist revolution wasn't abandoned, by any manner of means, but Connolly did put it on the long finger. *The Workers' Republic* sees his attempts, week by week, to grapple with this problem: desperately trying to seize the opportunity, and forcing the republicans to do likewise. After succeeding in reaching agreement with them in January, his articles prepare the popular mind for rebellion against British imperialism and its war.

Parallel with this, Connolly kept up a tremendous fight to maintain and improve the position of the working class. While his 'Notes on the Front' dealt usually with the war and the national question, his editorials usually fought on the trade union front. Strikes, in Ireland and abroad, and defence of the workers' conditions generally, form a central preoccupation in

Connolly's work during the war. Right to the end, the idea that the rebellion of the working class is the hope of saving the world from barbarism and building a truly human society is at the forefront of Connolly's message.

Although the authorities threatened *The Workers' Republic*, and a Citizen Army guard was required to protect its press, the paper stood its ground. The last issue appeared on 22 April 1916. Two days later, Connolly marched from Liberty Hall to the GPO to take the great leap in the dark that was the Easter Rising.

OUR POLICY

[29 May 1915]

On the appearance of our first number in such a time of tension and excitement, our readers, we are sure, expect some sort of declaration of policy. This we hasten to give.

The policy of this paper will be to implant in the minds of its readers a correct understanding of the position and needs of Labour in Ireland and abroad. To do this we shall devote most of our space to the Labour movement in this country, and whatever articles or reprints we shall publish dealing with conditions and developments elsewhere, will be published because they serve to shed a light upon some of our home problems, or because they show how people else-where have mastered some difficulty with which we are still grappling. Thus in the present issue we quote from a German trades union writer an article giving particulars of how the German municipal authorities have grappled with the problem of the increase of the price of food – a problem which is no less acute in Ireland than it is in Germany, but which in this country has not yet been grappled with in any statesmanlike manner. In the article on 'The Problem of the Child' we show how the care of children is taken up in Hungary, which seems to have solved the question that the much talked of 'War Babies' have produced in these coun-tries – to the apparent destruction of all our conventional ideas of sex-morality.

At a time when everybody is talking of military matters, it would be mere affectation, or worse, to attempt to exclude such from our columns. Hence we keep in the fashion by our Citizen Army notes, which deal with the lessons of military science as exemplified in campaigns of similar bodies of armed citizens in other countries in the past.[1]

We pass no verdict upon the great War now raging. That part of our work was done in the columns of our predecessors, and any Irishman who has not made up his mind as to his duty must just make it up as best he can without our assistance. The Defence of the Realm Act is very far-reaching,[2] and we are not yet in a position to prevent its enforcement, were we ever so willing.

We regret nothing in our former action. The work we did then had to be done at all risks or costs, to save the honour of our class and our country we did it, and in such an emergency we should so act again.

Our great work now is to consolidate our ranks, to educate our members, to lay broad and deep the foundations of a great Labour movement in this country, and to think out and propound the plans by which we hope to make it possible for that movement to enter into the possession of a regenerated Ireland.

From time to time we shall do our best to present to our readers an understanding of the true magnificence of the Labour movement; we shall tell how the workers of Ireland have suffered in the past, how they are winning their way to emancipation, and we shall do our endeavour to make this country realise that all those strivings after better wages and better conditions, all those squabbles over half-pennies and pennies per hour, squalid and sordid as they seem, are nevertheless in their essence beautiful and spiritual strivings of imperfect human souls for the cleansing of the environment in which they are placed.

In the long run the freedom of a nation is measured by the freedom of its lowest class; every upward step of that class to the possibility of possessing higher things raises the standard of the nation in the scale of civilisation; every time that class is beaten back into the mire, the whole moral tone of the nation suffers. Contemned and despised though he be the rebellious docker is a sign and symbol to all that an imperfect civilisation cannot last, for slavery cannot survive the awakened intelligence of the slave.

To increase the intelligence of the slave, to sow broadcast the seeds of that intelligence, that they may take root and ripen into revolt, to be the interpreter of that revolt, and finally to help in guiding it to victory, is the mission we set before ourselves in the columns of the *Workers' Republic*.

A RAILWAY THIEF

[26 June 1915]

There is a strike of shopmen and other workers on in the Midland and Great Western and Dublin and South Eastern Railways in Dublin. The employees are out on strike because no answer has been given to their repeated requests for an increase of wages to meet the abnormal increase of prices resulting from the great war. That is the central fact of the situation. But arising out of that fact there comes that inevitable touch of humour, such as never fails in Ireland to light up the most serious situation. The General Manager at the Broadstone depot is a man named Keogh. That gentleman writes to the Press and with the most owlish gravity informs all and sundry that there is no dispute between the railway company and their employees, that he does not recognise the Transport Union, and that he never heard of any complaint on the part of the men now on strike. Then he adds, as if it were an unimportant matter, that he had received two communications from the Union, one of them three months ago, and another a week before the strike, but this notwithstanding the men left work without giving notice. After tying himself up in a black knot in this fashion Mr Keogh sent out the Chief Engineer to tell the strike pickets that if they would send in a deputation on the following day he would arrange for them to meet a body of the directors. The men reported this to their Union, and at a mass meeting of all the men on our advice a deputation was appointed to hear what the directors had to say and to lay the facts before them. When the deputation attended on the following day they were ushered into the Board Room where they met – Mr Keogh and the Chief Engineer. Not a director was present. Seeing they had thus been inveigled in by a lying promise the men stood on their dignity and retired. In chagrin at this the Management stopped the Week's Pay due to the men, in the hope that the unexpected loss would lead to demoralisation. To put it more plainly,

Mr Keogh Stole the Wages of the Men

just as truly as does the less respectable but more honest thief who picks a pocket in the street.

The Transport Union immediately paid the men a week's strike pay, and ordered the stoppage of all coal destined for the Midland. Three boats were held up on Sunday night.

Is it not a humorous situation to hear an incompetent jack-in-office, on a railway notorious for its muddling inefficiency and rotten service, say that he will not recognise the right of the men to negotiate through a Union of their own choosing? At the present moment the Government of Great Britain has recognised the right of its working class citizens to speak through their unions, and at every crisis the responsible minister calls together the heads of Unions to consult with them and profit by their advice. In every European country it has been recognised that national organisation on an effective scale is only possible through the co-operation of organised Labour, but this poor derelict manager of an almost derelict railway, a railway made more derelict by his poor managership, with his head full of eighteenth century ideas refuses to recognise the rights of his fellow countrymen to organise in an Irish Union.

Imagining he is another William Martin Murphy[3] he swells his chest to repeat the war cries of the employers during the great lock-out; swells himself like the ox in the fable – and will either burst himself, or cause others to die laughing.

He need not imagine that the world to-day, in 1915, is interested in his attempt to restart a conflict like that of 1913–14, or in his attempt to become another disrupter of the public peace. The men must get their increase. *That* is the vital point, and all squirmings and dodgings about recognition do not affect the issue. Through their Union they have put in a request that their wages be so advanced that they may maintain the same standard of life as heretofore. That modest request must be acceded to, and all the rest of the palaver from Mr Keogh may be dispensed with.

As serious men we cannot afford to turn back in our march to consider the babblings of another age even from the lips of a General Manager.[4]

DUBLIN TRADES COUNCIL

[31 July 1915]

The fortnightly meeting of the Dublin Trades Council was held on Monday evening, Mr T. Farren, President, in the Chair. Also present: Messrs Edward Lyons, Brass Founders and Gasfitters; R. Carroll, TC, Brick and Stone Layers; John Lawler, Cab and Car Owners; J. Simmons, Carpenters (Amal); Matthew Callanan, Central Ironmoulders; M. Culliton, Carpenters (Gen. Union); T. Murphy, Carpet Planners; Francis Farrell, Coachmakers; A. Kavanagh, P. Bowes, J. Bermingham, Corporation Labourers; C. Woodhead, Electricians; J. Bowman, Engineers; B. Drumm, Farriers; Joseph McGrath, Irish Clerks' Union; J. Metcalfe, W. P. Partridge, TC, T. Foran, PLG, James Connolly, Irish Transport Workers; James Courteney, Marble Polishers; J. Lennon, Mineral Water Operatives; J. Kelly, National Union Assurance Agents; Jos. Farrell, M. Smith, Painters (Amal); F. Davidson, Dyers and Cleaners; W. Shanks, Packing Case and Box Makers; Peter Macken, John Bermingham, Painters (Metropolitan); D. Holland, M. A. Brady, Printers (Typo); A. Doyle, Saddlers; G. Paisley, Sawyers; P. D. Bolger, Slaters; W. J. Murphy, Smiths (White); J. Flanagan, P. Carey, Stationary Engine Drivers; Thomas Farren, Stonecutters; John Farren, Sheet Metal Workers; John Duffy, Iron Dressers; J. F. O'Neill, Irish Grocers' and Purveyors' Assistants Union; Winston, National League Blind; Jeremiah Kennedy, Smiths (United).

Messrs Lawler and Farren (Representatives on the Asylum Board) reported that a resolution had been adopted by the Board forbidding the taking in of apprentices in any of the Board's workshops, as in their opinion such boys were not given full facilities to learn their trade, and rarely turned out good workmen. The Board had also agreed to give its labourers coal at cost price.

The President said the report proved the utility of having representatives on such public bodies.

Mr Partridge complained of the attempt by Mr Watson, of the Great Southern and Western Railway, to commandeer the machinery of the Bolton Street Technical School for the manufacture of war munitions, while Mr Watson's own machinery was lying idle all night, and not all of it was worked on munitions in the day time.

Mr J. Murphy was astonished to hear of such an application, and thought the Education Committee were justified in refusing. In his opinion the boys in the school might be taught to do this work.

Mr Connolly said there was more in the matter than that suggested by the last speaker. The machines were originally acquired for educational purposes, and would be spoiled by the application to such work as it was now suggested to put them, and the citizens should not submit to it. He proposed a resolution protesting against the granting of such machinery for the munitions of war. They should be only employed in teaching the arts of Peace.

Mr Macken seconded the resolution, which he said would strengthen the Technical Education Committee in its refusal to grant the machines, and suggested that copies be sent to the Committee and the Department.

The resolution was passed unanimously.

Mr Macken referred to the forthcoming funeral procession of O'Donovan Rossa,[5] which was now definitely known would leave the City Hall on Sunday next at two o'clock, and urged all working people to attend.

Mr Lawler asked that the trades should keep together, and suggested that they meet in Capel Street.

Mr Partridge expressed the hope that every Irish man in Dublin and its vicinity would attend, and advocated the closing of the public houses.

Messrs Holland and Simmons disagreed with the suggestion on the ground that it would cause great inconvenience to the travelling public.

Mr T. Murphy suggested Stephen's Green as the rallying point of the various Trades.

Mr Connolly supported the suggestion, which was adopted.

The Chairman urged all present to do their utmost in making the procession worthy of the man and creditable to the nation.

It was decided to send a subscription to the Committee having charge of affairs in connection with the procession.

Mr Connolly said that the result of the South Wales Miners' Strike[6] was another signal proof of the strengths and invincibility of Labour when united. Here we had the greatest and strongest government that these countries had ever seen in modern times – a government vested with powers that a few years ago no one present would ever have dreamt would be vested in a modern British Government. We had a Coalition Cabinet of all the virtues; a military commander with almost unlimited power, and a civil population that had become hardened to the sight of the exercise of arbitrary authority by that power; we had an army and navy of unprecedented size and efficiency, and as against all that on the one side we had on the other a body of workers in control of nothing but their labour power. But when that body of workers declared that they would stop the process of production it was found that they were more powerful than all the mighty civil and military forces arrayed against them. What a lesson was this for Labour! It showed that Labour already possessed the power, all that it needed was the united will to exercise it. But we had been cursed with leaders without faith in their own class, without vision, without moral courage – leaders who were always preaching about our weakness instead of teaching us to rely upon our strength. Had we had the right kind of leaders this war would never have taken place. If the working class soldiers of Europe had but had the moral courage to say to the diplomats that they would not march against their brothers across the frontiers, but if they were going to fight they would rather fight against their enemies at home than against their brothers abroad, there would have been no war, and millions of homes that were now desolated would be happy (applause).

The Chairman said that it would be a pity to spoil such a magnificent speech by adding anything to it. He took that as the opinion of the Delegates.

The meeting then adjourned.

TO ALL LABOURERS' SOCIETIES

[14 August 1915]

FELLOW WORKERS, –

This is a day of great Organisations. Whether it be on the side of Labour or of Capital, in the realm of peaceful industry or in the arena of warfare, this is a day in which victory goes to the force that is most thoroughly organised. For this reason we of the Irish Transport and General Workers' Union have resolved to invite you, and all other

Irish Societies organising the Workers engaged in general labour, to a Conference to be held in Dublin on some date to be mutually agreed upon, for the purpose of bringing about an amalgamation of all our Unions into one Great Irish Organisation of Labour.

There are few who have not noticed and deplored the large number of small Unions in this country, and still fewer who have not seen that each of those small Unions is much weaker and more helpless than it would be if it was united to the others. They are like companies and regiments on a battlefield, but like companies and regiments which have not united to form an army but persist in each fighting isolated in its own corner, although opposed to an enemy thoroughly united, disciplined and armed, and directed with skill and cunning.

Under such circumstances the local Unions of Labour have all the odds against them. The Capitalists are in control of vast masses of capital, they own all the newspapers, they own and control the Government, and they can use all the military and police forces as they choose as their obedient servants.

To oppose this odds Labour must Unite. It has been found by experience that mere Federation is not sufficient. The Federation of Unions is better than entire isolation, but it has the danger that each separate Union so federated, when its brother Union calls for assistance in a fight thinks of its own treasury and its own finances before it thinks that it should make its brothers' cause its own. We do not blame them, they must do so as long as they are separate Unions, but the necessity keeps them weak, and enables the Capitalist to attack and defeat them one by one.

It is the old tale of the Irish clans all over again. Each Irish clan when attacked by the English Invader was left to fight its battle alone, as all the others thought it was none of their business. United they could have crushed the invader, but they failed to amalgamate, and so he crushed them and stole their country.

Labour in Ireland must amalgamate if it would save itself from slavery. All the small unions must be fused into one, and that one must take over all the members, assets and liabilities of the whole. There must be One Card, One Badge, One Executive – One Front to the Common Enemy.

There will have to be rules to prevent members going from one department too readily to another – leaving a lowly paid occupation to rush into and flood a better paid one, and thus lower its standard. There must be rules to allow all local bodies sufficient self government and control; there must be provision made for taking over all the present officers and premises, so that no one will suffer by the change, but running through and inspiring all such rules and provisions there must be the guiding principle that all local bodies are to be fashioned into an army to be governed, and directed, from a common centre.

This can all be done if the right spirit inspires us all. The economy and greater effectiveness that would result from amalgamation, the ease with which men could maintain their membership in the most diverse occupations, instead of finding the necessity of joining a fresh union and abandoning the old one every time they changed their job or moved from one locality to another; the increased power of tracing members and keeping their cards in good trim which would result from the amalgamation, and above all the greater strength in face of the capitalist class, all, all are factors calling loudly for earnest consideration.

We therefore appeal to all Unions of General Labour in Ireland to communicate with us at Liberty Hall, Dublin,[7] or with the Secretary of the Dublin Trades Council informing us of their views on the matter, and letting us know whether they would be prepared to send delegates to a Conference to discuss this question, and frame a scheme to be submitted to the various bodies.

JAMES CONNOLLY.

COERCION IN ENGLAND

[28 August 1915]

The news which came to hand as we went to press last week that the offices of the *Labour Leader* had been raided in London and Manchester is of a gravity that cannot be minimised. Press prosecutions, and even ruthless suppressions of the press we are familiar enough with in Ireland – so familiar that we appear to have lost even the capacity of resenting it, so familiar, indeed, are we with it that when the *Irish Worker* was suppressed there was not a Labour or Socialist journal in Great Britain protested against the act, or thought it important enough to devote a paragraph to deprecating it.

But press prosecutions, raids upon printing offices in Great Britain, especially raids upon printing offices controlled by a

political party with hundreds of branches and widespread ramifications through the country, that is a fact of much more
sinister significance than any suppression in Ireland. We have
had before now governments which were openly tyrannical and
oppressive in Ireland, but which were nevertheless on the
general side of greater freedom in England; we have had governments which abolished the right of trial by jury in Ireland,
and at the same time extended the suffrage in England. Just as
it is said that there is seldom to be found a man wholly bad, a
man who has not some good points; as no ruffian is wholly
depraved, so there was seldom in modern times a British
Government which did not cover its evil deeds in Ireland with
a pretence at good deeds in England.

Therefore when we meet with the spectacle of a government which is brutally destructive of liberty – in Ireland,
which muzzles one part of the press and corrupts the other
– in Ireland, which abolishes the right of trial by jury – in
Ireland, which denies the sanctity of the home and gives the
right of search to every ignorant and insolent policeman – in
Ireland, which destroys Free Speech, gives untrammelled
licence to speakers of one political party and jails the spokes-
men of another – in Ireland, when we meet with the
spectacle of such a government actually daring to extend
some of those 'blessings of British rule' to England, to its
own dearly beloved 'God's Englishmen' we are stricken with
wonder and feel that the foundations of the world are being
swept away.

Either this government is mad, or else the panic cowardice of
fear has set its grasp upon it, and it is reeling stupidly to its
doom.

LABOUR AND THE BUDGET
Dublin Transport Workers' Protest

[2 October 1915]

A meeting to 'call upon all sections of labour to oppose the
attempt of the British Government to heavily tax the food of
the people to pay war expenses'[8] was held in Beresford Place
on Sunday September 26, under the auspices of the Transport
Workers' Union. ... [9]

Mr James Connolly remarked that before they were asked to
pay the blood tax of the war it was surely right that the Irish

race should have been asked to consent to waging war at all. Their representatives should have come to Ireland and laid before them a full and accurate statement of what led to it. Why were they asked to make war upon the German people, and believe that the Germans were their natural enemies – that it was a high and holy and righteous thing and pleasing in the sight of God that they should arm themselves and go out to slaughter men who never did them any harm – (hear, hear) – brothers of theirs in toil and labour, to kill them, to manure the soil with their corpses, and offer up their own lives in the attempt to do so (cheers).

Some had said that Labour should send a candidate forward in the Harbour Division as a protest against this Budget. Who cared about such a protest and what should it avail? One man's voice against that of 600 and more in the great House of Thieves in Westminster. He could tell them a more effective way of protesting. In the time of war Labour was weak politically, but strong industrially. Let them protest where they were strong. The Government was a rich man's Government, the Employers controlled it in their own interest. Then let them tell the employers that every increase of taxation upon the necessaries of life must mean an increase of wages, and when the employers learned that they would bring pressure to bear upon the Government to reduce the taxes upon the food of the poor. More taxes must mean more wages.

They were prepared to fight industrially or any other way that became necessary (cheers).

NOTES ON THE FRONT

[2 October 1915]

Now, everyone has a chance to be happy! All we have to do to support the Government in its prosecution of the war for Civilisation and Small Nationalities is to continue eating, drinking and smoking as usual.
THE BUDGET DOES IT.

The poor old mother, worn out by a lifetime of toil amid misery and wretchedness, need no longer weep bitter tears over her inability to help the war against the Huns. The kind British Government comes to her aid, and enables her to contribute to the successful prosecution of the war without moving

from her seat in the corner at the fire. Every time her son or grandson, daughter or granddaughter, wish to give her a cup of tea the kind British Government steps in and forbids the Christian act until they have first paid over to that Government a tax to enable it to buy something to kill Germans.
THE BUDGET DOES IT.

Your mother may be dying for want of a cup of tea to cheer her old age, your child may be in the last agonies of fever or ague, and fainting for a warm drink, your wife may long for a cheering cup to soothe her nerves after a day of trouble and sickness – no matter. The Government will forbid you doing your duty to these sufferers until you first enable it to push on the work of killing Germans – and pay the extra duty on the tea.
THE BUDGET DOES IT.

Your old father may be passing away and longing for a smoke to ease his last days, but he cannot get a smoke of tobacco until you pay the Government the extra tax to enable it to carry on the war. You may hate the war, and believe it to be a product of hell – conceived in sin, and begotten in iniquity – but pay for it you must before you can get a smoke, or the old father 'get a blast of the pipe.'
THE BUDGET DOES IT.

The food of the poor is taxed to pay for the wars of the rich. The tax that will be put upon the working man and woman will be equal to an increase of at least 6/8 in the £ in prices, and on many articles equal to 10/- in the £. This means that the wages of the working class will be reduced one third at least, and in some cases one half.
THE BUDGET DOES IT.

How can we pay it? Already the working class is staggering under the heavy prices put on all the necessaries of life since the beginning of the war; already the war has meant less food on our tables; less clothes on our backs; less coal on our fires; less boots on our own or our children's feet. More taxes on food means more starvation, more nakedness, more wretchedness and general misery. The working class has seen its best blood driven into the army by the compulsion of hunger and the threat of hunger, now it is to see the miserable relatives of those recruits and reservists, and those defiant ones who refused to be either driven or fooled, alike compelled to pay for the war in hunger and suffering by a tax upon its necessaries of life.
THE BUDGET DOES IT.

Up and down Ireland on every Monday morning there is to be seen outside the Post Office the spectacle of Irish wives and mothers and children standing patiently in line like criminals, waiting for the receipt of the blood money which the British Government allows them in return for the limbs and lives of their husbands, sons or fathers. Some have given the limbs and lives of their nearest and dearest with sorrow and reluctance, some with bitter protests and unavailing tears, a few with willingness and drunken joy, but the Government now reaches out its hand and takes back from all alike half of its blood money by a tax upon the food these poor people must buy in order to live.

The tax upon the food of the poor is equal to an increased tax of fifty per cent. Yet what a howl would go up if it were proposed to tax the rich with a fifty per cent tax. As it is the increased income tax will still not represent one tenth part of the income of a rich man, whilst the increased prices which will follow the tax on food will undoubtedly mean the loss to the worker of at least one half of his weekly income. In other words, it will soon take One Pound to buy the same necessaries of life as could have been bought for ten shillings before the war.

The purchasing power of your wages will be cut in half. THE BUDGET DOES IT.

Hurrah for the Budget. I don't think.

From the Huddersfield *Worker* we take the following parable written during the American Civil War by America's famous humorist, Artemus Ward. It reads as if it were written yesterday:

WILLIAM, A PATRIOT

RE-DEDICATED TO WAR EXPLOITERS

I.

'No, William Barker, you cannot have my daughter's hand in marriage until you are her equal in wealth and social position.'

The speaker was a haughty old man of some sixty years, and the person whom he addressed was a fine looking young man of twenty-five.

With a sad aspect the young man withdrew from the stately mansion.

II.

Six months later the young man stood in the presence of the haughty old man.

'What! YOU here again' angrily cried the old man.

'Aye, old man,' proudly exclaimed William Barker, 'I am here, your daughter's equal and yours!'

The old man's lips curled with scorn. A derisive smile lit up his cold features; when, casting upon the marble centre table an enormous roll of dollar greenbacks, William Barker cried:

'See! Look on this wealth. And I've tenfold more! Listen, old man! You spurned me from your door. But I did not despair. I secured a contract for furnishing the Army of the —— with beef –'

'Yes, yes!' eagerly exclaimed the old man.

'– and I bought up all the disabled cavalry horses I could find –'

'I see, I see!' cried the old man. 'And good beef they make, too.'

'They do! they do! and the profits are immense.'

'I should say so!'

'And now, sir, I claim your daughter's fair hand!'

'Boy, she is yours. But hold! Look me in the eye. Throughout all this have you been loyal?'

'To the core!' cried William Barker.

'And,' continued the old man, in a voice husky with emotion, 'are you in favour of a vigorous prosecution of the war?'

'I am! I am!'

'Then boy, take her! Maria, child, come hither. Your William claims thee. Be happy, my children! And whatever our lot in life may be, LET US ALL SUPPORT THE GOVERNMENT!'

That sounds home-like, does it not? We have a good many jingo patriots here (save the mark) who are making a fortune in the same way, and of course howling for the war as long as it pays them a good thumping profit.

The Americans coined the phrase to describe the Civil War that it was:

A RICH MAN'S WAR BUT A POOR MAN'S FIGHT.

It was a good phrase, terse and descriptive. But are all wars not rich men's wars, in the sense that they are made for the profit of the rich, and poor men's fights in the sense that it is the blood of the poor that is spilt in them all?

But some day the sons of the poor will determine to fight

only in their own interest, and against All the Ruling Thieves of Civilisation.

And then –

> The proud throne shall crumble,
>   The diadem shall wave,
> The Tribes of Earth shall humble
>   The pride of those who reign.
> And war shall lay its pomp away
>   The fame which heroes cherish,
> And glory born in bloody fray
>   Shall fade, decay and perish.

NOTES ON THE FRONT

[23 October 1915]

'Where the treasure is there the heart is also.' So said an old proverb, and its truth was never more apparent than it has been since the present war began. Since that witches' cauldron was stirred up we have seen the most extraordinary somersaults thrown by men and nations, and the most careful study of conditions cannot reveal any other reason for the somersaulting than the overmastering love of treasures.

Consider the case of France. France is the mother of European democracy, the apostle of the right of rebellion, the century-long sword of the revolution of peoples. England, which struts before the world as the home of the Mother of Parliaments, has in reality been chiefly engaged in evolving a system of government in which there should be the greatest semblance of freedom, and the least practical control by the democracy of the essentials of freedom. Witness the absolute power vested in the Cabinet, despite the fact that the Cabinet is quite outside the Constitution, and unknown to British Law.

America has since its own foundation as a nation, the United States, been ever opposed to all revolutionary movements elsewhere; and fettered the free development of its own citizens by means of a Supreme Court to which all laws are amenable. The decision of an overwhelming majority of the electors of the United States upon any particular question can be upset and rendered null and void by five members of the Supreme Court.

But France, the example of France, the free spirit of France, the human outlook of France, the glorious tradition of France – all combined to make France the beau ideal among the nations of all lovers of liberty.

Ever since the Revolution this has been the lot of France – to inspire and enthuse rebels everywhere, and everywhere to lend keenness to the blades of whosoever struck out for Freedom.

But since the great defeat of 1870 – a great defeat brought upon France by the rule of an unscrupulous despot and murderer, Napoleon III, brought upon France by that despot waging a criminal and foolish dynastic war upon a matter in which his subjects had no earthly interest, viz: the succession to the throne of Spain[10] – since then France has been gradually turning her back upon her glorious past, and uniting with forces that stood for all those things in warring against which her revolutionary children had made her name immortal.

France has been the incarnation of Freedom, Russia has been the embodiment of brutal and soulless despotism. They were as far as the poles asunder. But there came a time when Russia borrowed money in France, when French bankers coaxed thrifty French peasants to empty their stockings of the hoards of sorely accumulated coins, and lend them to the Czar's government at good rates of interest. And the peasants yielded to the lure – the thrifty republicans lent gold to the spendthrift despot.

If you lend money to a man you do not like to hear of him losing his job the next week; if you lend money to a business house you do not like to hear of it putting up its shutter and going into bankruptcy. No, until you get your money back you want that man to stop at his job, that house to keep its doors open, and its business flourishing.

England has flourished because she owed money everywhere, her national debt was the biggest in the world, and every one who had bought a share in that debt, or lent England money was anxious that the British Empire should not go down lest their money should go down along with her.

The Russian despot borrowed money from the French Republicans, and gradually the fear lest they should lose their money so worked upon the minds of the republicans that they dreaded the advent of a republic in Russia, and lent more money to keep the despot on his throne, and aid him in crushing in blood the aspirations of those who wanted in Russia the same Republican Freedom as the French enjoyed in France.

It was a situation to make the Devil grin. The great Russian Revolution of 1905 was only crushed by means of the monies lent to the Czar by the French Republicans; it was the children of revolutionary France that enabled the blood-soaked despot to overthrow the Duma, and fill his jails to overflowing with the bravest, best and most enlightened of his subjects.[11]

Out of that horrible situation has grown the participation of France in this War. The money-lenders of France force their nation into war that they might not lose the money they lent to the Czar to enable him to destroy the Russian Revolution. Gallant France, liberty-loving France, revolutionary France, with its free spirit, its human outlook, its glorious tradition does not make this war, although it suffers and fights in it. The France that makes this war is the France of the capitalists, the money-lenders' France whose one great enthusiasm and ideal is that their dividends upon Russian loans be paid though millions perish, and the child of Freedom be strangled in its cradle.

'Where the treasure is there the heart is also.' Over the Atlantic we are beholding the first stages in the similar process of corrupting the hearts of a people. America has taken up a Billion Dollar Loan to the Allies. Henceforth America is no passive onlooker at the struggles of Europe. Her heart will ever follow her treasures, and the splendid neutrality of the past will be followed by an excited and selfish interest in the fortunes of European wars.

The fathers of the American Revolution laid down the axiom that the United States should make no 'entangling alliances.' The last great message of George Washington[12] to his countrymen embodied that advice, and for over a century it has guided American statesmen.

Following that advice America remained the hope and the refuge of all European rebels against tyranny, and the shining example to the world of a nation seeking only a peaceful intercourse with others.

The greatest and most insidious enemy of that policy of America has ever been the statesmen of the British Empire. Without ceasing they have ever striven to lure the United States into an alliance with Great Britain – an Anglo-Saxon Alliance as they phrased it, coolly ignoring the fact that the

Anglo-Saxon strain in American blood is but a poor stream in a mighty ocean of many powerful currents.

But the real American spirit has ever been too strong for this attempt to succeed, and America has grown strong in peace, and mighty through the strength of her own industry and resources.

But the rulers of the British Empire have many strings to their bow, and in the attempt to snare a nation are the most sleepless hunters the world has ever known.

Where the politician could not succeed, where the most wily diplomat was worsted, the financier has succeeded. An appeal to the cupidity of American capitalists has resulted in these gentry betraying their nation's best interests, as capitalists will ever sell for gold any human or holy cause.

America lends money to enable the Allies to pay for war, as America made munitions to enable the Allies to make war.

Consider the hellish irony of it all! The All Lies buy munitions of war from America, and propose to pay for them with monies borrowed from America.

It is like as if you bought a suit of clothes and proposed to pay for them with money borrowed from the tailor who made them. Did you ever try it?

The result is that all the powerful financial interests in America – the Steel Trust, the Armament makers, the Bankers, the manufacturers of Army requirements, all will henceforth be pledged to keep America on the side of the Governments of France, England, or Russia in every war *or domestic revolution* in which these latter may be engaged.

And that means that all the small investors with whose money those great sharks are gambling will slowly, almost imperceptibility, but surely and inevitably have all their sympathies drawn from the side of freedom towards that side which makes for the security of the Governments to whom their money has been lent.

'Where the treasure is there the heart is also.' America is no longer free of entangling alliances: America is committed to the worst kind of an alliance, that alliance of sordid interests in whose grasp French Republicanism has surrendered its soul, to whose loathsome embraces American capitalism has committed the civilisation of the American Continent.

And yet, and yet – the forces of evil will not forever prevail.

THE RETURNED EMIGRANTS

[13 November 1915]

The pages of Irish literature are covered with references to
the returned Irish Emigrants. Especially do our poets revel
in describing the emotions of the Irish Emigrant returned to
the home of his or her ancestors. But the past week has
added to our knowledge another kind of returned emigrant.
The daily papers tell us with glee that a large number of
Irish emigrants, or would-be emigrants, have been refused
permission to board Atlantic liners at Liverpool and London-
derry, and forcibly compelled to return to their homes in
Ireland.

These emigrants we are further informed were all of military
age, and were suspected of a desire to leave the country in order
to avoid conscription. The *Daily Mail* gave on Monday a first
class picture showing these poor Irish lads standing in line at the
steamship company's office, surrounded by a jeering mob of
Englishmen. It is significant that every face shown on the picture
as belonging to the jeering mob is the face of a young man of
military age. Why did they not show the example of enlisting,
instead of loafing around the docks of Liverpool in the middle of
the day?

We learn also that all the British Steamship Companies
plying to the United States have issued notices declining to
book passages thither to any men of military age.

This is good!

Surely the issue could be made no clearer. These young
Irishmen have just brought in the harvest that is to feed
England and her armies, and now, their work done, they
seek to escape from the country, but are told that Irishmen
can only escape from Ireland by fighting for England as well
as feeding her.

In other words it is made plain to them (and to us all)
that to the Imperial mind an Irishman's destiny is to serve
England.

For that and for that alone did an All Wise Providence
create us.

But every day there is still pouring out of Ireland the good
food, in the shape of cereals and livestock, that is necessary for
the maintenance of these emigrants that England sent back,
that is necessary for them and for us all.

Some serious questions arise upon this.

We are told these emigrants are shirkers. Suppose they were. And then ask the question: What would happen if, as England has refused to let away the shirkers from Ireland, the Irish people were to refuse to let away the Irish food to feed the shirkers in England?

Or, why should Irish people allow their cattle and harvests to leave Ireland if the men who sowed and reaped the harvests, and tended the cattle, cannot go also? If the men are turned back shall we also turn back the cattle and foodstuffs?

The stokers of the *Saxonia* came out on strike rather than take Irish men *from* England. Should Dublin dockers go on strike rather than ship Irish cattle *to* England?

But the stokers in Liverpool had *their* nation behind them, with its armed forces if necessary.

Would the armed forces that recognise the Irish nation be behind the Irish docker should he take such action?

Would they?

Ah! That makes the difference!

THE DISPUTE ON THE DOCKS
Is it War?

[20 November 1915]

The fight of the employees of the City of Dublin Steam Packet Company against the attempt of that company to reduce them below the level of their fellow-workers[13] has produced some very interesting developments.

Late last week this office was honoured by a visit from a representative of the Irish Party in the person of a gentleman who most pompously announced himself as 'Mr Esmonde, MP.'[14] No one in Liberty Hall seeming very much impressed by this title the young man proceeded to unload himself of a large and varied assortment of threats as to what the Government and the Irish Party were going to do to the Transport Union. As he expressed it, they would 'wage war' upon us. Being told not too politely that he and the Government and the Irish Party could take themselves to a climate warmer than the Dardanelles or Flanders, the young gentleman (who, although an officer in the British Army, has no desire to go to any of the places specified or hinted at), looked a little pained and displeased, and suggested arbitration under the Munitions Act.[15] He was then informed that there was nothing to arbitrate about.

That every other company on the quays were paying at least as high, and some higher than the company involved, and it would have to pay the same.

Here followed another explosion of wrath, and some more threats, and eventually it was hinted to 'Mr Esmonde, MP' that his room was preferable to his company. To go – and he goed. He was a nice young man for an old maid's tea party, no doubt, but the most insufferable coxcomb that ever the wind blew into this office. There are queer things comes up with the tide, and certainly he was one of the quarest.

We can well imagine how those old Parliamentary hands, Joe Devlin and J. D. Nugent, winked at each other behind his back when they sent him off to an interview at Liberty Hall.

Following the interview we had telephone messages from the Lord Mayor of Dublin on the same subject. His Lordship got from this office the courteous answer any gentleman gets here to a message courteously put, and was a welcome change to the manners of our former interviewers. But, of course, although we were interested to learn that we were the subject of Conference at the Viceregal Lodge[16] and at Dublin Castle we still could not see that there was anything to arbitrate.

We were informed too that the Admiralty proposed taking the boats and using them as transports.

Well, the Admiralty has a legal right to take any boats it wants, but we hold that to take a boat that is involved in a strike, and pay the owners of that boat for its use during that strike is equal to assisting the company against the men. It is paying Government money to keep the owners from losing by the suspension of their business. It is like paying strike pay to the owners, and takes out of the hands of the men the only weapon they possess, viz, their power to inflict loss upon their late employer. Such an action by the British Government in a Dublin dispute could only be interpreted as an act of war upon Labour, and we would have no alternative but accept it in that light.

It would, we repeat, mean war.

We are going to win this fight. We are not going to allow Sir William Watson,[17] William Martin Murphy, nor the British Government to single out any body of workers for attack and destruction. We know that the destruction of that body of workers would mean an instant attack all along the line upon organised Labour in Dublin, and to prevent that destruction and avert that attack we will fight with 'all the resources of civilization.'

NOTES ON THE FRONT

[25 December 1915]

MORE POETRY.

> Watch and Wait, boys, watch and wait,
>   Let it be your motto, ever,
> Foolish zeal, unguarded hate,
>   Often baulks a brave endeavour.
> God ordains, boys, God ordains
>   That we pine a little longer,
> Ere we burst the galling chains,
>   Ere we crush the brutal wronger.

Did ever you read and ponder over these lines of Gavan Duffy?[18] They were written at a time in Irish history wonderfully similar to the present. At a time of unrest and longing for struggle, tempered by preachings of caution.

It was in the days of the Young Irelanders. Eloquent voices had been preaching of the glories of the sword and eulogising the rights of nations to take back their own with armed hand; sweet singers had been wedding the hope of Irish patriots to deathless verse in heroic measures; the hearts of the young men of the Irish race were swelling with the passions of hatred for oppression and ambition for freedom, and the Great Famine was lashing the most stolid into willingness to try any adventure that held out hope of food for the perishing millions.[19]

Ireland seemed, even to the most cautious and calculating foreign observer, to be on the point of great endeavours.

Instead of the great adventure Ireland witnessed the most sordid, squalid, meanest fiasco in all her history. Fintan Lalor,[20] in one of those biting sentences of his which seem to crystallise a whole volume of history, says:

> The soul of this country seems to sink where that of another would soar.

To tell how that fiasco took its place in Irish history instead of a Great Adventure like unto that of Tone and Emmet,[21] would be to give point and corroboration to the above analysis of the character of the soul of Ireland.

It is a hard tale to tell, and a harder one to understand, unless your own soul is attuned in harmony with the passions of the actors in that great squalid tragedy of our history.

As your soul is attuned in sympathy to one side or the other, so one side or the other is comprehensible to you – and the other an unsolved and insoluble problem.

As in all revolutionary movements there came a point when all agreed that force would have to settle the differences between Ireland and the British Empire. But immediately there arose a cleavage between the revolutionists who desired to strike, and the tacticians who counselled greater preparedness and the desirability of 'putting the Government plainly in the wrong.'

It was the clash between the outlook of revolutionists, and the outlook of politicians manoeuvring for a political advantage, and yet both sides were earnestly revolutionary.

You can grasp that fact if you study carefully the verse at the beginning of these notes. There is not a sentiment in them that at first glance would not be endorsed by every true nationalist, and yet practically every true nationalist deplores the fact that the counsel there given was taken by the Irish people at the time.

As a counsel of caution they ring true. As a historical fact it was such counsel that permitted John Mitchel to be carried off safely in chains, and stuck a dagger to the heart of the Irish insurrection of 1848.

The literature of the '48 Insurrection was beautiful; the story of the Insurrection itself reads like the book of a badly written burlesque.

Another poem of a similar character to that quoted above written at the same time and for the same purpose, viz: to restrain the revolutionary spirit of the people, is we think one of the finest revolutionary songs in the English language.

It breathes revolutionary feeling and democratic spirit in every line, yet the sum total of its effects at the time was to tighten the hold of the enemy upon this country, and to hold the people in leash until the opportune moment was passed.

Yet its author, M. J. Barry, with peculiar logic declared afterwards that as the Irish people had failed to make even a decent fight in 1848 he considered the cause of Ireland hopeless, and would thereafter accept the English connection with all its consequences.

The song in question is by its own merits worthy of a place in any nationalist or Labour Concert programme, but we do not remember hearing it sung at any such in Ireland, although it is a favourite in revolutionary circles elsewhere. Here it is:

BIDE YOUR TIME

I.

BIDE YOUR TIME, the morn is breaking,
    Bright with Freedom's blessed ray –
Millions, from their trance awaking,
    Soon shall stand in firm array.
Man shall fetter man no longer,
    Liberty shall march sublime;
Every moment makes you stronger,
    Firm, unshrinking, BIDE YOUR TIME.

II.

BIDE YOUR TIME – one false step taken
    Perils all you yet have done;
Undismayed, erect, unshaken –
    Watch and wait, and all is won.
'Tis not by a rash endeavour
    Men or states to greatness climb –
Would you win your rights forever
    Calm and thoughtful, BIDE YOUR TIME.

III.

BIDE YOUR TIME – your worst transgression
    Were to strike, and strike in vain;
He, whose arm would smite oppression,
    Must not need to smite again!
Danger makes the brave man steady –
    Rashness is the coward's crime –
Be for Freedom's battle ready,
    When it comes – but, BIDE YOUR TIME.

You will perhaps wonder at our statement that a certain section of the revolutionists of 1848 resolved not to strike, unless and until they saw an opportunity of 'putting England in the wrong.' The idea that this left it to the Government to choose the time, the place, and the circumstances for the fight doubtless did occur to them but was not allowed to alter their purpose. They grandly declared that they would not be driven before their time.

Eventually the Government, having leisurely made all its preparations – and preparations made by a government with untold millions at its disposal can always outmatch a thousand to one the preparations made illegally by a few thousand poverty stricken men and women – having made all its preparations the Government issued orders for the arrest of the Young Ireland leaders. They took to the country, and issued the call for insurrection. Smith O'Brien was the chief,[22] and in the course of his peregrinations he arrived at the village of Killenaule. Here it was reported that a body of Dragoons were approaching with a warrant for his apprehension. Instantly the people prepared to fight. They barricaded one end of the village and as the dragoons rode in at the other end the people raised barricades behind them. The soldiers were trapped, and Stephens[23] was about to fire upon the officer in command, when Smith O'Brien ordered him to lower his rifle. Then upon being assured by the English officer that he had no warrant for Smith O'Brien's arrest that gentleman ordered the people to clear a passage for the soldiers who thereupon rode safely away.

You see it would not put the government in the wrong to fire upon the army unless the army fired first, and government outraged their own constitution.

Now do you understand what we have meant when we said that Irish rebels had a constitutional frame of mind – wanted to conduct revolutions according to constitutional procedure?

They wanted to establish it as a fact in history that they were driven into rebellion against their wills. And regarded it as a disgraceful thing that they should be accused of eagerly seeking revolution, and as longing for a chance to begin the fight for freedom.

We do not know if there are any such to-day amongst us. If there are they are a danger. Ireland needs no legal excuses for revolution. The presence of English government in this country, be that government bad or good, is at all times provocation and outrage enough. It is not native, it rests upon no sanction but force, and it holds the interests of a foreign empire to be superior to the well-being of the Irish people.

But once again the old clash of opinions arises. Is the time here, or is it not? Who knows? Perhaps the writer of these 'Notes on the Front' is wrong.

Perhaps the writer of the following poem is right. At any rate, like its predecessors that we have already quoted, it is beatifully written, and worthy of a place. Read:

THE WATCHING HOUR

A steel grey dawn is in the sky,
 Above the watchers on each hill;
And you who live and you who die
 Shall *preach* a race unconquered still.

Tho' lingering wait may often tire,
 And idle critic's words may gall;
Keep watch upon the signal fire,
 Whose burning blaze is Ireland's call.

A soldier knows how to obey,
 To 'wait the word with arms girth;
Nor lag behind nor chide delay;
 Disciplined strength gives Freedom birth.

And you whose ardent souls now chide
 The hand that holds you from the fray,
Remember that a nation's pride
 A nation's life hangs on *the day*.
Then watch beneath the steel grey sky,

 Beside the watchers on each hill,
Till you who live and you who die,
 May *prove* a race unconquered still.

PATRICK HOGAN.

So we have given the other side a look in this time. This being the blessed Christmas season we do this in order to show our kindly Christmas feelings to our erring brothers. We have been given to understand that some of them do not appreciate our suggestions at their proper value, and even a few, a very few, are a little irritated, and say that we are not playing the game fair.

Well, all we can say is that our allegiance is not to the game, nor to the players of the game, but to Ireland and the cause of Freedom. To some people the Game has become more important than the Cause, and they as the players of the Game more important than either. It is not a new frame of mind in Ireland, witness the incident of Smith O'Brien who made the question of 'Insurrection or no Insurrection' turn upon whether an officer had or had not a warrant for his arrest, but there are few who share it. And these few can safely be ignored.

The needs of our time call for a frank recognition of the fact that our Slogan must be

All for the Cause

and

The Cause over All.

Shall we see another year and Ireland patiently bearing her Chains?

To all slaves in Revolt we wish A Merry Christmas!

CORRESPONDENTS [24]

[25 December 1915]

O'ROURKE (London.) – Thanks, comrade. We are more proud of the comradeship of toilers like yourself than you can well imagine. It is such loyalty as yours that keeps us hopeful of our class and country.

CÚ CHULAINN (Dundalk.)[25] – No! We do not believe that war is glorious, inspiring, or regenerating. We believe it to be hateful, damnable, and damning. And the present war upon Germany we believe to be a hell-inspired outrage. Any person, whether English, German, or Irish, who sings the praises of war is, in our opinion, a blithering idiot. But when a nation has been robbed it should strike back to recover her lost property. Ireland has been robbed of her freedom, and to recover it should strike swiftly and relentlessly, and in such a fashion as will put the fear of God in the hearts of all who connived at the robbery or its continuance. But do not let us have any more maudlin trash about the 'glories of war,' or the 'regenerative influence of war,' or the 'sacred mission of the soldier,' or the 'fertilising of all earth with the heroic blood of her children,' etc, etc. We are sick of it, the world is sick of it. And when combined with the cant about 'patience,' and 'waiting,' and the 'folly of rashness,' and the 'wisdom of caution,' and all the other phrases that are to be heard from the Irish eulogists of war we confess it gives us a feeling like sea-sickness – nausea.

No, friend! War is hell, but if freedom is on the farther side shall even hell be allowed to daunt us.

A HAPPY NEW YEAR

[1 January 1916]

We should in this issue wish all our readers a 'Happy New Year.' We do so wish them. But such a wish rings better when it is accompanied by a belief that the wish may be realised, and at the present moment the signs of a Happy New Year are none too plentiful.

Over all the world the shadow of war lies heavy on the hearts of every lover of humankind. Over a great part of the world war itself is daily taking its toll, and the gashed and mangled limbs of many thousands are daily scattered abroad, an affront to the sight of God and man. In the British Empire, of which we are unluckily a part, the ruling class has taken the opportunity provided by the war to make a deadly onslaught upon all the rights and liberties acquired by labour in a century of struggling; and found the leaders of labour as a rule only too ready to yield to the attack and surrender the position they ought to have given their lives to hold. Were the war to end tomorrow the working class of these islands would be immediately launched into a bitter fight to resist the attempt of the capitalist class to make permanent all the concessions the too pliant trade union leaders have been swindled into conceding upon the plea of war emergencies. In addition, the whole system of industry has been moulded anew in many of its most important branches. Division of labour has been pushed to an extent hitherto undreamed of. Women have been harnessed to the wheels of production in places and at operations hitherto performed solely by men – and so harnessed with none of the rights with which men safeguarded their positions – and the whole industrial population has been made accustomed to browbeating and driving from those set in authority.

The civil rights of the people have gone, and the ruling class has succeeded in so familiarising the multitude with thoughts of slaughter and bloodshed that the killing of

workers on strike will no longer send even a thrill through
the nation.

Peace will send home millions of men; will dislocate all
industry so that those millions will find little employment
and will thus be compelled to compete fiercely for work at
any price. The terrible taxation caused by the war will send
up and keep up the price of everything, whilst the misery of
the returned soldier looking for work will hammer down
wages.

Nationally Ireland has seen herself betrayed by one set of
politicians, her children bartered for sale as hired assassins in
the service of her ancient and present enemy. The coming year
may see her still linked to that enemy once more at peace with
the world, and the 'Irish Nation' finally relegated to the mere
status of a gallant tradition, as little useful politically as the
Jacobite tradition is to Scotland. With England at peace that
country will possess an army of at least one million men,
veteran soldiers of the greatest war of all the ages, and when
that time arrives the Irish question will trouble England as
little as the rivalries of Lancashire and Yorkshire.

With an army of two veteran soldiers for every adult male
in Ireland there will no longer be an Irish cause for any
uneasiness to the rulers of the British Empire.

A happy new year! Ah, well! Our readers are, we hope,
rebels in heart, and hence may rebel even at our own picture
of the future. If that is so let us remind them that opportunities are for those who seize them, and that the coming year
may be as bright as we choose to make it. We have sketched
out the future as it awaits the slave who fears death more than
slavery. For those who choose to advance to meet Fate determined to mould it to their purpose that future may be as
bright as our picture is dark.

A LESSON OF THE STRIKE

[8 January 1916]

The long-drawn out fight with the City of Dublin Steam
Packet Company is one of the most striking lessons yet offered
of the absurdity of our present social arrangements. Here we
have the spectacle of one man being able to upset the business
and destroy the happiness of a whole community, in order to

gratify his personal spleen against men who refused to be lowered beneath the level of their fellows. We find the Chamber of Commerce, representing all their fellow-business men; the Lord Mayor, representing the interests of the city at large; the Under Secretary for Ireland, representing the British Government in Dublin; and the Chief Industrial Commissioner, Sir George Askwith, representing the Government of Great Britain, all anxious to have the dispute settled and the business of the port resumed. And this one man is able to set them all at defiance, and proceed on his own way, wrecking their hopes along with his own business.

The social system we live under is held by its apologists to be the one that gives the greatest freedom to the individual, combined with the fullest service to the community.

The work of serving the public is not undertaken by a public authority but is left to the haphazard enterprise of individuals spurred by the desire of gain. People are not fed, clothed, housed, or warmed because the feeding, clothing, housing or warming is a public duty; but because certain individuals think that they can make a profit by so doing. If at any time these individuals think that they are not making enough profit by performing these functions, then they cease rendering this public service, and the whole life of the community is thrown out of gear. This dispute is a case in point. Every shipowner on the quays of Dublin has learned that he can pay the rate of wages asked by the City of Dublin Company strikers, and make a profit while doing so. Knowing this to be the case they keep their boats running to serve themselves and the public. The Chairman of the City of Dublin Steam Packet Company declares that he cannot make his boats pay under the same conditions as his competitors, and stops his boats accordingly. If his statement is true then it is a most lamentable confession of inefficiency and bungling mismanagement. Yet no power says to this man –

> Either run your boats, or resign and go out of business. You cannot be allowed to disarrange the business of half of the merchants in the city.

He as owner of the mail boat from Kingstown receives a large Government subsidy, and is thus in a better position than his competitors who have to make their business pay without any such aid. If he cannot make his business pay then he should be treated as he would treat a dock labourer who could not work under the same conditions as his fellows – he should be fired to make room for men who can.

But just there is the weakness of the present social system. His is not a public service, and he is not a public servant. It is a private service for private gain, and he is a private individual out for private profit, and willing to punish all his associates in the business world in order to make that profit – or in revenge for not making a profit big enough.

Some day the world will wake up sufficiently to recognise that the capitalist conducting business on his own account is just as much a nuisance, and as bunglingly inefficient at the job, as were the soldier chiefs of the past making war on their own account. And when the world does so recognise the fact it will reduce private business enterprises to the same level as private armies and private wars. The nation will take over the work of organising the industries of peace as it has taken out of private hands the owning of armies and the conducting of wars for private profit.

And when it thinks about that matter the recollection of the City of Dublin Steam Packet Company's war upon the interests of the port of Dublin will be of great service in educating the public mind to agree to the change.

NOTES ON THE FRONT

[5 February 1916]

THE TIES THAT BIND.
Recently we have been pondering deeply over the ties that bind this country to England. It is not a new theme for our thoughts; for long years we have carried on propaganda in Ireland pointing out how the strings of self-interest bound the capitalist and landlord classes to the Empire, and how it thus became a waste of time to appeal to those classes in the name of Irish patriotism.

We have said that the Working Class was the only class to whom the word 'Empire,' and the things of which it was the symbol did not appeal. That to the propertied classes 'Empire' meant high dividends and financial security, whereas to the Working Class that meant only the things it was in rebellion against.

Therefore from the intelligent working class could alone come the revolutionary impulse.

Recently we have seen the spread of those ties of self-interest binding certain classes and individuals to the Empire – we have seen it spread to a most astonishing degree until its ramifications cover the island, like the spread of a foul disease.

It would be almost impossible to name a single class or section of the population not evilly affected by this social, political, and moral leprosy.

Beginning with our parliamentary representatives, we see men so poisoned by the evil association of parliament and enervated with the unwonted luxury of a salary much greater than they could ever hope to enjoy in private life, that they have instantly and completely abandoned all the traditions of their political party, and become the mouthpieces and defenders of an Imperial system their greatest leaders had never ceased to hold up to the scorn of the world.

We see the ties of self-interest so poisoning those men that they become the foulest slanderers and enemies of all who stand for that unfettered Ireland to which they also once pledged their heartiest allegiance. For the sake of £400 a year they become Imperialists; for the sake of large travelling expenses and luxurious living they become lying recruiters.

Corporation after corporation elected to administer our towns and cities neglect their proper business, and make their city halls and town halls the scene of attempts to stampede the youth and manhood of Ireland out of the country to die inglorious deaths in foreign fields. And while those young and middle-aged men perish afar off the mayors and councillors who sent them to their doom scramble for place and titles at the hands of a foreign tyrant. We hear of a Mayor in a Western city drawing £5 per week as a recruiter, and a Councillor in Dublin prostituting himself for a paltry 17/6 per week for the same dirty cause.

Between those two there are all sorts of grades and steps in infamy. The western Mayor is reckoned by his associates as having got a good price for his soul, whereas the Dublin councillor who sells himself for 17/6 per week is generally despised as having made a sorry trade.

One councillor gets one thing, his colleague gets another. One Dublin city councillor has hired a number of his derelict houses to the Government for munition factories at a tidy sum, another is assured of good contracts, another is promised a reversion of a good salaried position in a few months.

There is nobody in a representative position so mean that the British government will not pay some price for his Irish soul. Newspaper men sell their Irish souls for government advertisements paid for at a lavish rate, Professors sell their souls for salaries and expenses, clergymen sell theirs for jobs for their relatives, business men sell their souls and become recruiters lest they lose the custom of government officials. In all the grades of Irish society the only section that has not furnished even one apostate to the cause it had worked for in times of peace is that of the much hated and traduced militant Labour Leaders.

But if the Militant Labour Leaders of Ireland have not apostatised the same can not be said of the working class as a whole. It is with shame and sorrow we say it, but the evil influence upon large sections of the Irish Working Class of the bribes and promises of the enemy cannot be denied.

We know all that can be said in extenuation of their mistakes, all that we ourselves have said and will say in condonation and excuse of their lapses from the path of true patriotism. But when all is said and done the facts remain horrible and shameful to the last degree.

For the sake of a few paltry shillings per week thousands of Irish workers have sold their country in the hour of their country's greatest need and greatest hope. For the sake of a few paltry shillings Separation Allowance thousands of Irish women have made life miserable for their husbands with entreaties to join the British Army. For the sake of a few paltry shillings Separation Allowance thousands of young Irish girls have rushed into matrimony with young Irish traitors who in full knowledge of the hopes of Nationalist Ireland had enlisted in the army that England keeps here to slaughter Irish patriots.

For what is the reason for the presence of the English army in this country? The sole reason for the presence of such soldiers in Dublin, in Ireland, is that they may be used to cut the throats of Irish men and women should we dare demand for Ireland what the British Government is pretending to fight for in Belgium.

For the sake of the Separation Allowance thousands of Irish men, women, and young girls have become accomplices of the British Government in this threatened crime against the true men and women of Ireland.

Like a poisonous ulcer this tie of self-interest has spread over Ireland corrupting and destroying all classes, from the Lord Mayor in his Mansion House to the poor boy and girl in the slum. Corrupting all hearts, destroying all friendships, poisoning all minds.

The British Government stands in the Market Places and streets of Ireland buying, buying, buying, buying *the souls* of the men and women, the boys and the girls, whom ambition, or greed, or passion, or vice, or poverty, or ignorance makes weak enough to listen to its seductions.

And yet the great heart of the nation remains true. Some day most of those deluded and misled brothers and sisters of ours will learn the truth, some day we will welcome them back to our arms purified and repentant of their errors.

Perhaps on that day the same evil passions the enemy has stirred up in so many of our Irish people will play havoc with his own hopes, and make more bitter and deadly the cup of his degradation and defeat.

But deep in the heart of Ireland has sunk the sense of the degradation wrought upon its people – our lost brothers and sisters – so deep and humiliating that no agency less potent than the red tide of war on Irish soil will ever be able to enable the Irish race to recover its self-respect, or establish its national dignity in the face of a world horrified and scandalised by what must seem to them our national apostasy.

Without the slightest trace of irreverence but in all due humility and awe we recognise that of us as of mankind before Calvary it may truly be said:

Without the Shedding of Blood there is no Redemption.

NOTES ON THE FRONT

[19 February 1916]

A GREAT ADVENTURE.

We wonder how many men have been led into the British Army by the lust for adventure. It seems to us that they must form no very inconsiderable proportion of the whole.

It is natural that the young should thirst for adventure; we would not think very highly of a boy who did not lust

after excitement, or be eager to do deeds the smug respectable property-respecting world would deem unlawful.

If he was our boy we might possibly spank him for doing
such things, but even whilst the spanking process was in full
swing we would be secretly proud that the boy – our boy –
had enough of the adventurous spirit in him to override conventional restraints.

It is the spirit of adventure that has carried the world
upward from savagery and ignorance into civilisation and
knowledge. It is the spirit of adventure that discovered new
continents, opened up ways over trackless waters, mapped and
charted snow-covered mountains and pathless forests, and
linked together territories and peoples seemingly destined by
nature to be isolated and alien.

It is the spirit of adventure that drove men to harness
the elements to the service of mankind, to utilise steam and
electricity, and all the wonderful secrets of nature that the
powers of man may be strengthened by the natural forces of
the world.

Beneficent has been the spirit of adventure in man, and
destructive also.

It is the spirit of adventure in man that enabled the
tyrants of the world in all ages to secure the services of the
stronger and healthier and least thoughtful of the race to be
armed bullies over and slayers of their more peaceful or
more freedom-loving fellows.

Given a state of hard and soulless bondage to labour, a
round of grinding, miserably-paid toil, with no outlook save
in the direction of more labour, and more toil as miserably
paid, and who can wonder if the spirit revolts at times, and
sets the feet of the labourer straying on the path of adventure that the life of a soldier in war time seems to open.

How often do we meet in life the tale of a labourer who
has served an employer, or a public board for 20, 30, or 40
years, and found at last that his faithful service had earned
him no security in his old age. Must not the thought
sometimes come to the younger generation who read such a
story that it would be better for them to 'break loose'
occasionally, rather than be such perfect machines for others
to exploit, and then throw in the rubbish heap.

Or even when peace in old age, and comfort, awaits these
patient plodders in industrial harness can high-spirited people
help speculating upon the question whether that life is really

worth living. Thirty years, forty years, in one job! Think of it. For thirty, forty years, to have no variety, see no new faces, break no new territory, adventure into no undiscovered grounds. For thirty, forty years, to be able to forecast a year ahead just what you would do on such and such a date. That you will get out of bed at such an hour, breakfast at such an hour, cease work at a definite moment, and so on from day to day, month to month, year to year, without a change until all the sap and vigour of life had gone out of you. And all in the hope that when you were grown too old to be useful you might be fed and sheltered, like a favourite dog, until you died.

'When we reach to a certain age,' says a French cynic, 'we think we have abandoned our vices, when in reality it is our vices that have abandoned us.'

The patient industrial plodder is a man who plods away in harness in the hope that he will have a good time when he is old, only to discover that when he is old he becomes incapable of enjoying a good time.

What wonder then that the tacit rebellion against such a fearful, drab existence – that rebellion which no man can permanently silence in his bosom – what wonder that sometimes that rebellion surges up triumphantly, and carries off the plodding slave into the adventurous path.

Ordinarily the means of escape into the alluring paths of adventure are awanting, and the slave plods on, and before the opportunity comes the adventurous surge within him has subsided. But the beating of the drums of war, the insistent call of the bugles to battle, continued for weeks and months, and aided by all the resources of a powerful and astute government anxious to dominate the imagination of its subjects, provides eventually for all such men the opportunity for escape and keeps it open long enough to catch the fancy at the proper moment.

The spirit of adventure then must be reckoned with among the many factors that help to drive men into the profession of hired assassins – as soldiering for pay has been well and fitly termed.

But it also must be counted amongst the forces that make for revolutions. The revolutionists of the past have ever been adventurous spirits, else they would never have been revolutionists. 'I perceive,' said Wolfe Tone in his Diary, 'that merchants make bad revolutionists.' And, as usual, Tone was right. The spirit of calculation which is the very essence of the spirit of a good merchant is the destruction of a good revolutionist.

For no matter how carefully you plan, how wisely you arrange your course of action, how astutely you have every-thing thought out, how admirably every contingency is provided against, there is always for the revolutionist the knowledge that a sudden move of the enemy may set all your schemes at naught, and force action along lines never even dreamed of by your wisest heads. In such a contingency the swiftest thought must be instantly followed by the swift-est action – the spirit of adventure then becomes the greatest revolutionary asset.

And just as the spirit of adventure sent hundreds, perhaps thousands, into the British Army, so it would send its thousands, and its tens of thousands, into the revolutionary ranks. Indeed it is safe to say that there are hundreds and perhaps thousands of young Irishmen serving in the British Army to-day, in obedience to the spirit of adventure, who would have served far more gladly in the revolutionary army of Ireland, had they been convinced that such an army was even a possibility of the near future.

Hard it will be in the future to apportion rightly the responsibility, the guilt, of allowing that splendid spirit of adventure in young Irish hearts to be perverted to the purposes of the foreign ruler, instead of being wisely handled for the Cause of Freedom.

The Irish Race is an old race – perhaps the oldest in Europe. But in its individual members the Irish Race is ever young. Amongst no other people do the old so readily sympathise with and share in the hopes, the joys, and the spirit of the young. The Irish Race rises responsive to the call of battle; the beat of the drums seems to set its blood tingling through its veins to feel its feet once more set upon adventurous paths. A thousand times defeated the Irish Race once more pants to challenge its destiny.

And this is the spirit in which we hear the Call to the Great Adventure of our generation.

NOTES ON THE FRONT

[4 March 1916]

TIGHTENING THE GRIP.

In our editorial last week[26] we pointed out that the pressure of economic forces were being brought to bear upon this country in order to compel the young manhood of Ireland to enlist in the British Army.

We also pointed out that this was also an astute move in the interests of the great capitalists. This latter point is so important, and so little understood in this country, that we feel moved to again revert to it in our Notes this week.

The first point scarcely needs any stressing. The Military Service Act now being applied to England has not been enforced in Ireland because, as has been confessed in the House of Commons by Mr Bonar Law, it could not be put in operation without the use of a 'considerable amount of force.'[27] The armed manhood of Ireland whom Messrs Redmond and Devlin failed to betray into the ranks of England's army forbade the attempt being made to force them in.

They had good 'reasons' for not being conscripted, and most of their 'reasons' were well provided with serviceable ammunition. More reasons of various calibres are coming in every day, and hence the Government concluded that it would be better to let Ireland alone – until after the war.

After the war England may compensate herself for her defeat at the hands of Germany by wreaking her armed vengeance upon Ireland, but for the present other means must be sought for finding Irish recruits. What are those other means?

Oratory has been tried, and failed. All over Dublin recruiting meetings are being broken up by the spontaneous action of the jeering crowds. Up and down the country the Khaki recruiting bands are marching in vain. The supply of corner boys and wastrels in our Irish towns and villages has fallen so low that the police magistrates have had practically nothing to do since the war fever swept up these undesirables in response to the oratory of Redmond and Devlin. In town and country the manhood of Ireland are thinking things about the Empire, and the things they think do not lead to soldiering *for* that institution.

The weeding out of young men of military age by the process of discharging them has been zealously recommended by the Empire builders, and adopted by many Irish employers. But many others whilst loudly proclaiming their zeal for recruiting have kept eligible young men in their own employment, and indeed insisted upon youth and physical fitness as a condition of employment in their service.

Newspapers have been bought, and journalists have freely prostituted themselves, in the service of recruiting, but few people in Ireland nowadays believe newspapers. We have been so long accustomed to their lying about what happened in Labour Wars at home that it has become impossible for us to credit what they say about other wars abroad.

So the British Government having used up all its light cavalry and infantry in vain now moves up its really heavy artillery to bring these Irish to reason. The heavy artillery in this case consists of the scientific employment of economic force.

Thus there will be served at one and the same time the interests of the British Government as such, and the interests of the great capitalists who own the British Government.

The material needed for the prosecution of every Irish industry which enters into competition with British industries will be interfered with either by totally prohibiting its importation, or by limiting it to such an extent that its cost will become almost prohibitive to those who do not possess large reserves of capital to call upon.

To make this still more effective in its power to cripple struggling industries, and bankrupt small employers, the Government issues secret orders to the banks to refuse all overdrafts to their business customers. At one blow this puts automatically out of business thousands of small employers who from week to week must trade upon the credit represented by those overdrafts.

There are thousands of small employers whose businesses are perfectly sound, but who have large sums owing to them not immediately realisable in cash, but nevertheless perfectly well secured. It is the perfectly legitimate custom of such employers to draw from their banks overdrafts upon their deposits in order to enable them to keep their businesses going, paying back to the bank the sums thus borrowed according as they themselves are paid by their debtors.

Large firms with unlimited capital to call upon do not need to pursue this practice, but in a country of small capitalists like Ireland nine-tenths of the business firms are kept going in this manner.

Observe well the deadly sequence of these moves of the Government. First, the restrictions upon imports create immediate financial troubles and precipitate an industrial crisis in which money is sought at a high premium. Next, the banks are forbidden to give their customers even the usual facilities to obtain this money, and thus when money is most needed it cannot be had.

Result. Will probably be widespread bankruptcy, the closing down of many places of employment in Ireland, and the consequent hunting of Irish workers into the British Army, or to England to be conscripted in the near future.

Only those capitalists in Ireland with large reserves to call upon will be able to carry themselves over the crisis. For the temporary strain upon them they will be rewarded by being enabled to absorb all the business of the smaller firms who will have succumbed.

The business of the smaller firms will thus be practically confiscated by their mammoth rivals, and the small capitalist will be allowed to go into the workhouse if he is old, or to the army if he is young. If he goes into the army he will have the honour of fighting for the plutocratic gang that planned and accomplished his ruin.

Many Irish firms have already turned their entire business establishments over to war work. These firms have been enabled to exist for years because of the patriotic self-denial of Irish Irelanders who pushed their goods in season and out of season, at home and abroad.

Now these firms so established and supported have given up all their customers in favour of war work. They have sent adrift all the customers secured for them by long years of propaganda by others. Where will they look for these customers when the war is over? Factories in England and America will have snapped up all or a majority of their customers, and they will have to begin all over again the weary work of looking for orders, and whilst they are so looking their machinery will rust and their workpeople starve.

All over the country it is the same. We believe the Blarney Tweed Company is solely engaged in war work. Who is supplying its customers? Probably some of its English competitors. Pierce's Iron Foundry in Wexford has turned from the manufacture of agricultural implements to that of munitions for the English Army, thus reversing the scriptural idea of turning swords into ploughshares. In Kilkenny, in Dundalk, in Sligo, in Newry, everywhere in Ireland the capitalist fools have thrown overboard their old customers, abandoned a trade built upon the permanent needs of the community, in favour of a trade consisting of the passing needs of a mad war.

The very moment peace is declared all their orders will stop. And the returning soldiers will buy their necessities for civil life from the shops who have been compelled to get their orders filled by English or American factories whose owners were too shrewd to throw away customers to please the British Government.

All the firms that will be thus ruined are small firms; all the firms that will benefit by their ruin are mammoth firms; the British Government is owned by the great mammoth capitalist firms.

Do you see the point?

Again we press the point home. This war is not only a war for the destruction of a great commercial rival abroad, it is also being manipulated by the great capitalists for the destruction of commercial rivals at home.

The capitalist class of Great Britain, the meanest, most unscrupulous governing class in all history, is out for plunder. The plunder of German trade by force, the plunder of Irish trade by economic scheming, the plunder of the small capitalist class by financial pressure, the plunder of the Irish Nation by a combination of all three.

The grip of the enemy upon Ireland is tightening. Perhaps the sword alone can loosen it. Wait and see!

TO THE SEAFARERS OF IRELAND

[4 March 1916]

We wish again to draw the attention of all thoughtful Labour men and women to the extraordinary attitude of the officials of the National Seamen's and Firemen's Union to the claims of their members in Ireland, and more especially in the port of Dublin.

As our readers are aware the seamen and firemen formerly engaged on the boats of the City of Dublin Steam

Packet Company, upon being ordered, refused to take the boats to sea after they had been worked by clerks and others scabbing upon the dockers out on strike.

These men refused, that is to say, to scab upon their mates who were members of the Irish Transport Workers' Union. For this refusal the National officials of the Seamen's and Firemen's Union declined to grant them any strike allowance, and for many weeks they have been dependent upon Liberty Hall for their weekly pittance. Now we find that the seamen of the London boats are also on strike for an increase of wages, and again the officials of the Seamen's and Firemen's Union refuse to grant them any support. Is it not time again to ask our Seamen and Firemen brothers the simple question: *For what reason do they pay into a Union that deserts them immediately they need its assistance?*

A Union that appears to hate the name of any Irishman that still clings to Ireland.

We would respectfully submit to all the seamen and firemen whose domicile is in Ireland that experience has proven to them that they cannot expect any justice from the national officials of the Union in question.

We also respectfully submit to them that the experience of the whole Trade Union world teaches that Labour should be organised as Capital is organised, viz, upon an Industrial basis. That the seaman cannot win without the help of the docker, and the docker is immensely strengthened by having the support of the seaman. That as they are both serving the one employer in the one industry they should be both organised in the one Union.

The only possible alternative to that system of organisation is the amalgamation of all unions of general labour into one body, such as was contemplated in Great Britain before the outbreak of war stopped all possibilities of immediate progress upon sane lines. Such amalgamation would make it possible to reorganise all the constituent bodies upon industrial lines as we have indicated above, and at the same time avoid the danger of crossing the interests of unions now sectionally organised. Those unions being first amalgamated their sectional interests would be eliminated from the problem. But the application of that solution to the shipping industry was rendered impossible by the fact that Mr Havelock Wilson and his Union[28] refused to join with a general labourers' organisation, and insisted upon remaining aloof as a sectional union.

As usual he preferred to play a lone hand, and to break up the labour ranks. It is only when he is in trouble that he remembers the principle of the Solidarity of Labour. At other times he only scoffs at it.

But his action in refusing to join an organisation that would have linked up the Seamen and Firemen in one Union with all the workers of the docks and harbours, and with the ranks of general labour everywhere, coupled with his persistent attacks upon the principle of solidarity in Ireland, clears the air sufficiently to permit of action being taken to properly deal with him. We believe that the Dublin seamen and firemen do not desire any longer to be members of such a strike breaker's union as the NS & FU is being made into. We believe that they wish to be enrolled in the ranks of organised Labour in Ireland, and to be a part of the militant movement of Labour in this country.

If they so desire, if we are correct in our estimate of their aspirations, we submit to them that it is time they took steps to organise a *Seafarers' Section of the Irish Transport and General Workers' Union*. Such a section should be open to all seafarers whose domicile is in Ireland. Linked up with the dock labourers as they would be their interests would be at once identical, and the motto, 'Each for All, and All for Each,' would become a reality, having immense influence upon their industrial progress. We are confident that we could secure recognition of their membership card in all the ports of the world, and that the new departure would mean a gain rather than a loss to those who prefer the deep sea boats.

We have been patiently watching the rake's progress of the NS and FU in its despicable attitude to its Irish branches. We believe that the time has come for the Irish seafarers to do what the Irish Dockers have done so well for themselves under our banner, viz, throw their lot together in an Irish organization, and by so doing increase their power as well as the power of the shore workers – and thus unitedly to form a force that would set the fighting pace for the Labour Movement of all the world.

NOTES ON THE FRONT

[18 March 1916]

A UNION OF FORCES.

Some issues ago we pointed out how the British Government was tightening its grip upon this country by a deft use of economic power. We wish again to recur to this theme in order to point out some more applications of this pressure upon the people of Ireland.

In the great industrial dispute of 1913–14 one of the most malignant firms upon the side of the employers was the firm of Messrs W. & R. Jacobs, Biscuit Manufacturers. No firm engaged in the dispute touched as low a depth of meanness as did this firm; so vilely used their power when the fight was over.

The helpless girls who had come out on strike from this firm in a noble effort to vindicate that right to organise upon which all our hopes of peaceful progress and higher civilisation are based, when they failed and had to re-apply for employment were subjected to every form of personal insult and dishonour that the foul minds of those in charge in the firm could conceive.

Hundreds were victimised and denied employment for ever, after being paraded before the jeering gaze of the poor lost creatures who had scabbed upon them; scores sank into hopeless wretchedness through being denied employment elsewhere because of the manner in which the Messrs Jacobs blacklisted them wherever they applied for work, and more than we care to recall were forced by the vengeance of Jacobs into the lost sisterhood of the streets.

As soon as the war broke out the responsible heads of this firm of pious sweaters and soul murderers joined hands with the recruiters in the attempt to swell the ranks of the British Army. They who had outrivalled the lowest in their methods of warfare upon the rights of the workers of Dublin became clamorous that the men of Dublin should go out to fight and die to protect them from the Huns.

By every means they could devise they strove to swell the British Army, and turned up their eyes in horror at the atrocities retailed in the newspapers – were as horrified at the atrocities supposedly committed by the Germans in Belgium as they had been happy and exultant over the atrocities committed by the police in Dublin.

For some time back this firm has had its reward by being kept going with Government orders, and its male employees mostly resisted the attempt to seduce them into the army that keeps the Messrs Jacobs upon the necks of Labour. But within the past two weeks the firm is reported to have summarily dismissed every man of military age.

Messrs Jacobs in 1913–14 used their power over the means of livelihood of their employees to coerce them out of the trade union of their choice on the pain of starvation; now that same firm is again using its power over the means of livelihood of the workers to coerce them into an army that stood ready to shoot them down in 1913–14.

In the course of the Board of Trade Inquiry at Dublin Castle this slimy firm of sweaters instructed Mr Timothy Healy, the counsel for the employers, to state before Sir George Askwith[29] that his firm was selected by Larkin to be attacked because it used Irish made flour instead of English. The statement was, of course, a double-barrelled lie, because the firm only uses a very small proportion of Irish made flour, and also because the place of origin of the flour had nothing to do with the dispute.

But at that time it suited Messrs Jacobs to pretend to a great hostility to things English, and a great love for things Irish. Now it suits Messrs Jacobs to throw off the mask, and come out in their true lights as being willing to use all their economic power to help England, by starving Irishmen into the British Army, and thus to ensure that death and misery will hang like a cloud over scores or hundreds of Irish homes.

A Rich Man's War and a Poor Man's Fight! Already there is formed in every ward in Dublin and in most Irish towns and cities a Recruiting Committee to devise means of bringing pressure to bear upon Irishmen to join the Army. One of the earliest moves in the activities of this pernicious Committee (which by the way is invariably composed of the veriest snobs and the worst employers in the district) lies before us as we write. It is a circular to Employers, and is headed by the following question.

Are you willing to permit Canvassers sent by the Department of Recruiting for Ireland to interview men of military age in your employment on your premises at a convenient time during business hours?

This is followed by a demand for the *Names and Addresses of men of military age in employment of above person or firm.*

This precious circular is being sent to every employer in Ireland, and from now on the Recruiting agents will descend like a flock of vultures upon every working man, and compel them in the presence of their employers and foremen to state their reasons for or against joining the British Army.

Thus there will be gained information invaluable for the spy system of our rulers. The employers or their agents will stand by and listen whilst the employee reveals his political convictions, and every man of advanced opinions will be marked out for early victimisation.

Not in Russia in its worst day was there any political terrorism exercised like this. Not anywhere in the world has it ever before been the case that the agents of the government and the agents of the capitalist stood side by side in workshop or factory, and compelled the wage-slave to reveal his inmost political thoughts.

The employer thus gets an accurate knowledge of the political opinions of his wage slaves, and the Recruiting Agent enters down the name and address and political opinion of every able-bodied Irishman, and turns the list over to the G Division (the political police) to be placed safely in the records of our British Rulers.

British rule in Ireland is thus revealed in its most loathsome aspects. It is seen nakedly as existing by terrorism, as recruited by hunger, as denying the most fundamental rights of political and social freedom. It is the perfect fruit of capitalism. The capitalist system came into this world covered with mud and blood, and dirt. It has its origin in the forcible theft of the common lands, the property of all, and the sanctification of that theft by laws made by robbers to legalise their robbery. At every stage of its progress it has been nourished upon the unpaid toil of the workers, and its state machinery is ever oiled with the blood of the poor.

The rise of capitalism and the rise of the British Empire were synonymous, and built upon similar crimes – the one is but the political embodiment of the meanest form of the other. Taking their origin in the plunder of the Catholic Church, each substituted the license of the strong and the unscrupulous for the economic security which with the growth of education would have eventuated in the greater freedom of the multitude.

The essential meanness of the British Empire is that it robs under the pretence of being generous, and it enslaves under pretence of liberating. The essential meanness of the capitalist system is that the capitalist pretends he is giving you a job when in reality he is securing you as a slave the fruits of whose labour he can legally appropriate.

The wages of the labourer is simply the modern equivalent for the rations of the slave – the fodder for the human beast of burden.

When the capitalist in Ireland wishes to drive you by hunger to enlist in the army to defend his property he deprives you of your means of living, and insults your intelligence by telling you that you are 'released for active service.'

The case of Messrs Jacob, and of the Recruiting Committee in its circular to the employers establishing a spy system to serve the double purposes of labour-hating employers and foreign rulers, is a sample of this natural union of the forces which make for the social and political enslavement of the people of Ireland.

We say this 'natural union,' for it is only natural that they who desire the industrial enslavement of the workers of Ireland should also desire the perpetuation of a form of Government as far as possible removed from the control of the people so enslaved. It is also very natural that the Government which keeps Ireland in subjection as a nation in order that it may prevent its industrial progress should also desire to prevent the growth of self reliance, and the spread of sound principles of industrial democracy, amongst the working classes of that subject nation.

Just as natural is it that those who desire the liberation of the Irish nation from foreign control should join hands with those forces of Labour whose ideal of industrial democracy cannot be realised as long as the economic future of their country is at the mercy of another country controlled by rival interests.

The abolition of the British Empire in Ireland is a necessary condition for the liberation of all the human factors making for the active intellectual life and political growth of democracy, as also it is a necessary condition for the utilization of all the natural powers of the soil of their country for the social enrichment of the country.

We are at the parting of the ways. All the forces of oppression, political and social, have joined hands to perpetuate our subjection. Shall not all the forces aspiring to social and political freedom unite to end our subjection?

WE WILL RISE AGAIN

[25 March 1916]

The celebrations of the past week in Ireland[30] are a welcome reminder of the indestructible nature of the spirit of freedom. Who would have thought in August, 1914, that in March, 1916, the principle of a distinct and separate existence for Irish Nationality would evoke such splendid manifestations of popular support and popular approval. In August, 1914, it seemed to many of the most hopeful of us that Ireland had at length taken its final plunge into the abyss of Imperialism, and bade a long farewell to all hopes of a separate unfettered existence as a nation.

Plans carefully laid for years before had been suddenly and relentlessly put in operation. A party of Parliamentary representatives elected to obtain Home Rule from England, and without any mandate expressing hostility to any other people, suddenly claimed the power and right to pledge the manhood of Ireland to battle with a friendly nation – a nation whose last public act towards Ireland had been an attempt to open the port of Queenstown when shut by English intrigue.[31] The same Parliamentary Party publicly renounced all hope and desire that this country should ever attain the status of nationhood, and expressly limited the ambitions of Ireland to such freedoms as the British Government would judge to be not incompatible with the British Empire. Having so limited the claims and renounced the hopes of Ireland this Parliamentary Party consummated its treason by calling upon their fellow countrymen to go out to die, in order to win for Belgium those national rights and powers they had just renounced the right to claim for Ireland.

The public press, the vaunted guardians of public liberty, sold themselves in a body to the Government that had publicly pledged itself not to interfere with an Orange-cum-militarist conspiracy against the liberties of Ireland, and immediately became the foulest slanderers and vilifiers of all who stood by the national cause they had deserted.

The few papers that refused to be bullied, or to be bought, were ruthlessly suppressed by military force.

All over Ireland the public representatives whom a lifetime of political intrigue, vote-hunting and job-hunting had debased and demoralised, yielded at the first onset of the new Irish Imperialism, and joyfully, eagerly, exultantly sold their country and their country's cause.

August, 1914, and the months immediately succeeding it, were months of darkness and of national tribulation. If the darkest hour is that before the dawn, then the dawn should not be far off, for surely no darker hour could come for Ireland than that we passed through in the beginning of this English war upon Germany.

But slowly, gradually, but persistently, the forces standing for the social and national freedom of Ireland won the people back to greater sanity and clearer visions. Despite imprisonment, despite persecution, despite suppression of newspapers, despite avalanches of carefully framed lies, the truth made headway throughout the country. The people saw clearer and clearer that nothing had been changed in Ireland, that Ireland was still denied every prerogative that makes for true nationhood, that her interests were still subject to the interests of a rival country, that the Home Rule Act expressly declared for the subjection of Ireland as a permanent condition, that the Redmond–Devlin party had sold the birthright of their country in return for the valueless promise of a Government that did not even keep faith with its own countrymen or women, that the British Empire and the freedom or prosperity of the Irish people were two things that could not exist together in Ireland, and that therefore one or the other must forever and utterly perish.

All through Ireland last week the manhood and womanhood of the nation have gladly, enthusiastically proclaimed their realisation of those truths. This 17th of March will be forever memorable for that reason. The magnificent parades of Volunteers under arms, the overflowing meetings, the joyous abandon of the Irish gatherings of all descriptions, and above all the exultant rebel note everywhere manifest, all, all were signs that the cause of freedom is again in the ascendant in Ireland.

The Cause is not lost, this 17th of March has assured us that despite all the treasons of all the traitors Ireland still remains as pure in heart as ever, and though Empires fall and tyrannies perish

We Will Rise Again.

A CHEAP BARGAIN

[1 April 1916]

The Capitalist Press this week announced with great exultation the settlement of the Seamen's Strike on the City of Dublin Steam Packet Co. None have however given the facts of the case, and as these facts are worth repeating we propose to supply the deficiency caused by that omission.

The seamen and firemen employed on the boats of the above Company came out on strike because they were asked to sail the boats while the dock labourers were on strike, and in spite of the fact that these boats had been loaded by scabs or clerks acting as scabs. The Seamen's and Firemen's Union ordered them to scab, and they refused to scab. That was all. There was no question of money, or of a demand for an increase of wages involved in the matter. It was simply a strike upon a point of honour.

Now according to the daily press *these same men are returning to work because the Company has promised them an increase of five shillings in their weekly wages.* They have accepted this as a satisfactory settlement upon the advice of their officials – and return to work accordingly.

Do you understand that? Do you understand how the payment of five shillings per week can buy men to do a thing that they had declared was a dishonourable, unclean thing to do? They did not come out for an increase, they came out upon a point of honour. But for the payment of five shillings per week per man they have sold their honour, and betrayed their comrades in the hour of victory. In the hour of victory, for negotiations for an all-round satisfactory settlement were in progress when the seamen and firemen, prompted by their English officials, sold the pass upon their Irish brethren.

It is not hard to understand that. We see it every day. But it is hard to write temperately about it. So we will stop writing – and go on thinking.

FORCES OF CIVILISATION

[8 April 1916]

We have already pointed out in these columns that in the midst of the present world horror the forces of Organised Labour are the only forces still consciously and painstakingly pushing on the work of upbuilding a saner and juster civilisation. Each day confirms this view of matters. We receive in our office newspaper exchanges from all parts of the world, and it is noteworthy that in them all, next in importance to the news of the war, we always find prominence given to the efforts of Organised Labour to maintain the standard of living of the workers, and to secure their position against present and potential attacks. The Organised Labour Movement in effect says that no matter what the outcome of the war may be from a military standpoint it is essential that its finish shall see the working class of the world deprived of none of those rights and liberties they had won before its outbreak.

The full realisation of that wish we must regretfully say is in many countries an utter impossibility. In Great Britain, for instance, the Labour Leaders have so shamelessly sold the hard won position of their members that it is quite certain that the end of the war will see the capitalist class securely entrenched in possession of economic power greater than this generation has ever seen. It matters little what legal guarantees the Government may have promised or even given to the Labour Leaders. Legislation does not control the Lords of Industry; it is the Lords of Industry who control legislation. As we have often put it: The Class which rules industrially will rule politically.

The end of the war will find the British worker utterly demoralised by the advent of new conditions in the workshop. The apprenticeship system smashed, the Division or Dilution of Labour everywhere introduced, women and girls thoroughly expert in the work of performing certain processes hitherto part of the work of men, new machines installed, and the whole system of labour completely revolutionised in administration, in technique, and in outlook. All the old safeguards will be broken down, and in his efforts to erect new ones more in conformity with industrial development the worker will be hampered and baffled by the existence of vast masses of unemployed derelicts from the disbanded armies – unemployed derelicts making a reserve for the Capitalist Class with which to break strikes and enforce their will.

Every force that seeks to maintain for the labourer the position he had before the war, and to improve upon that position is for that reason a valuable force for the preservation of civilisation. The civilisation of any country to-day is judged by the position of its working class. A degraded working class means a degraded country, and a country weak against its foreign enemies. A working class upon a high plane of intelligence, in possession of social rights and strongly entrenched upon the political and economic field means a country dignified, respected, progressive, and powerful against foreign attack.

Reasoning from the foregoing the reader who has been attentively observing the trend of events in Ireland will appreciate the fact that the strikes and Labour struggles now on in this country are not mere isolated phenomena without bearing upon the progress of the race. Rather he will see that all of them – the prolonged fight of the City of Dublin Dockers,[32] the campaign of the Dublin Building Trades for an increase of wages, the continued and successful agitation for the betterment of conditions in the Gas Works, the spread of the Transport Workers' Union through the South of Ireland (of which the report of the meeting in Listowel in this issue is further evidence), the increases gained by the same Union in Cork, Sligo, Tralee, Kingstown, and Fenit, and all the other manifestations of activity on the part of Organised Labour, are so many evidences of the resolve of the workers to preserve and extend their heritage of freedom, despite the madness of the rulers of the world.

Germany has shown a lesson to the world in this respect. That country had the best educated working class in the world, the greatest number of labour papers, daily, weekly, and monthly, the greatest number of parliamentary and local representatives elected on a working class platform, the greatest number of Socialist votes in proportion to the entire population. All this was an index to the high level of intelligence of the German working class, as well as to their strong political and industrial position. This again was an infallible index to the high civilisation of the whole German nation. Germany had builded well upon the sure foundation of an educated self-respecting people. Upon such a foundation Germany laid her progress in peace, and her success in war.

Let Ireland learn this lesson. The labour fights the public
hears of in Ireland are not signs of mere restlessness – they are
the throbbing of the hearts of the worker aspiring after a
civilisation that shall make the Irish nation of our time a
worthy representative of the free Ireland of the past.

NOTES ON THE FRONT

[15 April 1916]

A MIXTURE OF ALL SORTS.

> Sydney Barker, the publisher of the Australian organ of the 'Indus-
> trial Workers of the World,' has been fined £100, with the alternative
> of a year's imprisonment with hard labour, for publishing statements
> likely to prejudice recruiting.

Thus we read in a Labour paper published in England. In a
Labour paper published in Scotland we read confirmation of
the news published in the capitalist dailies that about a dozen
prominent members of the working class movement – trade
unionists – have been seized in the middle of the night in
Scotland, and deported without any form of trial.[33]
     In Ireland we see prominent organisers of the Irish
Volunteers arrested and sentenced to deportation for feebly
endeavouring to imitate Sir Edward Carson;[34] we see newspapers raided and printing machinery seized by the military
amid a chorus of approval from all the enemies of militarism;[35] and in the rural districts we see every day arrests of
men for passing the most ordinary comments upon the war.
     Free speech and a free press no longer exists. The Rights of
Labour have been suppressed; to strike is an offence against
the law whenever the authorities choose to declare it so; and
all over these countries bands of soldiers and sailors are being
encouraged to invade and break up meetings of civilians.
     Gradually the authorities have been making successful war
upon every public right, gradually the mind of the unthinking
has been accustomed to see without alarm the outraging of
every constitutional liberty. That arbitrary exercise of power
which two years ago would have evoked a storm of protest is
now accepted with equanimity and even with approval.
     Tyranny grows with what it feeds upon, and the slave soon
grows accustomed to the bearing of chains which when first

applied seemed worse than death itself. The state of these countries to-day is a sad proof of the truth of these maxims.

That brilliant revolutionist, Tom Mann, speaking at Sheffield said that

> the termination of the war at this moment would result in serious disaster,

and that other trade union leader, Ben Tillett, has a constant job on the recruiting platform. These two men were before the war the greatest of internationalists, and rather despised our Irish love for our own nationality, as being mere sentimental slop and entirely out of date. Now they are raving jingoes, howling for the blood of every rival of the British capitalist class.[36]

In the speech above mentioned Mr Tom Mann quoted some figures which serve to show the wonderful fight being made by the Germans against odds. He said that:

> Official figures showed that the enemy had 19,800,000 men of military age. Russia alone had 19,719,000, and of these 10,000,000 had not been touched. The allies, excluding Britain, had 31,997,000.

Yet in spite of these enormous odds it is freely admitted by every competent military authority that the superiority lies undoubtedly with the forces of the Central Powers.

More than once we have pointed out this disparity of forces, more than once we have shown that Russia alone has a greater population than Austria and Germany combined, and therefore the fact that the German armies still remain immovably fixed on the soil of her enemies proves either of two things: Either the military forces of the Allies are hopelessly led by bungling incompetents. Or, the German Nation is incomparably superior to any nation in Europe.

But to read the accounts of the war published by the British press, and by the foresworn traitors who run in Ireland the pro-British press, one would imagine that the only real army on the field of battle was the British army, that the Germans were cowering in fear of a British attack, and that the French were in the rear of the British lines somewhere in France, and principally engaged in writing letters urging the British Tommies on.

An American writer, Irvin S Cobb, writing a humorous

sketch recently in the *Saturday Evening Post*, of Philadelphia, tells how he was interviewed by a bore who was an enthusiastic adherent of the Allies, and – but we will let him tell the story himself. In his Americanese he says:

> He cruelly impaled me in the lance tips of his steely relentless glance, and while I wriggled in feeble agony demanded of me, as one intrepid Anglo-Saxon to another, whether I agreed with him that the Anglo-Saxon was waging a magnificent struggle for the liberties and civilization of the world. And if not, why not? Hearing him one got a mental picture of a small determined Anglo-Saxon licking, single-handed, practically all the rest of creation.
>
> I might, I suppose, have told him that my Anglo-Saxon strain wouldn't bear the acid test, some of my ancestors having been the kind of Anglo-Saxons who came from the North of Scotland and spoke Gaelic; and others were the kind of Anglo-Saxons who hailed from the South of Ireland and disliked any mention of the late Oliver Cromwell coming up in the course of social conversation.
>
> I might have added that, after a cursory view of the situation, I was rather of the opinion that, in his struggle against the embattled foeman, the Anglo-Saxon, from time to time, was receiving some slight assistance from Frenchmen and Italians and Russians and Poles and Belgians and Japanese and Hindus and Sikhs and Ghurkas and Turcos and Canadians and Serbians and Australians and New Zealanders and Montenegrins and Algerians and Boers and South Africans and Americans – yes, quite a few Americans – and Celts and Slavs and Walloons, and various other allied branches of the Anglo-Saxon breed. But I didn't.
>
> I waited until he lowered his guard for a precious moment, and then I wrested myself free and fled, leaving him still rendering a favourite selection of airs on the Anglo-Saxophone.

In much the same way does the British and Redmondite press work to distort the news and to impress upon the mind of its readers a totally distorted view of events.

For instance there is one paper in Holland, the *Telegraaf*, owned and controlled by Englishmen, and when the *Freeman's Journal* or the *Irish Times* wishes to make us believe that the people of Holland are enthusiastic for the Allies they always quote this English-owned paper, and nearly always ignore every other.

From Italy the only papers quoted are those that support the Government, the others are either ignored or misrepresented.

In America papers like the New York *Sun*, which even in normal times is notorious for its snobbery and devotion to English interests and its contempt for American, are the favourites to which the *Freeman's Journal* turns when seeking American opinion on the war.

Even on the matter of the recent Irish Convention[37] it is the editorials of this lickspittle journal that the *Freeman's Journal* quotes to show the trend of Irish opinion upon this historic gathering. Never did the *Sun* in recent years show anything but contempt and hatred for all sincere Irish movements against English rule, but nevertheless on Monday, April 10, the *Freeman's Journal* gravely cites the paper in question in the defence of John E. Redmond against the angry denunciations of the American Irish.

And so the tale goes on, *ad infinitum*, a carnival of tyranny, a saturnalia of military license, an orgy of well-paid falsehoods. These are the everyday accompaniments of present day British rule in Ireland, and in the world.

Well, we must endure it, we suppose. At any rate we are not leaving Dublin until the Whit Trade Union Congress at Sligo. After that if the worst comes to the worst we can take our courage in our hands and –

PASS A STRONG RESOLUTION.

Notes

INTRODUCTION

1. *Edinburgh and Leith Labour Chronicle*, 1 December 1894: James Connolly, *Selected Political Writings*, ed. Owen Dudley Edwards and Bernard Ransom. (Writings of the Left' series, London: Jonathan Cape 1973).
2. Introduction to 1909 edition of *Erin's Hope – The End and the Means*, included in *Selected Political Writings* p. 167.
3. *The Socialist*, June 1904: *The Connolly–De Leon Controversy* (Cork: Cork Workers' Club 1976), p. 21.
4. *Irish Worker*, 14 March 1914: James Connolly, *Collected Works* (Dublin: New Books 1987 and 1988) I, p. 393.
5. *Irish Worker*, 8 August 1914: *Collected Works* I, p. 416.
6. *Collected Works* I, pp. 96–7.
7. In *The Attempt to Smash the Irish Transport and General Workers' Union* (Dublin: ITGWU 1924), pp. 162–5; and *Some Pages from Union History: The facts concerning Larkin's departure to America* (Dublin: ITGWU [1924]), pp. 8–12.
8. *A Socialist and War 1914–16*, ed. P. J. Musgrave (London: Lawrence and Wishart 1941).
9. All published At the Sign of the Three Candles, Dublin: *Socialism and Nationalism* in 1948; *Labour and Easter Week* in 1949; and *The Workers' Republic* in 1951. *Labour in Ireland* was also republished as part of the set.
10. *James Connolly: His Life Work & Writings* (Dublin: Talbot 1924).
11. Volume 1 was *Press Poisoners in Ireland* (1968); Volume 2 was *Yellow Unions in Ireland and other articles* (1968); Volume 3 was the *Connolly–Walker Controversy* (1969). Although not in the series, *Socialism & the Orange Worker* followed in 1969, published, like the others, by Connolly Books, Belfast.

12. *Revolutionary Warfare* (Dublin and Belfast: New Books 1968).
13. *Socialism Made Easy* (Dublin: Plough Book Service 1971).
14. See note 1.
15. Owen Dudley Edwards, *The Mind of an Activist – James Connolly* (Dublin: Gill and Macmillan 1971).
16. 1972, 1972, and 1976 respectively.
17. *The Best of Connolly*, ed. Proinsias Mac Aonghusa and Liam Ó Réagáin (Cork: Mercier 1967).
18. P. Berresford Ellis, *James Connolly: Selected Writings* (Harmondsworth: Penguin 1973).
19. Edward MacLysaght published a handful of Connolly's letters after O'Brien's death as an appendix to *Forth the Banners Go: Reminiscences of William O'Brien* (Dublin: Three Candles 1969)
20. *The Words of James Connolly*, ed. James Connolly Heron (Cork and Dublin: Mercier, 1986).
21. See note 4.
22. *What Connolly Said*, ed. Proinsias Mac Aonghusa (Dublin: New Island 1995).
23. Articles, portions of which Ryan relegated to footnotes, have of course been included, but none of the articles from which he, or other editors, took extracts appear here. The only exception is 'The National Danger' (see pp. 138–42), two paragraphs of which appeared in the 1975 edition of *Ireland upon the Dissecting Table* (p. 72) under the title 'No Compromise – No Conciliation'. But this exception is more than justified: first, because the Cork Workers' Club managed to find the least significant section of the article; and second, because 'The National Danger' is indispensable to an understanding of Connolly's reaction to the war, and the fact that previous editors have passed over it is unforgivable.

Part 1 – The Workers' Republic *1898–1903*

1. In 1798 the Society of United Irishmen organised an uprising to establish an independent Irish republic; Theobald
   Wolfe Tone (1763–98) was the most outstanding of the
   United Irish leaders. The '98 Executive was set up to commemorate the centenary of the rising, and had chosen the
   feast of the Assumption to lay the foundation stone for a
   monument to Tone in Dublin. It was Connolly himself who
   had criticised the move in the preceding *Workers' Republic*.
2. The building workers of Dublin were out for four months
   in 1896 in an unsuccessful attempt to increase their wages
   and reduce their hours.
3. John Mitchel (1815–75) was a leading figure on the radical
   wing of the Young Ireland movement, which organised an
   abortive republican insurrection in 1848. For his part in
   the Young Irelanders' agitation Mitchel was deported to
   Tasmania.
4. That is, the financial relations between Ireland and Britain. Irish politicians of all stripes agreed that Ireland had
   been over-taxed down through the years, and was entitled
   to be recompensed by the Exchequer.
5. The Land Courts were set up by the 1881 Land Act to
   arbitrate fair rents for tenants.
6. The story goes that British soldiers occupying Kilkenny in
   1798 used to amuse themselves by tying cats together by
   the tails and watching them fight.
7. Connolly is referring to the pawnshop, of course.
8. The Mansion House is the official residence of the Lord
   Mayor of Dublin; the banquet was in commemoration of
   the United Irishmen.
9. O'Leary, president of the '98 Executive, was a veteran of
   the Fenian movement, which fought for Irish independence from 1858 onwards. He would have been 68 years of
   age at this time.
10. T. M. Healy was a leading light in the Home Rule party,
    which had been trying to achieve limited independence for
    Ireland within the British Empire since 1870.
11. Timothy Harrington, John Dillon, and T. P. O'Connor
    were also leading Home Rulers, and John Redmond was
    the party's official leader. Dublin Castle was the seat of
    the British administration in Ireland.

12 'Spailpín' is Irish for a migrant labourer, but more commonly has the connotation of a disrespectful rascal. Connolly's choice of the word as a pen name obviously plays on the two meanings.

13. The seat of Dublin Corporation.

14. The *Workers' Republic* had published details of nationalists who had participated, or at least acquiesced, in toasting the British queen at '98 banquets. *United Ireland* was edited by Timothy Harrington.

15. The Lord Lieutenant was the British queen's official representative in Ireland.

16. The Employers Federation of Engineering Associations locked out their workers throughout Britain and Ireland from July 1897 to January 1898, and defeated the engineers' demand for the eight-hour day.

17. Where the *Freeman's Journal* was located.

18. The international peace conference summoned by the Russian government had been sitting from 18 May, but had failed to agree any limitation to the build-up of armaments. Tsar Nicholas II had just asserted his right to proclaim laws for Finland without regard to the country's assembly.

19. Britain did launch a war on the Boer settlers in South Africa in October.

20. The US took the Philippines from Spain in the war of 1898, following which they put down Filipino resistance to their rule.

21. President of the Irish TUC, whose advocacy of harmony between workers and employers had incurred the ire of Spailpín in *The Workers' Republic* of 3 June.

22. The Local Government Act of 1898 established a system of county councils, as well as urban and rural district councils, in Ireland, elected on a relatively wide franchise and with wide-ranging powers.

23. The demand for the public loan of agricultural machinery, quoted by Connolly later in the article, was among ten immediate demands put forward in the ISRP's programme in 1896 (see *Collected Works* I, pp. 466–7).

24. To the 1872 edition.

25. This is Connolly's blow-by-blow account of a fortnight of protest against the Boer War.

26. The Home Rulers' absence left the meeting without a quorum.

27. The Boers inflicted a serious defeat on the British at Stormberg on 10 December. It was soon followed by Boer victories at Magersfontein and Colenso, in what the British called 'Black Week'.
28. *Laager* is Afrikaans for a military encampment.
29. *Kopje* is Afrikaans for a small hill.
30. Michael Davitt was a former Fenian who had played a leading part in the Land War of 1879–82, a popular movement which broke landlordism and won major concessions for the tenant farmers. O'Brien and Willie Redmond (brother of John) were Home Rulers.
31. Gonne was a leading republican. Arthur Griffith, as editor of the *United Irishman*, called for the election of nationalist MPs who would boycott Westminster, establish an independent Irish parliament (albeit under a dual monarchy with Britain), and build up Irish industry.
32. The demonstration against the British queen's diamond jubilee was organised by the ISRP.
33. Lords are not allowed to sit in the British House of Commons.
34. Ireland's main university, Trinity College, was a Protestant institution, and the turn of the century saw a growing demand for a Catholic counterpart.
35. A Dublin magistrate at the time.
36. *Pisreoga*: superstitions.
37. A *seanchaí* is a traditional Irish storyteller.
38. 'Good health': an Irish toast.
39. Sam Woods, Thomas Burt and Ben Pickard were 'Lib-Lab' MPs: trade unionists run by the Liberal Party to catch the working-class vote.
40. Connolly pointed this much out in the editorial 'English Socialists and the Home Rule Party' in the March 1901 issue.
41. The Independent Labour Party, established in 1893 to secure independent representation for the working class in parliament.
42. James Keir Hardie was the ILP's leader, and the *Labour Leader* was the party's paper.
43. William McLoughlin was an ISRP member.
44. A Liberal MP with a reputation as a radical.
45. The ISRP candidate William McLoughlin got 371 votes (35 per cent) in the North City Ward, and Connolly himself got 431 votes (22 per cent) in the Wood Quay Ward.

46. Jean Jaurès had been a prominent figure in the French socialist movement for the past decade, and was at this time leader of the Parti Socialiste Français, the non-Marxist wing of French socialism.

47. In 1899 Alexandre Millerand, a Socialist deputy, accepted a ministerial post in a right-wing government, sparking a huge controversy in the socialist movement internationally.

48. The Home Rule party was also known as the Parliamentary party. J. P. Nannetti was one of its first 'Lib-Lab' representatives.

49. The Socialist Labor Party's trade union wing, set up in 1895.

50. The Parti Ouvrier Français (French Workers' Party) had represented the Marxist wing of French socialism since 1879. In 1902, it had changed its name to the Parti Socialiste de France (not to be confused with Jaurès's organisation) after absorbing other socialist groupings.

51. Eduard Bernstein was a trusted comrade of Friedrich Engels in his last years, but initiated the 'revisionist controversy' in international socialism when he published *The Prerequisites of Socialism and the Tasks of Social Democracy* in 1899, claiming that Marxism was out of date and that the social-democratic parties should openly proclaim themselves to be no more than parties of social reform.

52. Britain's Social Democratic Federation was set up in 1884, and counted Henry Mayers Hyndman and Harry Quelch among its leaders.

53. At the 1900 congress of the Socialist International in Paris, the Millerand affair was the main issue of debate. The majority, including the SDF, backed a resolution which condemned Millerand for not consulting his party first, but left open the general question of participation in right-wing governments. The ISRP delegates E. W. Stewart and Tom Lyng lined up with the revolutionary left in voting against the fudge.

54. The Land League led the Land War of 1879–82. At the turn of the century, Home Rulers in the west of Ireland were engaged in a campaign to divide big estates among the tenant farmers.

55. An Irish nobleman who went over to the side of the English, and played a leading part in the Norman invasion of 1169.

Part 2 – The Socialist *1902–1904*

1. *Justice* had functioned as an SDF paper since the organisation's foundation, but – as Connolly points out in the
   course of this article – it was controlled by an independent
   company, the Twentieth Century Press, rather than by the
   SDF's membership. The treatment of de Leonite malcon-
   tents applauded by the paper here was the expulsion of
   supporters of the *Socialist* from the SDF at its conference
   in April. Connolly's impressions of the US socialist movement were gathered on his speaking tour there in the last
   three months of 1902.
2. De Leon had edited the SLP's paper, the *People*, since
   1891.
3. Or Labour Representation Committee, set up in 1900 and
   a forerunner of the British Labour Party.
4. In 1896.
5. The Pullman rail strike of 1894.
6. The SLP habit of branding reformists 'kangaroos' seems to
   have arisen from the notion of them jumping around oppor-
   tunistically from one betrayal of the workers to another,
   much as the kangaroo courts of the American Civil War
   jumped around from one town to another.
7. In 1901.
8. Émile Loubet had been president of France since 1899.
9. From 1793 to 1815 Britain led a series of wars against
   revolutionary, and later Napoleonic, France.
10. It was not the Third, but the Second Empire that fell
    when France was defeated by Prussia in 1870, and the
    Third Republic established. Paris's mainly working-class
    National Guard took over the capital on 18 March 1871,
    establishing the Paris Commune, after the republican
    government attempted to disarm them as part of its
    capitulation to the Prussians. The Commune was brutally
    crushed in the last week of May, with the help of
    prisoners of war released by the Prussians.
11. A leading SDFer.
12. Following the suppression of the I Ho Tuan (or Boxer)
    rebellion in China in 1901, Russia occupied Manchuria.
13. Joseph Chamberlain, Britain's colonial secretary, had pro-
    posed earlier in the year that Britain erect a tariff wall
    around its empire.

14. A strike movement across Russia between 1901 and 1903 faced brutal repression from the Cossacks.

15. The Taff Vale judgment in 1901 made unions liable for employers' losses during strikes; together with another judgment in the same year severely restricting picketing, it had a crippling effect on trade unionism. The attack in Dublin seems to refer to the baton charges on those demonstrating against the visit of the British queen in 1900.

Part 3 – The Harp *1908–1910*

1. The Vikings made repeated forays into Ireland from the year 795 onwards.

2. The Edict, which guaranteed religious freedom to Protestants, was revoked in 1685.

3. In 1688 William of Orange invaded England, taking the throne from James II, who threatened to turn the clock back to old-style Catholic monarchical rule. James fled to France, and the following year to Ireland, where he attempted to take his stand again. The war became part of a general European power struggle before the Williamite forces won in 1691.

4. In 1314.

5. Oliver Cromwell landed in Ireland in 1649, and within three years his forces brutally suppressed an Irish uprising, which could have strengthened the royalists who wanted to roll back the English revolution. Most of the vanquished were given the option of leaving Ireland, and thousands became soldiers in various European armies.

6. O'Neill led the defeat of the English at the battle of the Yellow Ford in 1598.

7. O'Malley plied her trade in the late sixteenth century.

8. At the 1907 congress of the International, Gustave Hervé proposed that the working class should meet the threat of war with an immediate general strike and mutiny. The German delegation, whom he attacked for their conservatism, opposed him with a resolution proposing that socialists continue to do all in their power to prevent war, without committing themselves to specific tactics. In the end a compromise resolution was adopted unanimously, affirming the inevitability of war under capitalism, the

duty of the working class to use whatever means necessary to prevent it, and, if unsuccessful, to use the crisis to hasten capitalism's overthrow.

9. In 1898, when the US succeeded in taking over Spain's colonies in Latin America.

10. Crawlers, toadies.

11. The American Federation of Labor.

12. Very roughly translated, 'Learned Man of Ireland'.

13. This manifesto was issued by the ISRP, and was first published in *Reynolds' Newspaper* on 4 October 1896.

14. Having won the 1895 general election.

15. The Brehon laws, written down in the eighth and ninth centuries, codified the legal relations of pre-Norman Ireland, based – formally – on the common ownership of land.

16. A movement in mid-nineteenth-century America which violently opposed immigrants, and Catholic immigrants in particular. The name arose from their unconvincing denials of involvement in anti-immigrant activities.

17. That is, a delegate to the Socialist Party convention.

18. Astray.

19. Sinn Féin had been set up by Arthur Griffith in 1905.

20. The Act was actually passed in 1898, but the first elections under its terms were held in 1899.

21. The Irish National Union of Workers appears not to have lasted very long. Its members were likely absorbed into the Socialist Party of Ireland, or the Irish Transport and General Workers' Union, both founded soon after.

22. The International Working Men's Association, founded in 1864.

23. The painter John Butler Yeats had been speaking to American audiences of the great spirituality of the Irish, and drew Connolly's wrath in the March 'Harp Strings'.

24. See p. 51 above.

25. Priest.

26. 1580–c.1644.

27. The Uraiceacht was a treatise of Irish grammar.

28. Luigi Galvani's researches into electricity in the latter half of the eighteenth century later became the foundation for the invention of the battery. William Kelly invented the pneumatic process of steelmaking around 1850. Lord Kelvin was a pioneering physicist in the late nineteenth and early twentieth centuries. 'Isaac Watt' seems to be a mistake on Mac Néill's part: the reference

is probably to Isaac Newton, the discoverer of gravity, and James Watt, the inventor of the steam engine.

29. The *Irish Peasant* conducted a discussion in 1907 on the role of the Catholic Church in the management of schools. The cardinal wrote to the paper's owner demanding the editor's dismissal and a change in editorial policy, or the paper would be denounced from the altar. The owner acquiesced, but the editor, W. P. Ryan, stood his ground and published a successor paper.

Part 4 – The Irish Worker *1911–1914*

1. Larkin was organising in Belfast for the National Union of Dock Labourers during 1907.
2. On 5 August railworkers in Liverpool came out unofficially in support of the dockers. Within three days the port of Liverpool was closed, and reinforcements of police, army, and navy (including gunboats in the Mersey) were brought in. After two workers were shot dead by soldiers, the Amalgamated Society of Railway Servants (ASRS) called out all railworkers in Britain and Ireland. Dublin dockers refused to handle strikers' work, some were locked out, and clashes with the police took place. On 22 August the Belfast employers settled with the dockers, and the rail strike was called off.
3. Carpenter was imprisoned for distributing a manifesto, written by Connolly, against a royal visit (see *Collected Works* I, pp. 480–3).
4. Better known as Fianna Éireann, a republican youth organisation.
5. Dublin Metropolitan Police.
6. Helena Molony had also been imprisoned for insulting the British king.
7. The report has 'bailiffs' here, but Connolly obviously said 'bayonets'.
8. The dock and rail strike across Britain and Ireland.
9. Connolly was followed by speeches from Carpenter and Molony, from fellow SPI member Tom Lyng, Sinn Féin member Seán Milroy, and from Jim Larkin. A letter of support from Keir Hardie was read out as well.
10. A prominent figure in the British labour movement at the time.

11. The workers at Pierce's iron foundry in Wexford joined the ITGWU in the autumn of 1911, and were promptly locked out and replaced by scab labour. The dispute grew bitter, with the union's organiser, P. T. Daly, being assaulted by two local employers, and later imprisoned. Connolly took his place, and in February 1912 got Pierce's to recognise a new organisation, the Foundrymen's Union, which was affiliated to the ITGWU.

12. On 18 September 1867, the Fenians rescued two of their comrades from a prison van going through Manchester, and a policeman was killed in the process. From the many Irishmen rounded up, five were found guilty of murder. Two were reprieved, but on 23 November, William Allen, Philip Larkin and Michael O'Brien were hanged in Salford gaol. They soon became known as the 'Manchester martyrs'.

13. Connolly and Larkin were speaking to raise support for the Dublin workers locked out since the middle of August for refusing to sign a document repudiating the ITGWU.

14. The General Federation of Trade Unions was basically a committee set up by the TUC in 1899 to co-ordinate mutual financial support among unions. It never included more than a minority of them, however.

15. A resolution deploring Larkin's attacks on British trade union leaders was taken first.

16. Michael McKeown had been an official of the ITGWU since the union's foundation.

17. Secretary of Dublin No. 1 branch of the union.

18. A resolution demanding a refusal to handle Dublin goods if the employers refused to settle was defeated, officials representing two million members voting against, and officials representing 200,000 in favour.

19. Paper of the Sinn Féin party.

20. The enquiry did in fact exonerate the police, concluding that they 'discharged their duties throughout this trying period with conspicuous courage and patience'.

21. Justice Swifte proclaimed a public meeting on Dublin's O'Connell Street on 31 August. Larkin defied the ban, and the police ran amok, killing one and injuring 400 on what became known as 'Bloody Sunday'.

22. The delegates to the Irish TUC which assembled on 1 June.

23. The bill granting Home Rule to Ireland was due its third and final parliamentary reading in 1914; and the Dublin

lockout came to an end in January when the workers
drifted back to work.

24. The bill as introduced by the British government in 1912
denied the proposed Irish parliament any effective financial
powers, as well as control of foreign affairs and defence,
social welfare, the police, and a host of other matters. But in
March 1914 the government – with the support of the Home
Rule party – proposed amending its bill to allow Ulster
counties to vote themselves out of its provisions.

25. The text is illegible here.

26. The Ulster Volunteer Force was set up in January 1913,
under the leadership of Edward Carson, to prevent Home
Rule and maintain the union with Britain.

27. In 'Our Duty in this Crisis', his first response to the
outbreak of the world war, Connolly had dismissed both
the Home Rulers and the radical nationalists, and put his
faith in 'the working-class democracy'. If Germany were to
invade Ireland, he wrote, the workers of Ireland would
have every right to join any attempt to defeat the British
Empire; and if the European working class were to rise up
against the war, they should follow their example. In the
meantime the Irish working class should use whatever
means necessary to prevent the export of food and possible
famine during the war. (See *Collected Works* I, pp. 412–16.)

28. The Gaelic League was set up in 1893 to promote the
Irish language. At this period its members were also
prominent in nationalist politics.

29. The Irish Volunteers, set up in November 1913 to defend
Ireland's right to independence.

30. On 26 July the Irish Volunteers pulled off a successful
gun-running coup at Howth, Co. Dublin. Crowds in the
city jeered at the humiliated British troops, who opened
fire on an unarmed crowd on Bachelor's Walk, killing
three and injuring thirty-eight.

31. After losing the Battle of the Boyne, a symbolically important battle in the Williamite war, in 1690, James's
commander Patrick Sarsfield apparently offered to change
kings with the victorious Williamite officers and fight the
battle over again.

32. In June, Redmond demanded that the Provisional Committee of the Volunteers admit enough of his nominees to
give the Home Rulers a majority. The Provisional
Committee agreed.

33. Parnell (1846–91) was leader of the Home Rulers from 1879 to 1890, the party's most effective period.
34. William Ewart Gladstone was the British prime minister Parnell faced up until 1886.
35. Herbert Henry Asquith had been British prime minister since 1908.
36. Louis Antoine Léon de Saint-Just (1767–94) was a Jacobin leader in the French Revolution.
37. A regular column on the labour movement in Belfast, written by Cathal O'Shannon, a local member of both the ILP of Ireland and the ITGWU, under the pseudonym 'Crobh Dearg' (Red Hand).
38. William McMullen also spoke, and the meeting had to contend with the opposition of the police and supporters of the war.
39. Like Griffith, Councillor Seán T. O'Kelly (as he was more commonly known), Milroy, and Peadar Macken were Sinn Féiners, the latter also being a well-known trade unionist; Scollan represented the Ancient Order of Hibernians (Irish-American Alliance); MacBride was a veteran nationalist who had fought for the Boers against the British; and Constance Markievicz, having long since abandoned her aristocratic origins, was prominent in the labour and women's movements.
40. Cumann na mBan, set up in April 1914, and Inghinidhe na hÉireann, set up in 1900, were both republican women's organisations; the Irishwomen's Franchise League had been fighting for the vote since 1908.
41. Royal Irish Constabulary.
42. Connolly was followed by the others on the platform.
43. Augustine Birrell had been Chief Secretary for Ireland since 1907.

Part 5 – The Worker *1914–1915*

1. Labour maintained its representation of three on Dublin Corporation.
2. On 2 December 1914, the socialist Karl Liebknecht became the only deputy in the Reichstag to vote against war credits for the government.
3. A manifesto which demanded nationalisation of food supplies, credit and transport, in order to 'starve the war' and feed the American people.

4. The only other socialist parties in Europe to oppose the war.
5. Larkin had been speaking out against the war in America, and at a mass anti-war meeting in New York in November, attacked the British labour leaders' support for the war effort.
6. The paper is damaged here, but the meaning can be reconstructed fairly easily.

Part 6 – The Workers' Republic *1915–1916*

1. Connolly wrote the Citizen Army notes up until the 24 July issue of *The Workers' Republic*, after which the Army's chief of staff Michael Mallin took over. Connolly's notes, in which he analyses various examples of street fighting, are available in *Collected Works* II, pp. 451–83.
2. The Defence of the Realm Act (known affectionately or otherwise as DORA) gave the British government and army widespread powers to suppress anti-war opinion.
3. Murphy was Dublin's leading capitalist, and spearheaded the employers' attack on the ITGWU in 1913.
4. The union ran out of money for strike pay, and the men returned to work at the end of July.
5. Jeremiah O'Donovan Rossa (1831–1915) was a Fenian veteran, who had been elected to the British parliament in 1869 while serving a prison term. His funeral, on 1 August, became a great republican demonstration.
6. The miners had gone on strike for a wage rise. The government proclaimed the strike illegal and sent in the troops, but were forced to climb down.
7. Headquarters of the ITGWU.
8. The British government had announced a special budget increasing taxation on consumer goods to pay for the costs of the war.
9. There followed speeches by William O'Brien, William Partridge, Thomas Lawlor, and P. T. Daly – all of them ITGWU organisers – and by Helena Molony of the Irish Women Workers' Union.
10. A relative of the Prussian king was offered the Spanish throne in 1870, and the French empire protested at what it saw as Prussian encirclement. The candidacy was with-

drawn, but the Prussian chancellor, Otto von Bismarck, published the diplomatic correspondence on the affair in such a way as to insult the French, who declared war. Prussia won within six weeks.

11. Throughout 1905, strikes, mutinies and insurrections threatened to overthrow Tsarism, but the revolution was beaten by 1907. The Duma was the Tsar's excuse for a parliament, in which one landowner's vote was worth 15 peasants' votes, or 45 workers' votes. Such as it was, it was convened in April 1906, but dissolved three months later.

12. Washington (1732–99) led the American revolutionary war, and became first president of the United States.

13. Unlike the other shipping companies, this firm had refused to pay the increases demanded by the ITGWU to offset the war budget, and so its workers had been on strike since 8 November.

14. Sir Thomas Esmonde MP, no less. The Home Rule, or Parliamentary Party was also known as the Irish party.

15. The Munitions of War Act 1915 allowed for the compulsory arbitration of trade disputes.

16. Residence of the Lord Lieutenant, Lord Wimborne.

17. Chairman of the City of Dublin Steam Packet Company.

18. Charles Gavan Duffy (1816–1903) was one of the founders of the *Nation* newspaper in 1842, and a leading Young Irelander, although his arrest prevented him from taking part in the failed insurrection. He became a leader of the Tenants' League in the 1850s before emigrating to Australia, where he became prime minister of Victoria and was knighted.

19. The famine broke out in 1845, and by its end in 1849, over a million people had been killed, and at least twice that number forced to emigrate.

20. James Fintan Lalor (1807–49) was the most outstanding figure on the revolutionary wing of the Young Ireland movement, who insisted on the need to link the fight for independence with the people's fight for land.

21. Robert Emmet (1778–1803) led an unsuccessful republican insurrection in Dublin in 1803.

22. William Smith O'Brien (1803–64), the inveterate moderate who led the Young Ireland rising, was deported for his trouble.

23. James Stephens (1825–1901), who went on to become one of the founders of the Fenian movement.

24. Connolly would use this column to answer letters to *The Workers' Republic* – real or imaginary.

25. Cú Chulainn was a warrior in Irish mythology. Whether this particular Cú Chulainn existed or not, Connolly was replying here to an article by the leading republican Pádraig Pearse, which claimed that 'The last six months have been the most glorious in the history of Europe .... The old heart of the earth needed to be warmed with the red wine of the battlefields.'

26. Under the title 'Unemployment in Ireland'.

27. The Military Service Act had introduced conscription in Britain in January. Andrew Bonar Law, the Conservative leader, had been made Colonial Secretary in June 1915.

28. J. Havelock Wilson was leader of the National Seamen's and Firemen's Union.

29. Who headed the official enquiry into the 1913–14 lockout.

30. Celebrations of St Patrick's Day.

31. When British mail boats stopped calling at Queenstown (now Cóbh) the Hamburg–Amerika line planned to make it a port of call on its Atlantic sailings, but pressure from the British government prevailed upon the German government to prevent the plan.

32. Which went on until 17 April, when the company agreed to dismiss blacklegs, and the workers returned pending arbitration.

33. In late March the authorities arrested leaders of the Clyde Workers Committee, which organised the fight of Glasgow munitions workers to defend their conditions during the war, and deported them from Glasgow to Edinburgh.

34. Liam Mellows, a leading Volunteer, had been deported to England within the past week. Soon after the appearance of this issue of *The Workers' Republic*, however, he had been smuggled back (with the help of Nora Connolly) and went on to lead the Easter Rising in the west.

35. Earlier in the year the press of the British SLP – which printed Connolly's *Worker* and had been printing a paper of the same name for the Clyde Workers Committee – was raided and closed down by the police.

36. Mann and Tillett were both leaders in the London dock strike of 1889, and had been on the left of the British labour movement ever since. But Tillett had turned against the ITGWU at the TUC special conference of 1913, proposing the motion defending the British trade

union leaders, and both had supported the British war effort in 1914.

37. Two thousand delegates attended the Irish Race Convention in New York on 4–5 March, called by Clanna Gael, the American support group of the republican movement. The Convention launched the Friends of Irish Freedom to agitate for Irish independence.

INDEX

Index by Aindrias Ó Cathasaigh